THE BIOSYNTHESIS
OF MACROMOLECULES

BIOLOGY TEACHING
MONOGRAPH SERIES

CYRUS LEVINTHAL, *Editor*
Massachusetts Institute of Technology

Vernon M. Ingram, *Massachusetts Institute of Technology*
THE BIOSYNTHESIS OF MACROMOLECULES

Albert L. Lehninger, *Johns Hopkins University* BIOENERGETICS

James D. Watson, *Harvard University* THE MOLECULAR BIOLOGY
OF THE GENE

VERNON M. INGRAM
Massachusetts Institute of Technology

THE BIOSYNTHESIS

OF MACROMOLECULES

1966

W. A. BENJAMIN, INC. New York Amsterdam

THE BIOSYNTHESIS OF MACROMOLECULES

Library of Congress Catalog Card Number 65–11196
Manufactured in the United States of America

The final manuscript was put into production on May 21, 1964;
this volume was published March 3, 1965; second printing, with
corrections, March 8, 1966

W. A. BENJAMIN, INC.
New York, New York 10016

� TO MARGARET

EDITOR'S FOREWORD

GREAT CHANGES HAVE TAKEN PLACE RECENTLY IN THE TEACHING of undergraduate biology. To some extent, these changes are due, as they are in many other sciences, to the upgrading of high school science education. However, the major factor for biology would seem to be the change which has taken place during the last twenty to thirty years in the science itself. Biology, which has in the past been taught primarily as a descriptive subject, is now changing to one which is primarily analytical. One result of this change is that the undergraduate biology courses are becoming more and more dependent on physics, mathematics, and chemistry in order to enable the student to achieve a deeper understanding of his subject. Biochemistry, which until recent years has been a subject for advanced biology students and for medical students, has become an increasingly important part of the undergraduate training for all biology majors. In addition, the developments in molecular biology have not only become a part of the undergraduate biology curricula, but are increasingly necessary for a general understanding of our scientific culture.

This textbook series is designed to aid those biology teachers who are developing new programs for undergraduate biologists. We do not imagine a program lacking in the subject matter of "classical biology." Rather, we are thinking of a program in which the teaching of many of the more classical biological subjects will be firmly based on the student's background in biochemistry and molecular biology. We would hope that it will not be necessary to repeat the discussion of macromolecular synthesis in each of the more advanced books. A thorough and detailed discussion of these problems is included both in the sequence for the introductory course and in that for the biochemistry course so that the more advanced books, like the more advanced courses, can be based on the assumption that the students know, or at least have access to, complete treatments of this material.

This book, which is designed to be used for that part of the biochemistry course dealing with macromolecular synthesis, is the first of this series to be published, and it is hoped that it will be useful as a complete book in itself and also as part of the series.

CYRUS LEVINTHAL

Cambridge, Massachusetts
December 1964

PREFACE

THIS BOOK IS DESIGNED FOR THE STUDENT OF BIOCHEMISTRY OR
biology who has had some exposure to the basic principles of
organic chemistry and biochemistry. It can easily be used by
people who have not had this experience, if they first read the
relevant portions of a short introductory book on biochemistry,
such as, for example, *Cell Structure and Function* by A. G.
Loewy and P. Siekevitz (Holt, Rinehart & Winston, New York,
1963).

The main purpose of this book is to acquaint the reader with
the present state of our knowledge in the biochemistry of the
biosynthesis of macromolecules, such as the nucleic acids (both
DNA and RNA), proteins, and polysaccharides. It is hoped that
the material covered is sufficiently detailed and up-to-date to
enable him to follow and discuss advanced seminars, lectures,
research conferences, and research papers in the relevant areas
of molecular biology and modern biochemistry.

Specifically, this text is intended to cover the area of biochemistry dealing with the synthesis of macromolecules in living cells
and with the properties of nucleic acids. Many references to the
original literature are given, so that the book should be useful
both to undergraduate and graduate students and also to re-

search workers. In a field as vast as the one suggested by the title, inevitably a drastic selection had to be made, but it is hoped that the essential aspects have been covered.

VERNON M. INGRAM

Cambridge, Massachusetts
May 1964

ACKNOWLEDGMENTS

I WISH TO ACKNOWLEDGE WITH GRATEFUL THANKS THE HELP which I have received through the detailed criticism of two reviewers. Most of their suggestions were incorporated, but any faults which remain are entirely my own. During the fall term of 1963 I taught the *Biosynthesis of Macromolecules* to a class of junior, senior, and first-year graduate students at the Massachusetts Institute of Technology as part of a general biochemistry course. This experience was most important to the development of the book. I feel indebted to these students for their criticisms, questions, and reactions and to Dr. Bernard Moss for helping me plan and conduct the course of lectures. In particular, I would like to thank Mr. Alan Haberman, a member of the class, for reading and criticizing the whole manuscript. Thanks are also due to my colleague Dr. Phillips Robbins for commenting on Chapter Seven. Many other colleagues and friends have helped me, on numerous occasions, with the collection and the sifting of material.

Particular thanks are due the various people who have so kindly supplied me with copies of photographic material. They are specifically acknowledged with each figure. I wish to thank also the many publishers and authors who gave me permission to reproduce their illustrations. The origin of such material is given in each case.

It is a pleasure to thank Mrs. Marilynn Sovka, who prepared the manuscript, for her excellent and cheerful cooperation. I am grateful to Mr. Norman Davies who collected bibliographical material and to my secretary Miss Suzanne Choules for dealing so competently with the details of producing this book. Finally, I wish to thank the staff of W. A. Benjamin, Inc., for their help, efficiency, and patience.

V. M. I.

CONTENTS

ONE §§ INTRODUCTION

IN JUNE 1963 AN INTERNATIONAL CONFERENCE ENTITLED *Synthesis and Structure of Macromolecules* was held at the Cold Spring Harbor Laboratory for Quantitative Biology, New York. For six days and nights 315 scientists from many different countries discussed the biochemical and genetic control over the "holy trinity" of molecular biology—DNA, RNA, and protein—often until the small hours of the night. Fully two-thirds of what was said at the meeting is directly applicable to the subject area of the present book: the biosynthesis of macromolecules. It is therefore clear that a selection of topics had to be made to meet the size limitation; the author has chosen to treat some subjects in depth, rather than to survey the whole. To help the reader who is new to the subject matter, a glossary of terms will be found at the end of the book.

It is the aim of this volume to provide enough information and explanation to students with an elementary knowledge of biochemistry and organic chemistry so that they might then be able to understand and participate in the current excitement in molecular biology.

1

GENERAL SCHEME FOR DNA, RNA, AND PROTEIN SYNTHESIS

In the over-all scheme three key processes may be distinguished:

1. the exact *replication* of DNA, which is perhaps catalyzed by the enzyme DNA polymerase to be discussed in Chapter 2,

2. the *transcription* of the information contained in DNA into information in messenger RNA by the DNA-dependent RNA polymerase (Chapter 3) and

3. the *translation* that takes place when the information in messenger RNA is translated into the amino acid sequence of the newly synthesized peptide chain (Chapter 5).

The exact replication of DNA (Figure 1–1) ensures that all the cells in a multicellular organism will have the same genetic information and the same potential ability to synthesize specific protein molecules. Furthermore, this mechanism provides for the passing on of this information from generation to generation in all types of organisms. In other words, the exact copying of the DNA nucleotide sequence by DNA polymerase makes certain the genetic continuity of protein structure. It is against this background of continuity that we must place the occurrence of mutations as rare events that change a portion of the chemical structure of the DNA and therefore a part of the information carried by the DNA. In turn, there is an alteration in the structure of that protein which corresponds to the region of DNA that has been affected by the mutation. Mutations may occur spontaneously or they can be induced by the effects of chemical mutagens, such as nitrous acid, acridine dyes, or alkylating agents, and through the agency of physical mutagens, such as ultraviolet light or radiation. The altered DNA will be subject to the usual exact replication process; this means that the mutation is inherited and will be passed on to future generations of the organism. It follows that the altered protein will also be inherited. Some examples of the chemical expression of mutations and of how one can correlate the genetic event with the consequent alteration in protein structure will be found in Chapter 6.

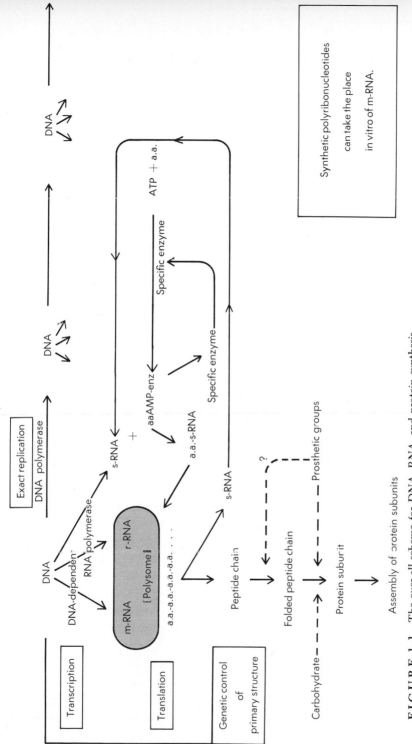

FIGURE 1-1   The over-all scheme for DNA, RNA, and protein synthesis.

The *transcription process* (Figure 1–1) takes the genetic information from the DNA in the nucleus and places it in the active ribosome fraction—the polysomes—in the cytoplasm of the cell where the actual process of protein synthesis takes place.

In the unicellular bacterium, where DNA and ribosomes are close together, the process of messenger-RNA formation on DNA and the subsequent assembly of the active ribosome, the polysome, from the messenger RNA and inactive ribosomes appears to be straightforward. In the nucleated metazoan cell, it appears that messenger RNA is also made on the DNA, but this is located in the nucleus.[1] It is not quite clear, however, whether the assembly of messenger RNA and ribosomes to form the active polysomes takes place in the nucleus or in the cytoplasm (see Figure 1–2). In the former alternative, the

FIGURE 1–2   *A schematic diagram of how some of the structural elements within a metazoan cell might be organized. Note the folded endoplasmic reticulum with ribosomes, probably polysomes, attached to it. Possibly the reticulum, with its polysomes, streams continuously from the site of synthesis of the polysomes, the nucleolus, into the cytoplasm.*

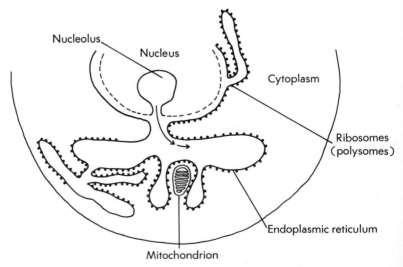

active polysomes would have to move out of the nucleus through holes in the nuclear membrane into the cytoplasm, and indeed it is possible that this is what happens. In the second alternative, the unprotected messenger RNA would find its way out of the nucleus into the cytoplasm and there would complex with inactive ribosomes to form the active polyribosome.

The transcription process is catalyzed by the enzyme DNA-dependent RNA polymerase discussed in Chapter 3. This is also an exact mechanism in the sense that the enzyme repro-duces the DNA nucleotide sequence in the messenger RNA.[2] Although in in vitro experiments with subcellular fractions both strands of the DNA molecule are transcribed into RNA, it seems that in vivo only one strand of the DNA is copied.[3,4] The mechanism by which the cell distinguishes between the two strands of DNA so that only one should be copied is at present unclear. Conceivably, both strands are copied in vivo, but the m-RNA copy of one strand of DNA is very rapidly degraded so that it is not found in the messenger-RNA fraction. However, this seems an unlikely process. It is more probable that a positive control exists in vivo that prevents the polymerase from copying one of the DNA strands.

The translation process (Figure 1–1) in the active ribosome[5] or polysome fraction involves the arrival of amino acids in the form of activated amino acyl-s-RNA molecules, their assembly in sequence on the messenger-RNA template in the polysome, and the combination of amino acids to form the peptide bonds of the finished peptide chain, together with the release of s-RNA. The s-RNA is used again and may be viewed as having a catalytic function in the whole process.

The process of translation in vivo is an exact one in the sense that very few mistakes are made. One of the best demonstra-tions is the synthesis of human hemoglobin in human immature red cells, the reticulocytes. Human hemoglobin is unusual in not containing any isoleucine, although other proteins, which do contain this amino acid, are made in the same cell. By incubating human reticulocytes with radioactive isoleucine of high specific radioactivity, it was possible to estimate the number of isoleucines mistakenly inserted into the newly synthesized hemoglobin.   One might reasonably expect isoleucine to be mistaken for the amino acid leucine or, more likely, valine, to which it is quite close structurally.[6]   Both these amino acids are found with high frequency in human hemoglobin.   The fact that the amount of radioactive isoleucine recovered in the newly synthesized hemoglobin was below the level of detection places the likelihood of such an error much below 1 per cent.   At the moment we do not know where this exact control over the accuracy of translation lies.   Each amino acid that is activated has its own specific activating enzyme and its own specific s-RNA molecule.   However it is known[6] that, during in vitro experiments, appreciable amounts of the "wrong" amino acid can be activated and can be transferred to an s-RNA molecule. Possibly control is tighter in vivo and perhaps some additional control exists also at the polysome assembly line.

In this connection the recent experiments of Davies, Gilbert, and Gorini[7] are of great interest.   They found that streptomycin and other related antibiotics cause extensive and specific alterations in the in vitro coding properties (see Chapter 5) of synthetic polynucleotides (synthetic messenger RNA).   It seems that the genetic code can be altered at the level of the polysome by streptomycin.   Thus it appears that the ribosomes control the accuracy of the reading of the information in messenger RNA.

Subsequent to the assembly of the peptide chain, a number of other steps are required before we have the finished protein molecule.   The peptide chain has to be released from the polysome, and it is possible that a specific enzyme is involved in this process.   The peptide chain, particularly that of a soluble protein molecule, must be folded into its correct secondary and tertiary structure.   It is not clear whether this happens on the polysome, as the peptide chain grows, or after the peptide chain is released into free solution.   From the elegant studies of Anfinsen and his colleagues[8,9] it seems that the primary structure of a polypeptide chain has enough information to direct to a considerable extent the three-dimensional folding of the molecule, a subject treated more fully in Bernhard's forthcoming book.[10]

$$...CO.NH.CH.CO.NH... \quad .CO.NH.CH.CO.NH...$$
$$\underset{\underset{...CO.NH.CH.CO.NH...}{|}}{\overset{\overset{...CO.NH.CH.CO.NH...}{|}}{\underset{CH_2}{\overset{CH_2}{\underset{SH}{\overset{SH}{|}}}}}} \xrightarrow[\text{[O]}]{} \underset{\underset{.CO.NH.CH.CO.NH...}{|}}{\overset{\overset{.CO.NH.CH.CO.NH...}{|}}{\underset{CH_2}{\overset{CH_2}{\underset{S}{\overset{S}{|}}}}}} \quad + H_2O \qquad (1\text{--}1)$$

Also involved in this process of folding may be the formation of disulfide from cysteine residues in different parts of the peptide chain (Equation 1–1, Figure 1–3). The formation of these disulfide bonds would help stabilize the secondary and tertiary structure of the folded peptide chain, and the two processes, the inherent preference of a given amino acid sequence for a certain tertiary structure and the formation of the stabilizing disulfide bridges, finally result in a fully folded protein subunit.

If the final protein is one containing prosthetic groups in addition to polypeptide chains, these must be inserted into the tertiary structure either during the process of folding or after folding is complete. If the prosthetic groups are attached covalently as they are in cytochrome c (from cysteine residues in the peptide chain to the vinyl groups of the heme group), these covalent bonds may be formed through the action of yet another enzyme. If, however, the prosthetic group is not held by covalent bonds but only by electrostatic interaction or by coordinate valencies, as in hemoglobin, the insertion of such prosthetic groups may not require a special enzyme. In proteins that contain also carbohydrate residues in addition to the polypeptide chain, these are usually attached covalently, presumably by special enzymes. We can speculate that the attachment occurs at the stage in protein synthesis when the peptide chain is already folded in its correct secondary and tertiary structure.

Many proteins are composed of more than one subunit, that is, of more than one peptide chain. The assembly of subunits into the final protein molecule is the last step in the synthesis of such a protein. It may or may not be accompanied by the

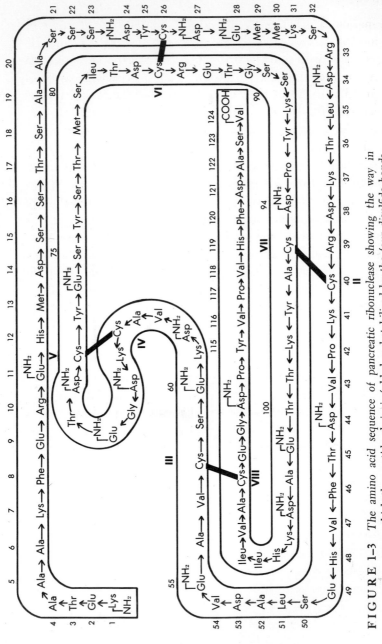

FIGURE 1-3 *The amino acid sequence of pancreatic ribonuclease showing the way in which the peptide chain is folded and stabilized by the four disulfide bonds.*

8

formation of disulfide bonds between subunits. In the case of hemoglobin, the subunits are held together by electrostatic interaction, with some hydrogen bonding and specific surface fit between the subunits; we assume that no special enzyme is required to carry out this assembly, but that the subunits come together in free solution. The subunits of the insoluble protein molecules keratin or collagen are, however, held together by covalent bonds, disulfide bonds in the case of keratin and ester bonds in the case of collagen. Although we know a considerable amount now about the various stages in the synthesis of a soluble protein, we know very little about the final stages of protein synthesis of structural and insoluble proteins. We assume that the assembly of the primary amino acid sequence of structural proteins is the same as for soluble proteins, but the mechanisms by which these are placed in position, bound to carbohydrate or lipid components, and assembled into such structures as cell membranes are almost completely unknown.

OUTLINE OF THIS BOOK

In the subsequent chapters we shall take up the various processes outlined above, beginning with replication of DNA in Chapter 2. Next we move on to the mechanism of biosynthesis of RNA and related topics (Chapter 3), followed by a brief account of the methods available for investigating the sequences of proteins, DNA and particularly RNA (Chapter 4). This brings us to a discussion of the mechanism of protein synthesis (Chapter 5) and of the genetic control of protein structure (Chapter 6). Finally, the biosynthesis of some polysaccharides (Chapter 7) is considered as an example of the biosynthesis of a macromolecule that does not carry information in unique sequences.

REFERENCES

1. Summarized in Cannellakis, E. S. (1962), "Metabolism of Nucleic Acids." *Ann. Rev. Biochem.*, **31**, 276.
2. Hurwitz, J., Evans, A., Babinet, C., and Skalka, A. (1963), "On the Copying of DNA in the RNA Polymerase Reaction." *Cold Spring Harb. Symp. Quant. Biol.*, **28**, 59.

3. Hayashi, M., Hayashi, M. N., and Spiegelman, S. (1964), "DNA Circularity and the Mechanism of Strand Selection in the Generation of Genetic Messages." *Proc. Natl. Acad. Sci.*, **51**, 351.

4. Spiegelman, S., and Hayashi, M. (1963), "The Present Status of the Transfer of Genetic Information and Its Control." *Cold Spring Harb. Symp. Quant. Biol.*, **28**, 161.

5. Summarized in Watson, J. D. (1963), "Involvement of RNA in the Synthesis of Proteins." *Science*, **140**, 17.

6. Loftfield, R. B., Hecht, L. I., and Eigner, E. A. (1963), "The Measurement of Amino Acid Specificity of Transfer RNA." *Biochim. Biophys. Acta*, **72**, 383.

7. Davies, J., Gilbert, W., and Gorini, L. (1964), "Streptomycin, Suppression and the Code." *Proc. Natl. Acad. Sci.*, **51**, 883.

8. Anfinsen, C. B. (1962), "Amino Acid Sequence as the Major Determinant of Structure and Function in Proteins" in "Basic Problems in Neoplastic Diseases" (edited by A. Gellhorn and E. Hirschberg, Columbia University Press, New York).

9. Epstein, C. J., Goldberger, R. F., and Anfinsen, C. B. (1963), "The Genetic Control of Tertiary Protein Structure: Studies with Model Systems." *Cold Spring Harb. Symp. Quant. Biol.*, **28**, 439.

10. Bernhard, S. A. "The Structure of Proteins," W. A. Benjamin, New York, in production.

TWO ∬ DNA

FOR A DETAILED DISCUSSION OF THE CHEMICAL STRUCTURE OF DNA the student is advised to look at a full description such as might be found in the reading list at the end of this book. Certain features of the structure will however be emphasized here for the purpose of making clear our discussions of the biosynthetic mechanisms by which DNA is synthesized.

DNA STRUCTURE

Native DNA is an exceedingly long molecule, very thin, yet rather rigid. Cairns[1] has shown that the molecule of DNA that makes up the genome of *E. coli* is up to 1.1 mm in length, corresponding to a molecular weight of 2.8×10^9. This molecule is rigid by virtue of the fact that it is composed of two strands of polynucleotides coiled around each other in a helical manner and held together by hydrogen bonds (see Glossary) between pairs of nucleotide bases (see Figures 2–1, 2–2, 2–3, and

11

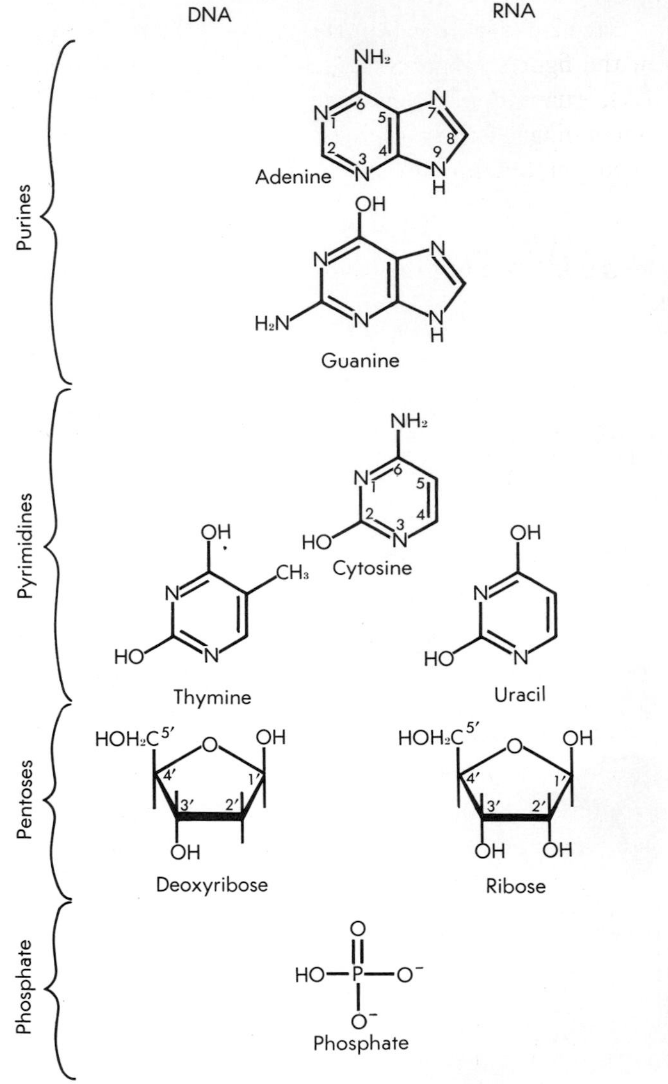

FIGURE 2–1   *The building blocks of DNA and RNA.*

2–4). It should be noted that the backbone of each of the two chains making up this double helix is composed of alternating 2-deoxyribose sugar residues linked by 3′,5′-phosphodiester linkages (Figure 2–2). This backbone is uniform throughout the enormous length of the molecule; it apparently carries no genetic information.

Each 2-deoxyribose is linked to one of the four bases, as shown in the figures (Figures 2–2, 2–3, and 2–4), which are adenine (A), guanine (G), cytosine (C), and thymine (T). Corresponding bases in each of the two strands form a pair by hydrogen bonding in the well-known Watson-Crick double-

FIGURE 2–2   *The structure of DNA and RNA polynucleotides.*

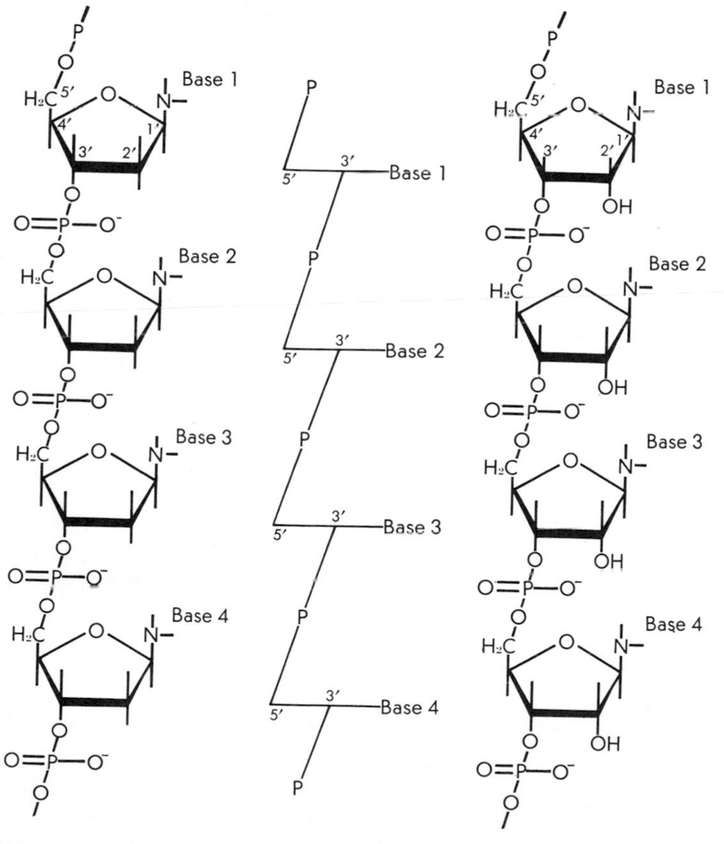

| DNA polynucleotide | Schematic form of DNA and RNA polynucleotides | RNA polynucleotide |

helical structure (Figure 2–3). Analysis of DNA from many different sources, performed originally by Chargaff and his colleagues, showed that the contents of the purines $(A + G)$ always equaled the contents of pyrimidines $(C + T)$. Furthermore, the bases with an amino group in position 6 (A and C) were equal in total amount to the bases having a 6-keto group (G and T). On the basis of these findings and of the X-ray structure data, Watson and Crick proposed their double-stranded helical model for DNA in which each adenine was paired with a thymine base and each guanine with a cytosine (Figures 2–3 and 2–4). In this way the analytical results were explained and reconciled with the X-ray-structure information, since the space between the two backbones is too small to accommodate two purine bases, too large for two pyrimidine bases, but just right for one of each kind. The equivalence of the bases in a total analysis of DNA is expressed as $A = T$, $G = C$, or $A + G/C + T = 1.0$. The genetic information carried by the DNA molecule is then contained in the sequence of the bases along one or other of the two strands that make up the double helix, or it may be carried by the sequence of base pairs acting as base pairs (Figures 2–4 and 2–5).

It should be emphasized that the Watson-Crick structure for

FIGURE 2–3 *Base pairs in the Watson-Crick structure of DNA. Note that guanine:cytosine can form three hydrogen bonds, but adenine:thymine only two. The sugar residues are those of the 2-deoxyribose units in the back bone of the polynucleotide chains. The long axis of the DNA helix is at right angles to the plane of the paper. Note the tautomeric forms of the cases involved in these pairs.*

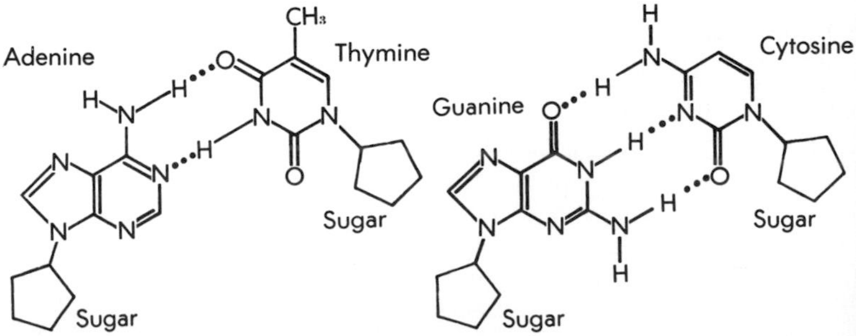

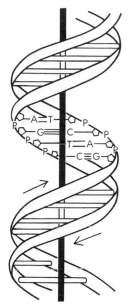

FIGURE 2–4 *Diagrammatic representation of the double helix of DNA. The arrows indicate the polarity of the 3′,5′-phosphodiester linkages in each strand.*

DNA, with its immediate suggestion for a biochemical mechanism for replicating genetic information carried in base sequences, has been a mainspring of much of recent molecular biology. On the other hand, the idea that genetic information is carried in DNA and that it must be stored in the base sequence is considerably older.

Recent work[2] indicates that the regular Watson-Crick structure applies to nearly the entire length of each DNA molecule. In solution, the mass:length ratio of both bacterial and animal DNAs agrees well with the formulation of the crystalline structure according to Watson and Crick. Furthermore, X-ray evidence indicates that the same pattern applies to DNAs from many different sources.[3] It seems safe to assume that this structure is widely representative of DNA and accounts for the configuration of each molecule.

The isolation of such a very long molecule is technically difficult, because of the relative ease with which a long rigid rod

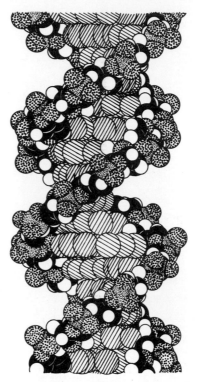

FIGURE 2–5   *Molecular model of the Watson-Crick-Wilkins struc-*
ture of the DNA molecule.

may be broken by hydrodynamic shear forces.[4]   Undoubtedly
many of the earlier preparations of DNA suffered such degradation.   Even the injection of a solution of DNA into the cell of
the analytical ultracentrifuge by forcing it through the needle of
a hypodermic syringe is sufficient to cause extensive breakdown
and a lowering of molecular weight by factors of two or four.
Since this danger was realized, experimenters have been careful
to avoid such degradation and this is why high molecular weights
such as the one just mentioned have been obtained, not

necessarily in the ultracentrifuge, but more specifically by measurements in the electron microscope and by radioautography of isolated DNA molecules.

Not only is the DNA of *E. coli* a very long molecule, but it is arranged, surprisingly, in the form of a ring. This structure essentially constitutes a circular chromosome[5], and similar circular structures have been postulated for the DNA of bacteriophages such as the lambda (Figure 2-6) and ϕX 174

FIGURE 2-6   *Electron micrograph of λ-phage DNA, phenol extracted, spread as a monolayer on a surface of water from a solution of the DNA and the basic protein cytochrome c. The arrow marks the discontinuity in the molecule, of which there is always only one. Perhaps this is the point where replication begins. (Ris and Chandler, Cold Spring Harbor Symposium, 1963, xxviii, p. 1, Fig. 1, reproduced with permission.)*

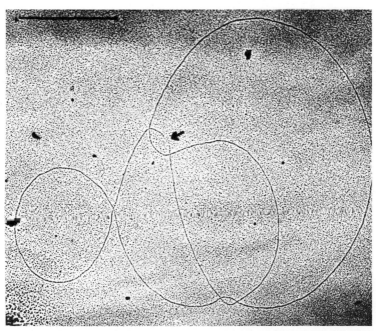

bacteriophages, the last being of particular interest because its DNA, in contrast to other naturally occurring DNAs, is single-stranded. As will be seen in a later section, the concept of a circular DNA molecule raises some fascinating questions when

FIGURE 2–7   (a) A diagrammatic representation of the replication of circular DNA, based on the assumption that each round of replication begins at the same place (the "swivel") and proceeds in the same direction. (b) Autoradiograph of the chromosome of E. coli (strain K12 Hfr) (p. 19), labeled with tritiated thymidine for two generations and extracted by treating the cells with lysozyme. The inset shows the same structure diagrammatically. The figure shows a predominantly half-hot chromosome that has completed two-thirds of the second round of duplication. Part of the still-unduplicated section is half-hot (from Y to C) and part is hot-hot (from C to X). This situation arises

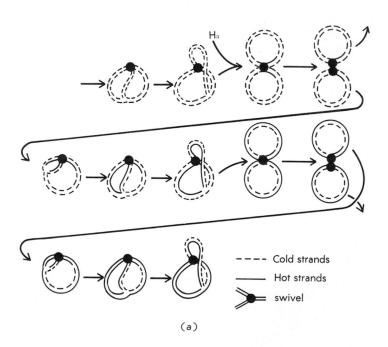

- - - - Cold strands

———— Hot strands

>—● swivel

(a)

we consider the replication of such a molecule (see Figure 2–7).

In solution, the shape of native DNA is rather insensitive to wide changes in ionic strength, a behavior unlike that of a typical

when the moment of introduction of the label does not coincide with the start of a round of replication. In the example shown one can identify one of the forks (X) as the starting and finishing point of duplication [see (a)] and the other (Y) as the growing point. (Reproduced with permission from Reference 5.)

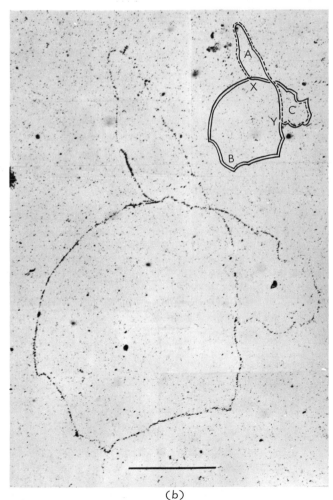

(b)

polyelectrolyte. This is presumably due to the existence of the double helix, which keeps the negatively charged phosphate groups at rigidly fixed regular spacings. On the other hand, denatured DNA such as heat-treated DNA or DNA, which has been subjected to acid, behaves like a flexible, loosely coiled polyelectrolyte chain. Under these conditions the double helix presumably has come apart and the hydrogen bonds joining base pairs have been broken. The molecular size and shape of such denatured DNA, as measured by its sedimentation coefficient in the ultracentrifuge and by its viscosity, are dependent on the ionic environment and are sensitive to changes in ionic strength. Denatured DNA behaves like RNA, which is usually found in the single-stranded form, and like the single-stranded synthetic polyribonucleotides. The DNA from the bacteriophage ϕX 174 mentioned above behaves in many respects like heat-denatured DNA.

DNA REPLICATION

A most appealing feature of the Watson-Crick structure for DNA was that it suggested a very reasonable mechanism for replicating a DNA molecule with preservation of its information content. This property is required of any molecule that plays a role as the genetic material. The information stored in such a molecule must be passed on extremely accurately from generation to generation. If the information is indeed contained in the sequence of bases in a chain of DNA, this sequence must be kept intact. Through the postulate that the sequence of bases in the two strands making up the DNA molecule are complementary to each other, we have a ready-made mechanism for ensuring such continuity. We can imagine that the strands of DNA will separate from each other and that a complementary copy of new DNA will be synthesized on each of the two separated parent strands (Figure 2–8). At the end of this process we shall have two DNA molecules, half of each is derived from the parent molecule, the other half being new DNA. Provided the base-pairing mechanism is accurate, and it seems to be so, the two new DNA molecules will exactly

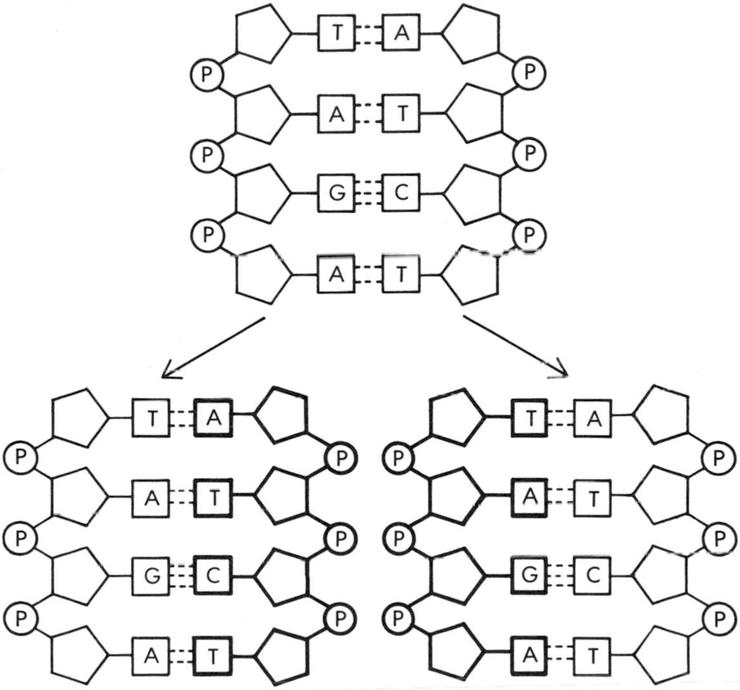

FIGURE 2–8 *Proposed scheme of replication of a Watson-Crick DNA molecule. The bold-lined polynucleotide chains are the newly synthesized daughter strands.*

resemble the original one. This mechanism of replication is called *semiconservative*; it is the currently accepted mechanism for which there is considerable experimental evidence.

Other models are possible, although there is no evidence for them at present. The *conservative* mode of replication would postulate that the two strands of the parent DNA molecule do not come apart but that, in some manner unknown, they transfer the information from the original strand to the daughter strand and thereby cause the biosynthesis of a new double-stranded DNA molecule. Alternatively, the two strands of the parent DNA molecule might temporarily separate, each of them acting as template for a complementary new DNA strand. Conservative replication, however, would demand that during or after this process the two original parent strands should rejoin to form a complete DNA molecule, and so should the two new daughter

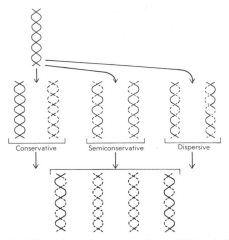

FIGURE 2–9   *Three hypothetical modes of DNA replication.*

DNA strands. There is, as we have said, no experimental evidence for this model.

A third theoretically possible mode of replication, the *dispersive* model, would involve the fragmentation of the DNA molecule in such a way that each single strand of the new daughter molecules contained sections of old and sections of new DNA. Each strand of DNA would therefore be a mixture of old and new (Figure 2–9). For this mechanism also there is at present no evidence.

Probably the most convincing experimental demonstration for the semiconservative mode of replication is the Meselson-Stahl experiment.[6] Bacteria (*E. coli*) were grown in a medium containing $^{15}NH_3$ as the only source of nitrogen. In this way all the nitrogen atoms of the bases in the DNA molecules were the heavy (^{15}N) atoms; as a result these DNA molecules were heavier and had a higher density than normal DNA molecules grown with $^{14}NH_3$.

The technique for measuring the density of DNA is as follows: By centrifuging a concentrated solution of cesium chloride in water, a density gradient is generated in the ultracentrifuge. It should be noted that this technique is an equilibrium method. At the start of the centrifugation the whole cell is filled with DNA solution in 7.7 M cesium chloride.

As the solution is spun, a density gradient forms and the DNA collects in a band in a position corresponding to its density; centrifugation is continued in the stable density gradient until the DNA band is in its equilibrium position and has its equilibrium width. In a typical experiment with 7.7 M cesium chloride, the density ranges from about 1.64 to 1.76 g/ml in a liquid column 1 cm high. The method is not suitable for proteins, because they have molecular weights of the order of 1 per cent, or less, of those of DNA and therefore form much broader bands in the density gradient. This is because the protein molecules, being smaller, diffuse much more rapidly. For DNA, the band will be narrow because the large DNA molecules diffuse slowly, so that the concentrating forces, which are those of buoyancy at the bottom of the band and centrifugation at the top of the band, overcome the diffusion forces. In fact, the higher the molecular weight the sharper the band, so that the width of the DNA band is a direct but not very sensitive method for measuring the molecular weight[7] of the DNA preparation. If a mixture of two DNAs is placed in the cell, one containing ^{14}N and one containing ^{15}N, two distinct separate bands are obtained at positions corresponding to the density of these two molecules.

This method is quite sensitive for distinguishing molecules with small differences in their densities; the DNA from E. coli has a (buoyant) density of 1.709 for ^{14}N-DNA and 1.725 for ^{15}N-DNA. Since the mean-residue weight per nucleotide is 300 and since the average nucleotide has approximately four nitrogen

FIGURE 2–10 *Ultraviolet-light photograph of ultracentrifuge cell containing DNA from the* ^{15}NH₃ *labeling experiment (see text) in a cesium chloride gradient. The dark bands show the location of DNA's of different densities. Density increases from left to right. (Photograph by courtesy of Dr. M. Meselson.)*

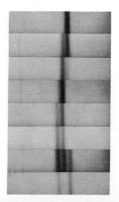

Generations after transfer

0

0.28

0.71

1.14

1.57

2.00

0 and 2 mixed

^{14}N and ^{15}N mixed for comparison

atoms, the molecular weight increases in going from ^{14}N-DNA to ^{15}N-DNA by a little more than 1 per cent.

In the experiment (see Figure 2–10), bacteria originally grown in ^{15}NH$_3$ were transferred to new medium containing ^{14}NH$_3$ and allowed to grow. DNA was isolated at various times and banded in the cesium chloride density gradient. As may be seen in the figure, at zero-generation time only a single band was obtained corresponding to ^{15}N-DNA. After a short time of growth, during which the DNA would partially replicate, a new lighter band was seen in the gradient, corresponding in density to a hybrid DNA molecule composed equally of chains carrying ^{15}N and, presumably, new chains carrying ^{14}N. By the time a whole generation had passed, all the DNA was in the form of this hybrid. This is exactly what we would expect from the semiconservative model illustrated in Figure 2–9.

After further growth until two generation cycles have been completed, two bands of DNA of equal intensity are found in the density gradient. These are the hybrid DNA containing ^{14}N and ^{15}N and also a lighter band corresponding to DNA having only ^{14}N and therefore being entirely composed of new DNA. Such completely light DNA after two generations must have been formed by the replication of the single ^{14}N-DNA strand present in the hybrid molecule after one generation. These results strongly support the semiconservative mode of replication of the DNA molecule.

It should be pointed out however that these results have also been interpreted[8] as being consistent with a model of replication in which the hybrid molecule is composed of two double helices, one entirely heavy (^{15}N) and the other entirely light (^{14}N); in other words the results are interpreted as consistent with conservative replication. Meselson and Stahl endeavored to cover this point in their experiments by denaturing the DNA hybrid and by showing that the molecular weight of the two single strands was half that of the original hybrid molecule. The point here is that, on heat denaturation, the two strands of the hybrid DNA molecule come apart and form two separate bands in the density gradient. These bands appear in new positions, because denatured DNA has a higher density than native DNA.

In semiconservative replication, the single strands of denatured DNA should have half the molecular weight of the native hybrid molecule. In the case of the conservative model mentioned above, the strands of denatured DNA should have a molecular weight one-quarter that of the hybrid molecule. The experimental results favored again the semiconservative model, but the experimental accuracy was not sufficiently high to make the results entirely clear-cut. However, put together, the evidence in favor of semiconservative replication is sufficient to allow us to accept this model.

In this connection (see also later) we should mention that the denatured DNA can reform to the native form[9] in spite of the fact that in denatured DNA the two strands have come apart.

PROPERTIES OF DNA

In the isolation of DNA a major difficulty is to keep such a long rigid molecule physically intact. It has been shown[10-12] that the shear forces set up when a solution of DNA is vigorously stirred are sufficient to break the long rigid DNA molecule. The molecules are first broken near the middle, then into quarters, and so on until a short-enough size is reached that the molecule will be relatively insensitive to breakage by shearing.

It is difficult to extrapolate the molecular weight of DNA found in solution to the actual molecular weight that exists in vivo because of the great ease of degradation by shear during extraction or by the inadvertent action of hydrolytic exzymes. Perhaps the best estimates are derived from radioautographic work in which the DNA is labeled with tritium. For example, in *E. coli*, Cairns[1] was able to detect DNA molecules up to 1.1 mm in length. This corresponds to a molecular weight of 2.8×10^9. Similarly the DNA from T2 bacteriophage has an average length of 49 μ, which would correspond to a molecular weight of 10^8. A rather smaller bacteriophage, called λ, has a DNA 23 μ in length. But even in the most carefully prepared samples of extracted DNA there is always 0.1 to 0.2 per cent of protein attached to the material. Therefore the possibility that a DNA molecule is actually made up of shorter lengths of DNA held together by protein or peptide-like materials cannot be completely ruled out (see review in Reference 13).

A method for isolating DNA almost free from protein and RNA was published, for example, by Marmur.[14] The walls of bacterial cells are digested with the enzyme lysozyme or broken with a detergent. Sodium perchlorate is used to dissociate protein and nucleic acid, and the solution is deproteinized by shaking it with a mixture of chloroform and isoamyl alcohol. RNA is removed with ribonuclease or by centrifugation in a density gradient of cesium chloride. In this gradient, RNA, which has a much higher density than DNA, is pelleted at the bottom of the centrifuge tube. The DNA may be selectively precipitated with isopropyl alcohol. Attack by deoxyribonuclease can be minimized if the operations are conducted in the presence of chelating agents or in the presence of a detergent such as sodium dodecyl sulfate. This procedure yields biologically active DNA such as, for example, transforming DNA. The DNA obtained however is somewhat degraded by the shear forces developed during shaking.

An alternate procedure for isolating highly polymerized DNA from animal tissues is the phenol-extraction method of Kirby,[15] in which proteins are denatured at the phenol-water interphase and the nucleic acids are extracted into the aqueous layer. RNA would be removed as mentioned above and the DNA precipitated.

For examination in the electron microscope, solutions of DNA are sprayed onto the grid and dried rapidly. Native DNA clearly gives long, stiff rod-like molecules, whereas the heat-denatured or otherwise-denatured (random-coil) molecules form "puddles."

Almost all the native DNAs in solution from a large variety of sources have the double-stranded structure as shown by the hyperchromic shift (see below) that occurs when a DNA solution is heated. On the other hand, denatured DNA is a flexible, loosely coiled, polyelectrolyte chain, very dependent in its hydrodynamic properties on the ionic environment. In fact, the denatured DNA in solution is rather similar to high-molecular-weight RNA, which shows some, but by no means complete, secondary structure. Closely similar also are the single-stranded synthetic polyribonucleotides made by the enzyme polynucleotide phosphorylase.[16] A naturally occurring example of randomly coiled DNA is found in the small bacteriophage ϕX 174. In general, the secondary structure of native DNA depends on its content of the bases guanine and cytosine (G + C). The higher the G + C content, the stronger the forces holding the two chains together. This is possible because guanine and cytosine can form three hydrogen bonds when paired in the DNA structure, whereas adenine and thymine can only form two (see Figure 2–3).

The *hyperchromic shift* is the increase in absorbency observed when double-stranded DNA is denatured to the single-stranded form. In an analogous case (Figure 2–11), the two polyribonucleotides polyadenylic acid and polyuridylic acid *when mixed together* have a lower absorbency at 260 mμ than that calculated for the two polymers measured separately. This is so because these polyribonucleotides can form base pairs A − T. Poly*deoxy*ribonucleotides can be expected to behave in a similar

FIGURE 2–11   *Absorption spectra of equimolar quantities of polyadenylic acid and polyuridylic acid. The upper curve refers to the mononucleotides obtained by alkaline hydrolysis.*

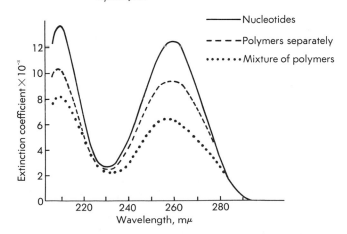

manner.   Another way of observing the hyperchromic shift is by destroying the double-stranded helical structure through the hydrolytic action of a nuclease (Figure 2–12).

There is in addition the *residual hyperchromism,* which is present even in the separately measured single-stranded polymers and which only becomes apparent when the polymer is broken down to mononucleotides.   Even di- and trinucleotides show residual hyperchromism.   It is presumably due to an interaction between bases linked to each other as oligo- or polynucleotides.

The native structure of DNA is stable in the pH range 2.7 to 12 and the molecule becomes denatured either below or above these pH values.   DNA configuration is unstable at room temperature at an ionic strength less than $10^{-4}M$.   If the optical density at 260 mμ is read at 25°C for T2 DNA (see curve *a* in Figure 2–13), it will be observed that there is no change in the absorbency when such a solution is heated until a temperature of around 75°C is reached.   If heating is continued, the optical density of the DNA solution increases by about 35 per cent over a range of perhaps 4°C.   Eventually the absorbency levels out at a value characteristic of the denatured form of DNA.   Denatured DNA may be detected by examination in the electron microscope or by the great decrease in the viscosity of the DNA solution.

FIGURE 2–12   *Increase in ultraviolet-light absorption at 260 mμ of natural and synthetic DNA upon digestion with pancreatic deoxyribonuclease.*

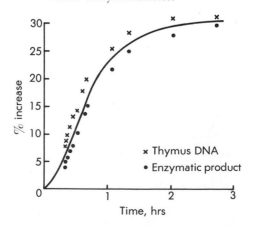

To describe the hyperchromic effect quantitatively, we may define it in terms of a temperature T_m at which the process is half complete. The value of T_m is characteristic for a particular species of DNA and it is dependent, to a first approximation, on the content of G + C in that DNA. In fact, Marmur and Doty[17] have deduced an empirical equation:

$$T_m = 69.3 + 0.41(G + C)$$

where G + C is the content of guanine plus cytosine as mole per cent of the total base content. The change in absorbency is characteristically and strikingly very sharp for DNA, indicating that the "melting out" of the double-helical structure of the DNA is a cooperative phenomenon. In other words, as soon as a few base pairs begin to come apart, there is an immediate corresponding facilitation of the melting out of neighboring base pairs. It also follows that the original DNA conformation must have been rather perfect and that most, if not all, of the bases are in their complementary Watson-Crick pairs.

If the heated solution is cooled rapidly, curve b (in Figure 2–13) is obtained, from which it is seen that the optical density does not return to its original value, even at 25°C. There is indeed a decrease in absorbency, but this is much less than the decrease to be expected, if the molecules of DNA returned to their original, highly ordered double-helical conformation. Preparations of DNA, which were heated and cooled rapidly, are still in the randomly coiled form at 25°C as may be seen by examination in the electron microscope and by the measurement of their relative viscosity.

If on the other hand the sample of heated DNA solution is cooled extremely slowly, taking perhaps 3 hr to cool from 91°C to 48°C, the absorbency of the DNA returns almost to its original value at 25°C; this is equivalent to saying that the double-helical structure with its exact base pairing is largely, if not completely, restored. Interestingly enough, Marmur, Doty, and their colleagues [9,18] have shown that, if this heating and slow cooling—this "annealing" process—is carried out with biologically active transforming DNA from D. pneumonia, it is possible to recover a considerable amount, perhaps 70 per cent, of the original biological activity. This high amount of reactivation of transforming ability indicates that the exact double-helical structure is reformed under these conditions, at least in some regions of the DNA molecule.

The optimum temperature for the renaturation of bacterial DNA is approximately 25° below its T_m, at 0.4M Na⁺ concentration. The DNA concentration should be kept low (at about 6 μg/ml) to minimize aggregation. Renaturation of DNA is a remarkable process, considering the very great length of the two randomly coiled single strands of denatured DNA which have to find their exact matching position to be able to reform an accurate double helix.

FIGURE 2–13   (a) *The hyperchromic shift on heating of native and of quickly or slowly cooled DNA from bacteriophage T2. Sample a was unheated; sample b was heated 15 min at 91°C and cooled quickly; sample c was treated like b, but then reheated and cooled slowly (165 min from 91° C to 48° C). Absorbancies were*

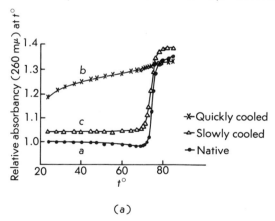

(a)

MECHANISM OF DNA BIOSYNTHESIS

During the replication of DNA, the sequence of nucleotides in the parent molecule must be accurately reproduced in the daughter molecules, since the genetic information contained in the sequence would otherwise be lost or distorted. Therefore it is likely than an enzyme system will exist that can synthesize double-stranded polydeoxyribonucleotides with Watson-Crick base pairing, but that also uses a primer DNA and reproduces the nucleotide sequence present in that primer DNA. It is generally believed that semiconservative replication occurs (see earlier); this implies that the two strands of the primer DNA molecule will separate at least locally where the enzyme is

measured on dialyzed samples after 15-fold dilution in 0.021 M Tris buffer, pH 7.5, containing 0.02 M NaCl. (b) Relation of guanine + cytosine content to denaturation temperature (T_m) for various DNA's in 0.15 M NaCl, 0.015 M citrate. [From J. Marmur, and P. Doty, Nature, **183**, 1427 (1959).]

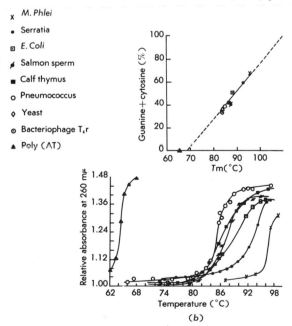

(b)

acting. A new single strand of DNA is then built up by the enzyme on each separate strand (see Figures 2–14 and 2–23).

Our knowledge of the in vitro enzymatic synthesis of DNA rests mainly on the work of Kornberg[19,19a] and his school in bacterial systems, and on Bollum's[20] work in a mammalian system. The original observation[21] was that crude extracts of *E. coli*, when incubated with radioactively labeled deoxynucleoside triphosphates, gave rise to a trace conversion of the soluble triphosphate into acid insoluble products. Out of 10^6 cpm added, some 50 cpm were incorporated. The result was interpreted to mean that a small amount of DNA had been synthesized, but that most of the product was broken down in these crude extracts by the nucleases that were undoubtedly present. Kornberg visualized the problem as one of enzyme purification, and

FIGURE 2–14 *Postulated mechanism for extending a DNA chain.*
(After A. Kornberg, Reference 19, chapter 2.)

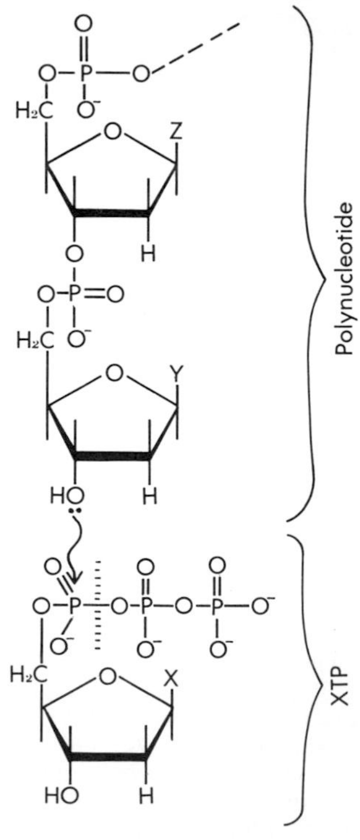

he and his colleagues spent the next years separating the DNA polymerase from contaminating nucleases. The enzyme is now several thousandfold purified, but still does not directly synthesize a biologically active DNA from a biologically active DNA primer that had transforming activity. Similar enzymes exist in other bacterial cells and in animal cells (see Bollum[20]).

REQUIREMENTS OF THE POLYMERASE

All four deoxynucleoside triphosphates must be present (dATP, dGTP, dTTP, dCTP), as given in Table 2–1.

$$
\left.
\begin{array}{l}
n \text{ dTTP} \\
n \text{ dGTP} \\
n \text{ dATP} \\
n \text{ dCTP}
\end{array}
\right\} + \text{DNA} \rightarrow \text{DNA}
\left\{
\begin{array}{l}
\text{dTP} \\
\text{dGP} \\
\text{dAP} \\
\text{dCP}
\end{array}
\right\}_n + 4n \text{ pyrophosphate} \qquad (2\text{–}1)
$$

DNA must be present as a *primer*. The DNA can be from animal, plant, bacterial, or virus sources. The priming DNA must have a high molecular weight and must be denatured to be efficient.

Synthesis may be obtained to the extent of 20 times or more of

T A B L E 2–1 *Requirements for deoxynucleotide incorporation into DNA*[a,b]

System	Deoxynucleotide incorporated, mµmoles
Complete system	0.50
Omit dCTP, dGTP, dATP	<0.01
Omit dCTP	<0.01
Omit dATP	<0.01
Omit Mg^{++}	<0.01
Omit DNA	<0.01
DNA pretreated with DNAase	<0.01

[a] From Reference 21.
[b] The complete system contained 5 µmoles of dTTP (dT^{32}P.PP, 1.5×10^6 cpm/µmole), dATP, dCTP, and dGTP, 1 µmole of MgCl$_2$, 20 µmoles of glycine buffer, pH 9.2, 10 µg of DNA, and 3 µg of "polymerase fraction V" in a final volume of 0.30 ml. The incubation was carried out at 37°C for 30 min.

T A B L E 2–2   *Liberation of inorganic pyrophosphate*[a,b]

Estimation	Control,[c] mμmoles	Experimental, mμmoles	Δ, mμmoles
^{14}C-DNA incorporation	1	25	24
^{32}P^{32}P released pyrophosphate	2	22	20
^{32}Pi released phosphate	7	11	4

[a] From Reference 21.
[b] The labeled substrate was dT^{32}P.^{32}P.^{32}P-2-^{14}C in the presence of the other three unlabeled triphosphates.
[c] dATP was omitted.

the weight of primer added until one of the substrates is exhausted. Inorganic pyrophosphate is released as shown in Eq. (2–1), in the reaction scheme of Figure 2–14, and in Table 2–2. The small amount of inorganic phosphate also released in Table 2–2 may be due to the presence of a pyrophosphatase.

If even one substrate is omitted, the extent of the reaction is diminished by a factor of 100 or so. Significant incorporation however is still obtained, but amounts to very little. In this so-called limited reaction (Table 2–3), the addition of only a few nucleotides occurs at the end of the primer chains, but this is also governed by base-pairing rules. The DNA-priming molecule may have ends of slightly unequal length; in such a situation we might suppose that the shorter chain would add a few nucleotides complementary to the nucleotides found in the longer sister chain, but there is no evidence for this. However, venom

T A B L E 2–3   *Incorporation of single deoxynucleotide into DNA*[a]

Additions	^{32}P-DNA, mμmoles
dCTP* + dGTP + dTTP + dATP	3300
dCTP* + dGTP + dTTP	15.7
dCTP* + dGTP	5.1
dCTP*	2.5
dCTP* (DNA omitted)	0.0

[a] The incubation mixture (0.3 ml) contained 5 mμmoles of dC^{32}P.PP (7.1 × 10^7 cpm/μmole), and of the other deoxynucleoside triphosphates, where indicated, 1 μmole MgCl$_2$, 20 μmoles glycine buffer, pH 9.2, 10 μg of DNA, and 3 μg of "enzyme fraction VI." The incubation was carried out at 37°C for 30 min. The DNA was isolated by precipitation. (From reference 21a.)

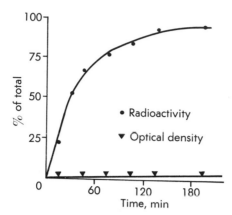

FIGURE 2–15   Action of snake venom phosphodiesterase on the product of the "limited reaction" of DNA polymerase.

phosphodiesterase, which removes nucleotides one at a time from the end of a chain, rapidly removes almost all the incorporated radioactivity while releasing only trace amounts of DNA as mononucleotides (Figure 2–15). This shows that the nucleotides added in the limited reaction were only added to one end of the DNA chain.

If we *omit the primer* DNA there is no synthesis at all. Presumably the necessary template is missing.

PHYSICAL PROPERTIES OF SYNTHESIZED DNA

As shown in Table 2–4, the new DNA has a sedimentation constant (see Glossary) of up to 25S, an intrinsic viscosity of up to 45 $(g/100 \text{ ml})^{-1}$, and an estimated molecular weight of up to 6×10^6 (Table 2–4). Of this material as much

T A B L E 2–4   *Physical properties of enzymatically synthesized DNA[a]*

Property	Primer	Product	Primer[b]	Product[b]
Sedimentation coefficient	25	20–25	20	14
Intrinsic viscosity $(g/100 \text{ ml})^{-1}$	40–50	15–45	<1	<1
Molecular weight	8×10^6	$4\text{–}6 \times 10^6$		

[a] From reference 21C.
[b] Heated at 100°C for 15 min.

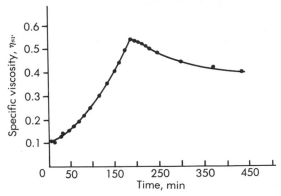

FIGURE 2–16   *The increase in specific viscosity of a solution during the synthesis of DNA by DNA polymerase.*

as 95 per cent is newly synthesized from the substrates supplied. Physically, the newly synthesized DNA is very similar to many preparations of native high-molecular-weight double-stranded DNA. Figure 2–16 shows the increase in viscosity during the enzymatic synthesis of new DNA molecules. With respect to its behavior on melting out (measured by increase in optical density) on heating, the usual hyperchromic effect is observed indicating the transition to the random-coil state. The synthesized DNA differs however from the original primer DNA in that it renatures readily after heating. The melting out occurs over a short range of temperature and is as sharp as with native DNA. The synthetic DNA is degraded by pancreatic deoxyribonuclease.

Heat-denatured DNA is an excellent primer for *E. coli* DNA polymerase. Denatured DNA, which is relatively nonviscous in solution, which forms a random coil, and which is single-stranded, promotes the formation of double-stranded DNA which has a very high intrinsic viscosity. When ϕX 174 DNA is used as the primer, double-stranded DNA is formed. Normal *E. coli* DNA polymerase *prefers* denatured DNA as a primer. However, after infection of *E. coli* with the bacterial virus (bacteriophage) T2, the formation of a new and different enzyme is induced (Chapter 4 in Reference 19), which *requires* denatured DNA as a primer[19a] (see Table 2–10). The same is true for the DNA polymerase prepared from calf thymus gland.[20]

ANALOG INCORPORATION

As can be seen from Table 2–5, deoxynucleoside triphosphates can be used in which the normal base is substituted by a chemical analog. For example, deoxy-UTP can take the place of deoxy-TTP, but not the place of any of the other three bases. The same is true of 5-bromo-dUTP and 5-fluoro-dUTP. The figures given in Table 2–5 were obtained in four separate experiments for each base analog tested. Each of the four columns represents an experiment where the particular deoxynucleoside triphosphate was omitted and replaced by the base analog triphosphate. This was done with each of the usual four deoxynucleoside triphosphates in turn. In many cases *E. coli* polymerase as well as T2 polymerase was tested.

The results are more or less those that would be expected on the basis of the chemical relationship between the base analogs and the naturally occurring bases. What was rather unex-

TABLE 2–5   *Replacement of natural bases by analogs in the enzymatic synthesis of DNA*[c]

Analog, used in form of deoxynucleoside triphosphate	Deoxynucleoside triphosphate replaced by analog, % of control value			
	dTTP	dATP	dCTP	dGTP
Uracil	54	0	0	0
5-Bromouracil	97(100)[a]	0(0)	0(0)	0(0)
5-Fluorouracil	32(9)	0(0)	0(0)	0(0)
5-Hydroxymethylcytosine[b]	(0)	(0)	-(98)	(0)
5-Methylcytosine	0	0	185	0
5-Bromocytosine	0(0)	0(0)	118(104)	0(0)
5-Fluorocytosine	0(0)	0(0)	63(67)	0(0)
N-Methyl-5-fluorocytosine	0	0	0	0
Hypoxanthine	0	0	0	25
Xanthine	0	0	0	0

[a] Values in parentheses were measured with T2-induced DNA polymerase; the others were measured with normal **E. coli** polymerase. Zero values represent those of less than 2% in most cases, and in all cases do not differ significantly from the background of this assay. Control values were measured as rates of radioactive deoxynucleotide incorporation into DNA in a standard assay system in the presence of dTTP, dATP, dCTP, and dGTP, with heated salmon sperm DNA as primer for T2 polymerase and calf thymus DNA for **E. coli** polymerase.
[b] This analog is quite inactive with normal **E. coli** polymerase. It was not tested with this enzyme in the experiment.
[c] From Reference 19.

pected, however, was to find that 5-methylcytosine-deoxynucleoside triphosphate not only replaced deoxy-CTP, but was utilized much more efficiently than the naturally occurring base. There is at present no rational explanation for this phenomenon. We note that at the level tested, no base analogs were able to replace any nucleoside triphosphate other than their natural analog. Of course a very small amount of substitution might not have been detected in these experiments. This is an important possibility, because it is frequently supposed that trace incorporations of analogs lead to changes in the genetic information and therefore to mutations.

CHEMICAL COMPOSITION OF SYNTHESIZED DNA

The enzymatically produced DNA has a base composition that shows A = T, and G = C, as did the primer DNA. The ratio A + T/G + C is equal to the ratio that is characteristic of the primer DNA (see Table 2–6). Moreover, this characteristic ratio is obtained in the product whether the extent of synthesis is small, say, 10 per cent or so by weight of the primer added, or whether synthesis is extensive and 10- to 20-fold. This last statement is equivalent to saying that, when only relatively short stretches of DNA molecule are copied, the base composition of such a region is essentially the same as that for the whole DNA molecule; even such a relatively short DNA region is, in terms of

TABLE 2–6 *Nucleotide composition of enzymatically synthesized DNA*[a]

Primer DNA	Ap	Tp	Gp	Cp	Product $\dfrac{A+G}{T+C}$	Product $\dfrac{A+T}{G+C}$	Primer $\dfrac{A+T}{G+C}$
Micrococcus lyso-deikticus	0.147	0.145	0.354	0.354	1.00	0.41	0.39
E. coli	0.248	0.254	0.249	0.249	0.99	1.01	0.97
Calf thymus	0.286	0.283	0.214	0.217	1.00	1.26	1.29
Bacteriophages T2, T4, T6	0.319	0.318	0.184	0.179	1.01	1.76	1.84
dAT copolymer (. . . ATATATA . . .)	0.500	0.500	0.002	0.002	1.00	>250	>40

[a] From Reference 19.

TABLE 2–7   *Effect of relative substrate concentrations on composition of synthetic DNA*[a]

Substrates, relative molar concentration				Net synthesis	Products	
dCTP	dGTP	dTTP	dATP		$\dfrac{A+T}{G+C}$	$\dfrac{A+G}{T+C}$
1.0	1.0	1.0	1.0	11-fold	1.98	1.00
1.0	1.0	0.2	1.0	6-fold	1.82	1.04
1.0	1.0	0.2	0.2	6-fold	1.82	0.97
T2 bacteriophage as primer.					1.92	0.98

[a] From Reference 21c.

nucleotide sequence, already exceedingly long. Alternatively, and perhaps more likely, during replication of double-stranded DNA, only a small proportion of molecules are copied, but completely. If this is so, they must resemble the rest of the primer-DNA molecules in terms of the ratio $A + T/G + C$. The reproduction of the characteristic $A + T/G + C$ ratio in the product is an important part of the experimental proof that the nucleotide sequence of the priming DNA is reproduced

FIGURE 2–17   *The synthesis of dAT copolymer in the unprimed reaction as measured by viscosity, absorbancy at 260 mμ and incorporation of ^{32}P radioactivity into acid-insoluble products. The lag period is slightly different in the two experiments. (From A. Kornberg, Reference 19, chapter 2.)*

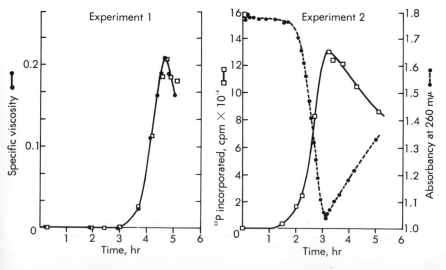

in the synthetic DNA. As can be seen in Tables 2–6 and 2–7, the ratios obtained are quite close to the expected ratios within the experimental error of the methods employed.

If one of the four nucleoside triphosphates is omitted from the incubation mixture, enzymatic synthesis of DNA by DNA polymerase stops almost completely. Only traces of nucleotides are incorporated under these conditions. When the purified DNA polymerase is incubated with deoxy-ATP and deoxy-TTP as the only nucleoside triphosphates, nothing happens for several hours. Later there is a fairly rapid formation of a DNA-like material (Figures 2–17 and 2–18); the reaction is self-primed and the duration of the lag period appears to be a function of the purity of the enzyme. The DNA-like material produced contains equal quantities of adenine and thymine incorporated into a DNA-like structure. The base sequence of this material is well defined, being composed of alternating A and T nucleotides:

...A.T.A.T.A.T.A.T...

...T.A.T.A.T.A.T.A...

FIGURE 2–18   *The effect of primer on the synthesis of dAT co-polymer by DNA polymerase.   (From A. Kornberg, Reference 19, chapter 2.)*

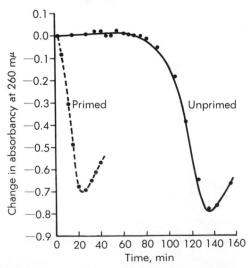

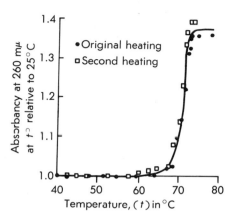

FIGURE 2–19 *Melting of the dAT copolymer. After the first heat-ing cycle the solution was cooled; before being re-heated the absorbancy at low temperature returned to its original value, indicating that the double helical structure had reformed. (From A. Kornberg, Ref-erence 19, chapter 2.)*

The polymer is highly viscous and of high molecular weight, indicating that it is probably double helical in structure and composed of two complementary strands. It has a lower melting-out temperature compared to DNA (Figure 2–19), although the transition of the hyperchromic shift is as sharp as in real DNA. The T_m of the dAT polymer in 0.2 M NaCl and 0.1 M sodium citrate is approximately 72°C, but at low ionic strength it can be as low as 41°C. In contrast to ordinary DNA, fast cooling allows a double-stranded structure to reform rapidly, and the solution returns to its normal absorbency at 25°C. A second heating of the same material produces a melting-out curve almost identical with the first one (Figure 2–19). Presum-ably it is the highly regular and very simple base sequence of this dAT copolymer that enables a double-stranded structure to reform with such great ease. It is easy for a base in one strand to find its correct partner in the other strand, and when it does, neighboring bases will automatically be "in register." Possibly these molecules fold back on themselves in order to obtain the stable double-stranded structure. The sedimentation coefficient of the dAT copolymer is approximately 17 S, which, together with a determination of the viscosity, gave a value for the molecular weight of 2 to 8×10^6. This, in other words, is very high-molecular-weight material. Another important property of the dAT copolymer is that it is capable of reducing the lag phase originally observed in the formation of the copolymer (Figure 2–18). dAT copolymer thus acts as an excellent primer in the DNA-polymerase reaction for the polymerization of dATP and dTTP. Even when the other two nucleoside triphosphates, dGTP and dCTP, are present, no trace of them is incorporated under these conditions.

There are however other conditions of much higher substrate and enzyme concentrations where, in an unprimed reaction, dGTP and dCTP polymerize to high-molecular-weight products in which two homopolymers—poly-dG and poly-dC—form a double helix (see later).

NUCLEOTIDE SEQUENCES OF SYNTHETIC DNA

The best proof that the newly synthesized DNA copies the nucleotide sequence of the original priming DNA was obtained by Josse, Kaiser, and Kornberg[22] through analysis of the nearest-neighbor frequencies of particular bases. The experimental approach is shown in Figure 2–20. A new nucleotide, Y-^{32}P-P-P, is added to the end of the nucleotide chain by means of the DNA polymerase. In this case, radioactive phosphorus occupies the phosphate nearest to the base in the incoming molecule:

Y—deoxyribose—O—(^{32}P)—O—(P)—O—(P)

Pyrophosphate is released during the reaction. The labeled phosphate group of the entering residue now forms the 3′–5′ linkage, which attaches the new nucleotide to the existing chain. Synthesis is allowed to proceed in the presence of three unlabeled nucleoside triphosphates and the one labeled nucleoside triphosphate. The DNA made in this enzymatic reaction is isolated and purified and then simultaneously degraded with micrococcal deoxyribonuclease and with spleen phosphodies-

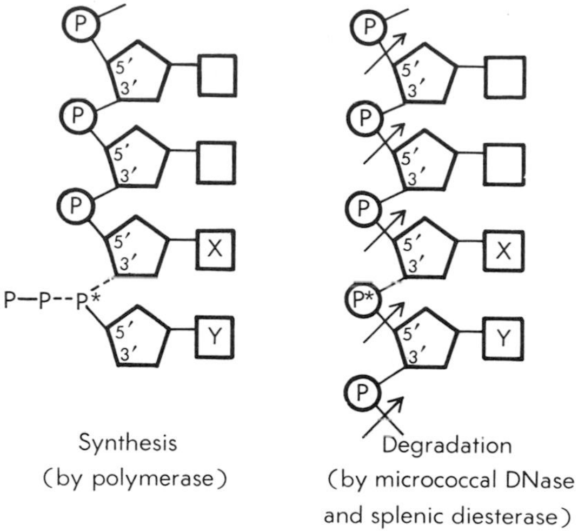

Synthesis
(by polymerase)

Degradation
(by micrococcal DNase
and splenic diesterase)

FIGURE 2–20   *Synthesis of a* ^{32}*P-labeled DNA chain and its sub-*
sequent enzymatic degradation to 3′-deoxyribonu-
cleotides. The arrows indicate the linkages cleaved by
micrococcal deoxyribonuclease and calf-spleen phos-
phodiesterase, yielding a digest composed entirely of
3′-deoxyribonucleotides. (From A. Kornberg, Refer-
ence 19, chapter 2.)

terase. As illustrated in Figure 2–20, this results in complete degradation of the DNA to mononucleotides, which all have the phosphate in the 3′ position. It can be seen that the radioactive phosphorus atom, which originally was covalently attached to base Y, is now attached to the neighboring base X. By measuring the specific radioactivity of the X-3′-phosphate mononucleotide obtained in the enzymatic degradation of the synthetic DNA, the proportion of XpY neighboring pairs may be estimated. By convention the abbreviation XpY stands for X-3′-(P)-5′-Y. If, for example, in this experiment the radioactively labeled triphosphate was deoxy-ATP, by measuring the amount of radioactivity in the 3′ phosphates of all four bases, the *relative* frequencies of all four possible neighboring pairs of the type CpA, GpA, etc., may be obtained (=C-3′-(P)-5′-A, etc.). From four such experiments in each of which a different nucleoside triphosphate is radioactively labeled, the frequencies of all 16 possible neighboring pairs can be estimated. This is done by multiplying each of the "frac-

T A B L E   2–8   *Radioactivity measurements in experiments with Mycobacterium phlei DNA as primer*[a]

Isolated 3′-deoxy-ribonucleo-tide	Sequence	cpm	Fraction
	Incubation with dAT^{32}*P*		
Tp^{32}	TpA	873	0.075
Ap^{32}	ApA	1,710	0.146
Cp^{32}	CpA	4,430	0.378
Gp^{32}	GpA	4,690	0.401
Total		11,703	1.000
	Incubation with dTT^{32}*P*		
Tp^{32}	TpT	1,665	0.157
Ap^{32}	ApT	2,065	0.194
Cp^{32}	CpT	2,980	0.279
Gp^{32}	GpT	3,945	0.370
Total		10,655	1.000
	Incubation with dGT^{32}*P*		
Tp^{32}	TpG	3,490	0.187
Ap^{32}	ApG	2,500	0.134
Cp^{32}	CpG	7,730	0.414
Gp^{32}	GpG	4,960	0.265
Total		18,680	1.000
	Incubation with dCT^{32}*P*		
Tp^{32}	TpC	4,130	0.182
Ap^{32}	ApC	4,300	0.189
Cp^{32}	CpC	6,070	0.268
Gp^{32}	GpC	8,200	0.361
Total		22,700	1.000

[a] From Reference 22.

tions" obtained for example in the incubation with dAT^{32}P by the mole fraction of A in the whole DNA. In this way all four columns of fractions together will add up to 1.00 (see Table 2–8). It should be noted that the incorporation of purine ^{32}P equals the incorporation of pyrimidine ^{32}P. In other words the Watson-Crick type of pairing is exact.

Once the nearest-neighbor frequencies of a specimen of synthetic DNA have been established by these techniques, this same DNA may be used as a primer in another round of DNA

synthesis by DNA polymerase in which the nearest-neighbor
frequencies in the product are again estimated. Obviously this
experiment would have to be done under conditions where
extensive replication occurred, so that the great bulk of the
newly synthesized material would be derived from the precursors
and not from the primer. If such an experiment is carried out, it
is found that the nearest-neighbor frequencies of the product
correspond closely to those of the priming DNA.

More importantly perhaps, this experiment enabled Kornberg
to distinguish between two possible models of the double-
stranded DNA structure, namely, *one* in which the two strands
were parallel with respect to the direction of their 3'-5'
linkages, and *second* a model in which the two strands are
antiparallel. Using the principle of Watson-Crick base pairing
and complementarity in the two strands, one would predict for a
model of DNA with *parallel* strands that a dinucleotide pair,
such as TpA, should occur with a frequency equal to that of the
complementary pair ApT. If on the other hand the structure of

FIGURE 2–21   *Comparison of a Watson-Crick model of DNA with
strands of opposite polarities and a model with strands
of similar polarities. The corresponding predicted
nearest-neighbor frequencies are different in the two
models. Values in parentheses are experimental results from the experiment in Table 2–8. (From
A. Kornberg, Reference 19, chapter 2.)*

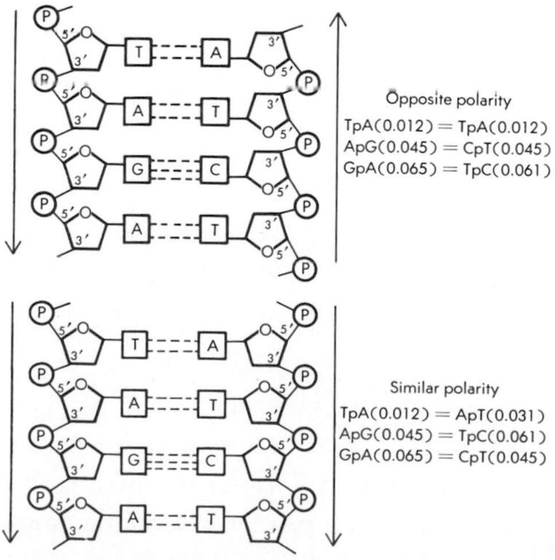

Opposite polarity

TpA(0.012) = TpA(0.012)
ApG(0.045) = CpT(0.045)
GpA(0.065) = TpC(0.061)

Similar polarity

TpA(0.012) = ApT(0.031)
ApG(0.045) = TpC(0.061)
GpA(0.065) = CpT(0.045)

the DNA has strands of opposite polarity (antiparallel), the complementary neighbor pairs are TpA equal TpA (see Figure 2–21). Other examples perhaps even more diagnostic are shown in Figure 2–21. The nearest-neighbor frequencies reported support the model in which the strands of the DNA molecule have *opposite polarity*. Of course not all pairs of neighbors are diagnostic in this connection, but all of those which are agree with the model of opposite polarity.

REPLICATION OF SINGLE-STRANDED DNA

In a hypothetical example (Figure 2–22) to test the replication of the single-stranded oligonucleotide TTCAGTG, the ratio A/T in this primer = 0.33, whereas the ratio A + T/G + C is 1.33. If such a primer were to be used with DNA polymerase in the presence of all four nucleoside triphosphates, after limited replication (20 per cent increase in DNA), the newly formed material will have the complementary base sequence of the primer. The ratio A/T is now the inverse of that in the primer,

FIGURE 2–22 *Scheme for replication of a hypothetical single stranded DNA (see text). The original primer sequence is in bold-face type. (From A. Kornberg, Reference 19, chapter 2.)*

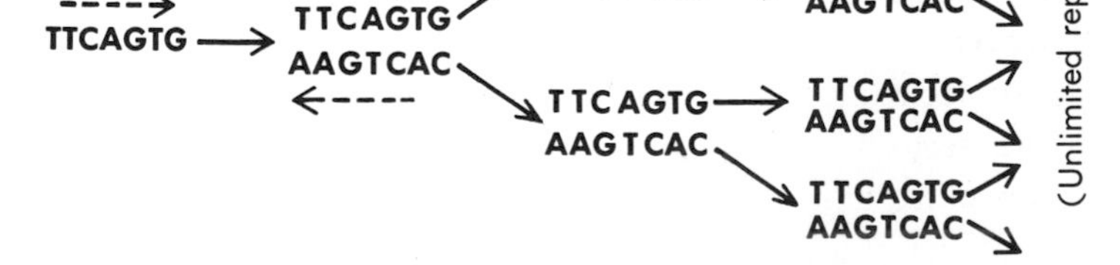

	Original primer	Limited replication	Extensive replicaton	
A/T	0.33	3.0 (new strands)	1.15 (new strands)	(1.00)
G/C	2.0	0.5	0.91	(1.00)
$\frac{A + T}{G + C}$	1.33	1.33	1.33	(1.33)

T A B L E 2–9 *Composition of products after limited and extensive replication of φX DNA*[a]

Base	Primer composition determined by chemical analysis[b]	20% synthesis		600% synthesis		
		Predicted from chemical analysis	Observed	Predicted[e] from chemical analysis	Predicted[e] from 20% synthesis	Observed
A	0.246	0.328	0.310	0.287	0.276	0.271
T	0.328	0.246	0.242	0.287	0.276	0.293
G	0.242	0.185	0.202	0.214	0.224	0.213
C	0.185	0.242	0.246	0.214	0.224	0.224

(The two 20%/600% synthesis groups share a common heading: **Composition of product determined by nearest-neighbor analysis**)

[a] From Reference 19.
[b] From Reference 23.
[e] Based on the replication of double-stranded DNA.

namely, 3.0; the ratio G/C is also the inverse, but the ratio A + T/G + C has remained unchanged at 1.33. If replication is allowed to proceed to a considerable increase, say sixfold, the ratios A/T and G/C will approximate to 1.0, but the ratio A + T/G + C, which is characteristic of the nucleotide sequence of the primer, will remain unchanged at 1.33. Taking as an actual example that of the single-stranded φX DNA, as illustrated in Table 2–9, 20 per cent synthesis gives a base ratio having the complementary composition of the input primer DNA; at this stage, the original single-stranded DNA, or rather portions of it, will have been copied, following the demands of the Watson-Crick specific base pairing.

It should be noted in passing that we are assuming that either 20 per cent of the molecules were each copied completely or that each molecule has been copied to the extent of only 20 per cent. In the second case we are also saying that the nucleotide sequence in that 20 per cent of the original primer-DNA molecule resembles the sequence of the whole molecule.

If synthesis is allowed to proceed to the extent of some 600 per cent, the base ratios approximate those of the regular DNA pattern in which A = T, etc.; as can be seen from the table, the results support this model. However, the ratio A + T/G + C remains unchanged, whether synthesis is limited or extensive. The explanation that, on the average, one-fifth of each molecule is replicated in the limited synthesis appears to be correct, because density-gradient-centrifugation experiments indicate that nearly all, i.e., more than 85 per cent, of the ϕX DNA is combined with some new DNA.[24]

Kornberg and his colleagues[19a] were able to show that the primer DNA is not covalently attached to the product DNA after extensive replication. The primer DNA may be recovered under conditions that do not involve the breakage of covalent bonds. The primer acts merely as a template providing the DNA polymerase with the necessary information for the desired nucleotide sequence.

In addition to the earlier description of the de novo synthesis of the dAT copolymer, it was observed that, if the DNA polymerase was incubated with deoxy-GTP and deoxy-CTP as the only triphosphates, after a lag phase of about 10 hr a highly viscous, that is, a high-molecular-weight DNA-like material, was produced. The initial product would serve to prime the reaction, thus drastically reducing the lag phase normally encountered. In contrast to the dAT copolymer, the polymer produced did not contain equal numbers of G and C nucleotides. It turned out that the structure of the dGdC polymer was made up of two types of chain, one of which was a homopolymer of G and the other of C. Of course, two such polymers would come together to form a double-stranded molecule, but presumably there is enough slippage between neighboring strands to make it unnecessary for them to be of equal lengths. Such slippage is prevented in the case of the dAT copolymer by the strictly alternating base sequence.

REMAINING PROBLEMS IN THE ENZYMATIC SYNTHESIS OF DNA

As can be seen from Figure 2–23, a problem is encountered when one considers the simultaneous replication of two anti-parallel strands of DNA. When a DNA molecule begins to replicate, it is assumed that the first step is an unwinding of the

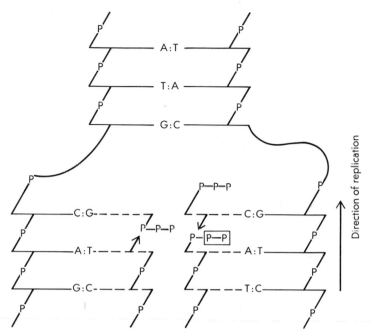

FIGURE 2–23 Diagram showing the "growing point" in a replicating DNA molecule, if both strands are duplicated simultaneously (see Figure 2–7a).

ends of such a molecule. Replication of each of the unwound portions of the chain could then proceed. It is also conceivable that replication could begin in the middle of a double helix, if there were a stretch of DNA that had loosened and untwisted. It then becomes immediately apparent that the direction in which these two chains grow would normally be opposite, just as the strands of the mother molecule show opposite polarity. However, from radioautographic studies it appears that, in fact, both chains of the DNA molecule replicate in the same direction. Therefore, in a model of *parallel chain growth*, one would expect (as shown in Figure 2–23) that there is nucleophilic attack by the 3′-hydroxyl group belonging to the end of the growing chain of one strand on the phosphate of the incoming nucleoside triphosphate. On the other hand, if the opposite strand is also growing in the same direction, the attacking 3'-hydroxyl group is that of the new, incoming nucleoside triphosphate. In that case pyrophosphate is derived from the end of the growing strand.

If this model of a simultaneous growth of two antiparallel chains in the same direction is correct, one should be able to detect the release of pyrophosphate from the growing point of the growing chain. Kornberg attempted to do this using label in the growing DNA molecule. Attack by cold nucleoside triphosphates should liberate radioactive pyrophosphate from the one strand of the growing chain, whereas the other chain should release cold pyrophosphate. Kornberg was unable to demonstrate that either of the growing chains can furnish a pyrophosphate group. Therefore we do not at the moment completely understand the mechanism whereby parallel growth of two antiparallel chains can take place.

What kind of priming DNA is required for the various DNA polymerase preparations is also not yet completely settled. It seems that the purest *E. coli* DNA-polymerase preparation is primed by heat-denatured or native DNA equally well[19a] (see Table 2–10), whereas earlier, cruder preparations preferred heat-denatured DNA. Recently, a special enzyme contaminant has been described in these preparations, which degrades one strand of native DNA, leaving single-stranded DNA the actual

T A B L E   2–10   *Rate and extent of DNA synthesis*[a]

DNA Polymerase	Heat-denatured DNA[b]		Native DNA[b]	
	Initial rate of incorporation[c]	Extent of synthesis[d]	Initial rate of incorporation[c]	Extent of synthesis[d]
E. coli	1.9	>10	1.5	>10
B. subtilis	1.0		0.8	2.5
T2 phage	5.2	0.7	0.2	<0.01

[a] From Reference 19a.
[b] Calf thymus DNA.
[c] mμmoles/μg enzyme protein/30 min.
[d] The extent of synthesis was determined in the presence of excess polymerase and deoxynucleoside triphosphates. The value for T2 phage polymerase with native DNA could not be increased by additions of more enzyme or more prolonged incubation.

primer. It is clear however that highly purified T2-induced DNA polymerase demands heat-denatured DNA for effective synthesis. The same is true for the mammalian DNA polymerase.

Another problem is the continued inability of the system to synthesize biologically active DNA. It is now unlikely that this is due to a hydrolytic or enzymatic destruction of the biologically active DNA molecules, which are used as templates in the reaction. Comparable preparations of RNA polymerase from *E. coli* do not degrade transforming DNA when this is used as a template, indicating that such RNA polymerase preparations are free of nucleases. It is hardly likely that the even more highly purified DNA polymerase would still contain nucleases not found in RNA polymerase preparations.

Another explanation has been put forward by Kornberg et al.,[10a] who observed that, in the electron microscope, synthetic DNA frequently showed branch points, whereas native DNA did not. In order to explain such possible branch points in the product (Figure 2–24), it was thought that, in the *in vitro* enzymatic reaction, there was sufficient slippage or sufficient inexactness of nucleotide complementarity that the newly formed DNA strands could form loops. Such loops would not necessarily continue to transmit the same genetic information on further replication. Moreover, the formation of loops would disturb the continuity of base sequences along the new strand. An alternative scheme can be proposed. By copying one strand of a DNA molecule and then crossing over and copying the partner strand, as shown in Figure 2–25, it is quite possible that branch points might arise. Either mechanism would result in a synthetic DNA that did not have the correct nucleotide sequence and was therefore biologically inactive. If branch points are formed on the original DNA molecules, even the original DNA would no longer be intact as far as its nucleotide sequence and base pairs are concerned.

In any case it is entirely possible that, during the in vitro synthesis of DNA by DNA polymerase, there may be a certain bias in base sequences synthesized which does not exist in vivo. Such bias is shown by the enzyme when it produces in vitro dAT copolymer and the polymers dGdC by unprimed reactions. Preferred synthesis of certain nucleotide sequences might result in a disordered sequence of a few nucleotides in the product, a defect which would be quite sufficient to destroy the biological activity of the material.

If these explanations are correct, it is not at all clear why DNA polymerase works so well in vivo. Is this due to the presence or the particular concentration of some crucial metal ions? We know that the specificity of the enzyme can be altered quite remarkably in vitro, because, in the presence of manganous ions (Mn^{++}), ribose ATP can be incorporated into a DNA-like

FIGURE 2–24   *Electron micrograph of the product of extensive synthesis (five replications) of B. subtilis DNA by E. coli DNA polymerase. This photograph shows a great increase of branch points compared to photos of the original primer. (Courtesy of A. Kornberg, see also Reference 19a, chapter 2.)*

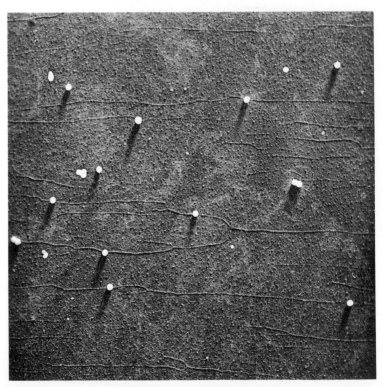

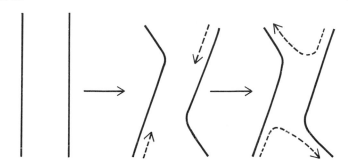

FIGURE 2–25 *Diagram showing a possible mechanism by which branch points may be formed during the synthesis of DNA by DNA polymerase. The dashed lines indicate the newly synthesized strands of DNA. (After A. Kornberg, Reference 19, chapter 2.)*

structure.[25] It may well be that the stereochemistry of the active site of the enzyme is different in the intact cell. In any case, in order for the enzyme to copy exactly a nucleotide sequence, more is required than the simple base-pairing requirements of the Watson-Crick structure. These by themselves would not be enough to hold the appropriate incoming nucleoside triphosphate in its correct place while synthesis takes place. We should think of the selection of the correct nucleoside triphosphate as the result of the restrictive stereochemistry of the active site of the enzyme *together with* the specific base-pairing requirements.

If it is true that in vitro as well as in vivo the actual template DNA is single-stranded DNA, and if the synthetic reaction produces double-stranded molecules only, the reaction should stop when the primer DNA has doubled. An increase beyond this point is only possible if the polymerase itself, or some other enzyme, can convert double-stranded DNA into the denatured single-stranded DNA form. The present enzyme preparations are not pure enough to observe such a limit. Impurities such as nucleases may in fact produce a conversion of the double-stranded primer to the active single-stranded form.[19a]

REFERENCES

1. Cairns, J. (1961), "An Estimate of the Length of the DNA Molecule of T2 Bacteriophage by Autoradiography." *J. Mol. Biol.*, **3**, 756.

2. Luzzati, V., Nicolaieff, A., and Masson, F. (1961), "Structure of DNA in Solution: Studied by Small Angle X-ray Scattering (article in French)." *J. Mol. Biol.*, **3**, 185.

3. Hamilton, L. D., Barclay, R. K., Wilkins, M. H. F., Brown, G. L., Wilson, H. R., Marvin, D. A., Ephrussi-Taylor, H., and Simmons, N. S. (1959), *J. Biophys. Biochem. Cytology*, **5**, 397.

4. Levinthal, C., and Davison, P. F. (1961), "Degradation of DNA under Hydrodynamic Shearing Forces." *J. Mol. Biol.*, **3**, 674.

5. Cairns, J. (1963), "The Chromosome of *Escherichia coli*." *Cold Spring Harb. Symp. Quant. Biol.*, **28**, 43.

6. Meselson, M., and Stahl, F. W. (1958), "The Replication of DNA in *Escherichia coli*." *Proc. Natl. Acad. Sci.*, **44**, 671.

7. Meselson, M., Stahl, F. W., and Vinograd, J. (1957), *Proc. Natl. Acad. Sci.*, **43**, 581.

8. Cavalieri, L. F., and Rosenberg, B. H. (1962), "Nucleic Acids: Molecular Biology of DNA." *Ann. Rev. Biochem.*, **31**, 260.

9. Doty, P., Marmur, J., Eigner, J., and Schildkraut, C. (1960), "Strand Separation and Specific Recombination in Deoxyribonucleic Acids: Physical Chemistry Studies." *Proc. Natl. Acad. Sci.*, **46**, 461.

10. Cavalieri, L. F., and Rosenberg, B. H. (1959), "Shear Degradation of Deoxyribonucleic Acid." *J. Am. Chem. Soc.*, **81**, 5136.

11. Davidson, P. F. (1960), "Sedimentation of Deoxyribonucleic Acid Isolated under Low Hydrodynamic Shear." *Nature*, **185**, 918.

12. Rosenberg, H. S., and Bendich, H. (1960) *J. Am. Chem. Soc.*, **82**, 3198.

13. Bendich, A., and Rosenkranz, H. S. (1963), "Some Thoughts on the Double-Stranded Model of Deoxyribonucleic Acid." *Progr. Nucl. Acid Research*, **I**, 219.

14. Marmur, J. (1963), quoted by Kit, S., *Ann. Rev. Biochem.*, **32**, 44.

15. Kirby, K. S. (1963), quoted by Kit, S., *Ann. Rev. Biochem.*, **32**, 44.

16. Grunberg-Manago, M. (1962), "Enzymatic Synthesis of Nucleic Acids." *Ann. Rev. Biochem.*, **31**, see on page 305.

17. Marmur, J., and Doty, P. (1962), "Determination of the Base Composition of DNA from Its Thermal Denaturation Temperature." *J. Mol. Biol.*, **5**, 109.

18. Marmur, J., and Lane, D. (1960), "Strand Separation and Specific Recombination in Deoxyribonucleic Acids: Biological Studies." *Proc. Natl. Acad. Sci.*, **46**, 453.

19. Kornberg, A. (1961), "Enzymatic Synthesis of DNA." John Wiley & Sons, New York.

19a. Richardson, C. C., Schildkraut, C. L., and Kornberg, A. (1963), "Studies on the Replication of DNA by DNA Polymerases." *Cold Spring Harb. Symp. Quant. Biol.*, **28**, 9.

20. Bollum, F. J. (1963), " 'Primer' in DNA Polymerase Reactions." *Progr. Nucl. Acid Research*, **I**, I.

21. Lehman, I. R., Bessman, M. J., Simms, E. S., and Kornberg, A. (1958), "Enzymatic Synthesis of Deoxyribonucleic Acid." *J. Biol. Chem.*, **233**, 163 and 171.

21a. Kornberg, A. (1959), *Harvey Lectures, Series 53*, p. 83.

21b. Lehman, I. R. (1959), *Ann. N.Y. Acad. Sci.*, **81**, 745.

21c. Lehman, I. R., Zimmerman, S. B., Adler, J., Bessman, M. J., Simms, E. S., and Kornberg, A. (1958), *Proc. Natl. Acad. Sci.*, **44**, 1191.

22. Josse, J., Kaiser, A. D., and Kornberg, A. (1961), "Enzymatic Synthesis of DNA." *J. Biol. Chem.*, **236**, 864.

23. Sinsheimer, R. L. (1959), "A Single-Stranded DNA from Bacteriophage φX 174." *J. Mol. Biol.*, **1**, 43.

24. Spiegelman, S., and Hayashi, M. (1963), "The Present Status of the Transfer of Genetic Information and Its Control." *Cold Spring Harb. Symp. Quant. Biol.*, **28**, 161.

25. Berg, P., Fancher, H., and Chamberlin, M. (1963), "Informational Macromolecules." Academic Press, New York.

THREE $\int\int$ BIOSYNTHESIS OF RNA

THE RIBONUCLEIC ACIDS IN A BACTERIAL OR MAMMALIAN CELL may be classified into three groups, as far as we know today (Table 3–1): (1) *ribosomal* RNA, the major RNA component of the cell, which is found in ribosomes, (2) *messenger* RNA, which is the template for protein synthesis and presumably the synthetically active part of polyribosomes, and (3) *soluble* RNA, whose function it is to act as amino acid-adaptor molecules

TABLE 3–1 *Types of cellular RNA (E. coli)*

	Amount, % of total RNA	Molecular weight
Ribosomal RNA r-RNA	75–80	1.2×10^6 and 0.5×10^6
Messenger RNA m-RNA	5–10	Up to 2×10^6 (heterogeneous)
Soluble RNA s-RNA (= transfer RNA or t-RNA)	10–15	25,000

carrying specific amino acids into their specific places on the
protein synthesizing template.

Ribosomal RNA (r-RNA) is the bulk of the RNA inside the
cell (Table 3–1). Characteristically, it is composed of two
major components, a larger molecule with a molecular weight of
1.2 million and a sedimentation constant of 23 S, and a smaller
molecule with a molecular weight of 0.5 million and a sedimentation constant of approximately 16 S (see Figures 3–1 and
3–2). Ribosomes from a wide variety of tissues and bacterial
cells always seem to contain both classes of r-RNA, although the
actual sedimentation constants vary slightly from species to
species. Its function in the ribosomal particle is not known at
all; a structural role has been ascribed to r-RNA for want of a
better understood function.

Messenger RNA (m-RNA) accounts for between 5 and 10 per
cent of total RNA inside *E. coli* and makes up a similar
proportion in most actively growing cells. In contrast to
r-RNA, messenger RNA is heterogeneous in its molecular size,
having molecular weights up to 2 million with a correspondingly
wide range of sedimentation constants (see Figure 3–2). In a

FIGURE 3–1   *Elution pattern of E. coli RNA on a methylated al-
bumin column. The RNA was extracted from a crude
extract with aqueous phenol.   The column was
eluted at pH 7.3 with a gradient of increasing NaCl
concentration.   [After Sueoka and Yamane, Proc.
Natl. Acad. Sci. (U.S.) 48, 1454, (1962).]*

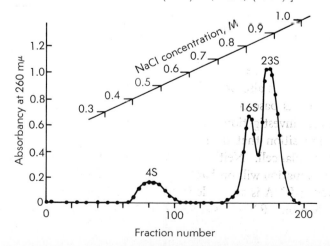

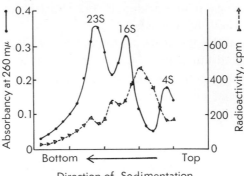

FIGURE 3-2   *Zone sedimentation of pulse-labeled RNA from E. coli growing with a generation time of 80 min. Pulse labeling with ^{14}C-uracil was for 30 sec. followed by phenol extraction of all RNA in the presence of the detergent sodium dodecylsulfate to inactivate ribonucleases. Zone-sedimentation analysis was carried out in a sucrose gradient of 5 to 20 per cent sucrose with contrifuging for 11 hr at 4°C. The absorbency at 260 mμ represents the distribution of r-RNA (16 S and 23 S) and of s-RNA (4 S). The radioactivity (the dotted line) indicates the sedimentation profile of the pulse-labeled m-RNA fraction.*

zone sedimentation analysis in a sucrose-gradient (see Glossary), ribosomal RNA will form two well-defined bands corresponding to the two molecular species, whereas m-RNA will often occupy a wide region forming a very broad band and therefore a straggling peak in the plot of amount of RNA vs. position in the sucrose gradient. For this reason the molecular definition of messenger RNA is not at all easy. It has been described as that RNA which gets labeled first[7] in an exposure of the intact cell to a *short* pulse of radioactive RNA precursors. Alternatively, m-RNA has also been defined[1] as an RNA fraction corresponding in its base composition to the DNA of the particular cell under investigation. In contradistinction, r-RNA has a base composition that does not resemble that of the DNA of the particular cell. Neither definition is completely satisfactory, and the situation will probably not be clarified until sufficiently purified m-RNA is available for direct chemical study.

Soluble RNA (s-RNA), also known as transfer RNA

(t-RNA), accounts for between 10 and 15 per cent of the total RNA of *E. coli*. Soluble RNA from a large variety of different cells is homogeneous in its molecular size having a molecular weight of approximately 25,000 and a sedimentation constant of 4 S (Figure 3–2). It appears that all molecules of s-RNA begin with the nucleotide sequence . . . pCpCpA and end with the nucleotide G, to which an additional 5′ phosphate is linked (Figure 3–3). The rest of the nucleotide sequence between these two ends varies widely. The over-all chain length of a typical s-RNA molecule is approximately 75 nucleotides.

The function of s-RNA is fairly well understood; the molecule acts as an acceptor for an activated amino acid and as an adaptor for carrying the amino acid to the site of protein synthesis on the m-RNA template in the polysome, ensuring that the correct amino acid is placed on the correct coding site. Thus for each of the 20 naturally occurring amino acids, there must be at least one, or possibly more, specific types of s-RNA molecule. It is likely that most of the s-RNA molecules in a given cell extract play this particular role.

Bulk RNA, containing all three kinds, is most conveniently extracted from broken cells with aqueous phenol. Proteins are denatured and rendered insoluble; most nucleases are inactivated. The aqueous solution that contains the nucleic acids may be freed of DNA by digestion with deoxyribonuclease, followed by dialysis to remove the fragments. Remaining traces of ribonucleases can be removed by adsorption onto specially treated clay particles, such as bentonite; this step is particularly important if undegraded very high molecular weight RNA (2×10^6) from, for example, tobacco mosaic virus is to be prepared. RNA from cellular extracts can be precipitated by the addition of alcohol; it can be fractionated into s-RNA and high-molecular-weight RNA (mainly r-RNA) by precipitation with 1 M sodium chloride in which the s-RNA remains soluble, as its name suggests. Also r-RNA and s-RNA can be fractionated on ion-exchange chromatography columns and by gel filtration, a process which sorts molecules primarily according to size.

Nobody has so far developed a satisfactory procedure for isolating messenger RNA in anything but trace amounts. The

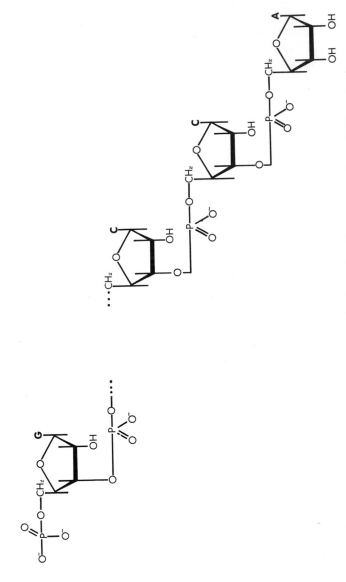

FIGURE 3–3 Schematic representation of the nucleotide structure of an s-RNA molecule.

m-RNA is usually detected by selective radioactive labeling (see Chapter 5). Some attempts to prepare m-RNA have centered on the dissociation of polysomes (believed to be aggregates of m-RNA with ribosomes) under conditions mild enough not to liberate the r-RNA from the ribosomes.

CONFIGURATION OF RNA IN SOLUTION

In distinction to double-stranded DNA, the various types of RNA do not have such a well-defined and stable secondary structure in aqueous solution. Of the three types of RNA, s-RNA has perhaps the best defined secondary structure, since there is now considerable evidence[2,3] that this molecule forms in large part a double helix of the Watson-Crick type. The X-ray evidence[4] of partially crystalline regions of s-RNA films indicates considerable double-helix content, with the repeating dimensions approaching those of the A helix of DNA. Although such preparations show over 90 per cent double-helix content as judged by the X-ray-diffraction pictures, there is now considerable doubt as to whether the intact s-RNA molecules themselves have as much helical character. This is because the preparations used for the X-ray work are partially degraded by heat or enzymatic treatment before they will form such partly crystalline films.

FIGURE 3-4   *Melting curve of E. coli s-RNA. Compare with the melting curve of DNA in Figure 2-13b and of high molecular-weight RNA in Figure 3-7. [After A. Tissières, J. Mol. Biol., 1, 368 (1959).]*

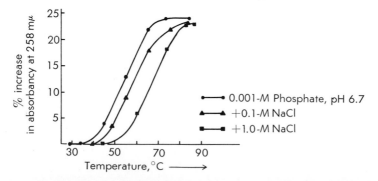

It is very likely that s-RNA in dilute salt solution contains regions of double-helical structure; at least it is possible to show the phenomenon of hyperchromicity on heating just as with DNA, even in preparations of s-RNA that are native and undegraded. Although in s-RNA, as in DNA, we can observe the phenomenon of melting out, the melting curves obtained are much less sharp than those of DNA (Figure 3–4); this indicates that the regions of helix content are much shorter and/or that the helix is not nearly so perfect. Perhaps it is interrupted by short unpaired regions or by the formation of loops[5] in the secondary structure of the molecule (Figure 3–5).

Ribosomal RNA in solution also gives some evidence for double-helix content and in particular for hyperchromicity. r-RNA shows a melting-out profile indicating a hydrogen-bonded structure with specific base pairing, or at least a regular stacking

FIGURE 3–5   *Scheme of a possible secondary structure of a poly-ribonucleotide chain of s-RNA. Note the "loops" containing unpaired bases. (After Reference 5.)*

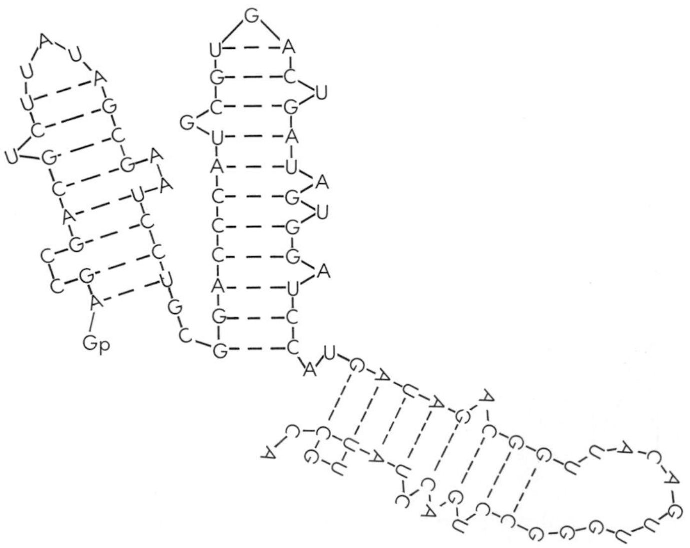

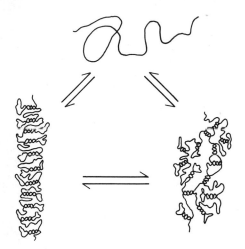

FIGURE 3–6 *The schematic conformations and transitions of high-molecular-weight RNA in solution, depending on pH, ionic strength, and temperature.* (*After Reference 6.*)

of the nucleotide bases, which is destroyed on heating (Figures 3–6 and 3–7). In r-RNA (as in s-RNA), the hyperchromicity is much more sensitive to changes in ionic strength than is the case with DNA. In other words, r-RNA and s-RNA in solution contain regions of double-helix structure with a regular stacking of bases and probably specific base pairing, but the extent of double-helix structure in either case is very much a function of the ionic environment, of pH, and of temperature. High pH destroys the regular configuration because it causes dissociation of the weakly acidic groups of uracil, cytosine, and guanine and thus places a negative charge on these bases. On the other hand, low pH causes adenine, cytosine, and guanine to acquire a positive charge. Such charged bases apparently do not form base pairs. Although high and low pH will also disrupt the regular structure of DNA, the values have to be more extreme than in the case of RNA.

Although the above may be the situation for ribosomal-RNA molecules in solution, the configuration of these molecules inside the ribosomal particle where they are combined with an approximately equal weight of basic protein may be of an

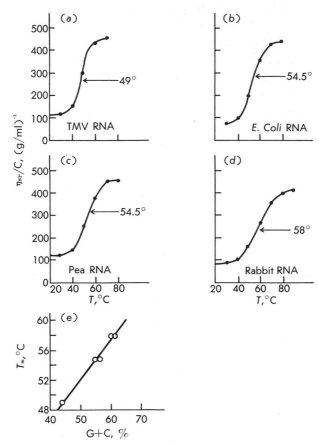

FIGURE 3–7 (a, b, c, d) *The temperature dependence of the viscosity of high-molecular-weight RNA from various sources. Solvent: phosphate buffer, pH 7.3, ionic strength 0.1, plus 0.01 M EDTA. TMV-RNA (tobacco mosaic virus RNA), concentration 1.6 mg/ml. Ribosomal RNAs, 2.5 mg/ml.* (e) *The dependence of T_m on the base composition $(G + C$ content) of the above samples of RNA.* (After Reference 6.)

entirely different nature. At this time we have no evidence for any regularity in the arrangement of the ribosomal RNA molecule within ribosomes. We also know little about the configuration of s-RNA when this is combined with the activating enzyme in the process of becoming charged with activated amino acid or when the s-RNA molecule is combined with the ribosomal particle at the time when the aminoacyl-s-RNA compound aligns itself on the protein-synthesizing template. Secondary structure of RNA as it exists in solution may or may not be relevant to the conformation of the functional RNA molecules in vivo. On the other hand, m-RNA does not appear to have any secondary structure at all when in protein-free solution. This agrees well with the supposed role of m-RNA in the polysome (see Chapter 5), where one requires a long stretched molecule in linear rather than coiled configuration, accommodating a number of ribosomes. In this connection it is interesting to note that the enzyme polynucleotide phosphorylase will not easily degrade s-RNA molecules or ribosomal RNA, but appears to attack messenger RNA. It is supposed that r- and s-RNA are resistant to attack by virtue of a certain amount of secondary structure.

DNA-DEPENDENT RNA POLYMERASE

The distribution of DNA-dependent RNA polymerase appears to be quite ubiquitous. The enzyme is in general associated with nucleic acid and sediments together with DNA when crude extracts are examined by sucrose-gradient centrifugation. The enzyme has however been isolated reasonably free from DNA. It was first characterized in rat liver by Weiss[7,8] and in extracts of E. coli by Hurwitz.[9] In rat liver the enzyme is apparently located in the cell nuclei. In plants it has also been shown that this RNA polymerase is associated with chromosomal DNA.

The *requirements* for the DNA-dependent RNA polymerase (Figure 3–8) are the simultaneous presence of the four ribonucleoside triphosphates: ATP (Figure 3–9), GTP, CTP, and UTP; a divalent ion which should be either magnesium or manganese (Mn^{++}); and native double-stranded DNA. In addition a sulfhydryl reagent must be present during the purification procedure, because the enzyme is easily inactivated by heavy metals or by specific sulfhydryl-inhibiting compounds such as pCMB (parachloromercuribenzoate). The inactivation

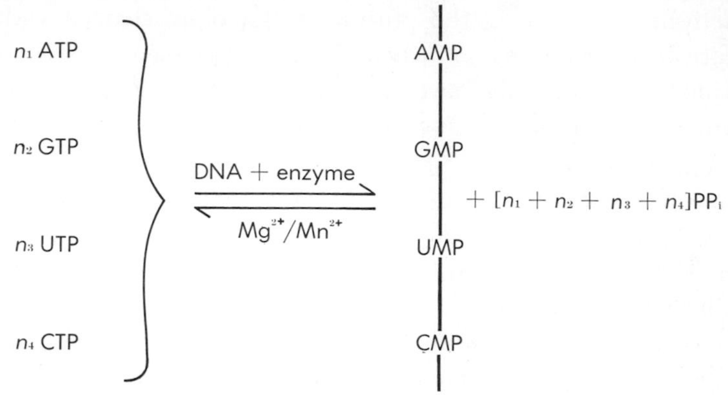

n_1 ATP

n_2 GTP

n_3 UTP

n_4 CTP

$$\xrightarrow[\mathrm{Mg^{2+}/Mn^{2+}}]{\mathrm{DNA + enzyme}}$$

AMP

GMP

UMP

CMP

$+ [n_1 + n_2 + n_3 + n_4]PP_i$

FIGURE 3–8   *The reaction scheme of DNA-dependent RNA polymerase.*

may be reversed by mercaptoethanol.   In the case of the *E. coli* enzyme, magnesium ions are only 30 per cent as effective as manganous ions in vitro, but the concentration of Mg^{++} inside the cell is at least one order of magnitude greater than that of Mn^{++}; therefore Mg^{++} is the effective metal in this reaction.   The K_m for magnesium is 5×10^{-3} M, whereas the corresponding constant for Mn^{++} is 1×10^{-3}.   The omission of one of the triphosphates reduces the incorporation of all others almost to zero.   The enzymatic reaction is very sensitive to deoxyribonuclease and to ribonuclease, as might be expected, since the former destroys the DNA that is required to prime the reaction and the latter destroys the RNA formed as the product.   As may

FIGURE 3–9   *The structure of ATP.*

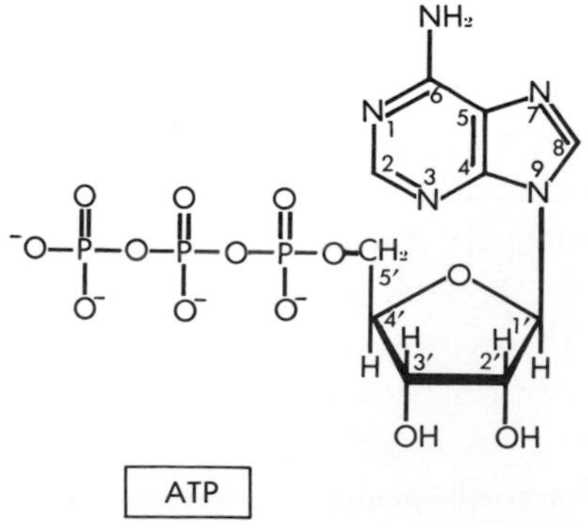

ATP

be seen in Figure 3–8, the enzymatic reaction produces pyrophosphate from each of the triphosphate substrates.

Pyrophosphorolysis of the RNA product[10] is the reversal of this enzymatic reaction in which inorganic pyrophosphate is incorporated into the triphosphate (see Figure 3–8). High concentrations of the enzyme are required and the pyrophosphorolysis is only a slow reaction. Pyrophosphorolysis is specific for the RNA produced by this enzyme; r-RNA and s-RNA are not attacked, possibly because they possess more secondary structure in solution than does the RNA produced in the enzymatic reaction. The presence of DNA is required for pyrophosphorolysis to recur.

The *DNA dependence* of the RNA-polymerase reaction is best illustrated by an analysis of the base composition of the product formed. As can be seen in Table 3–2, the base ratios of the product resemble, and are apparently determined by, the base composition of the DNA added to the reaction. This implies that during the in vitro reaction, both strands of the DNA are copied. It now seems likely that this is not the case in the in vivo situation.[11] However, the base composition of the RNA produced in vitro in the presence of *M. lysodeikticus* DNA is apparently constant over a thousandfold range of RNA synthesis. Yields of RNA up to 60 times the weight of DNA used

TABLE 3–2   *Base composition of the DNA-dependent RNA polymerase product*[a]

Source of DNA	RNA product, mμmoles incorporated				RNA product $\dfrac{A+G}{U+C}$	RNA product $\dfrac{A+U}{G+C}$	DNA $\dfrac{A+T}{G+C}$
	A	U	C	G			
B. subtilis	3.89	3.61	2.78	3.02	1.08	1.30	1.36
E. coli	0.94	1.03	1.07	0.98	0.90	0.96	1.00
M. phlei	0.45	0.52	1.09	1.18	0.99	0.43	0.49
Calf thymus	12.4	11.4	9.60	10.8	0.92	1.19	1.25
Calf thymus, heated	1.40	1.62	1.26	1.18	0.90	1.23	1.25
T2 phage	2.65	2.44	1.44	1.48	0.94	1.75	1.85
dAT Copolymer	18.6	16.9	<0.03	<0.03	(1.10)	>50	>50
Poly dT (synth.)	6.81	0.11	<0.10	<0.10			
(dG):(dC) Polymer[b]	<0.03	<0.03	1.90	0.23			

[a] After reference 12.
[b] After reference 12a.

to prime the reaction have been reported. The product is not linked covalently to the DNA, which may be recovered unchanged at the end of the reaction. For example, DNA with transforming activity remains active even after it has been used to direct the synthesis of 6 to 10 times its weight of RNA.[12,13] This is good evidence that the RNA-polymerase preparations used in this reaction are free of nucleases. Also the density of the DNA primer remains unchanged at the end of the experiment. Any combination or complexing with RNA would lead to an increase in density.[14] It is interesting to note that the single-stranded ϕX 174 DNA also directs the synthesis of RNA, although it is much less active in priming the reaction.

SIMILARITIES OF DNA POLYMERASE AND DNA-DEPENDENT RNA POLYMERASE (BOTH POLYMERASES IN VITRO)

1. All four nucleoside triphosphates are required.

2. Pyrophosphate exchange reaction occurs, dependent on the presence of DNA, but not on the simultaneous presence of all four triphosphates.

3. Base analogs are incorporated in a rather similar manner by both enzymes.

4. The base composition of the primer and of the product are complementary according to the Watson-Crick structure.

5. The two newly formed RNA strands have opposite polarity, just as do the newly formed DNA strands in the DNA polymerase.

6. The inhibition of polymerization by the antibiotic actinomycin D and by proflavin is qualitatively similar, but not quantitatively the same.

DIFFERENCES BETWEEN THE ENZYMES

Differences exist in the effectiveness of the DNA primers used, as shown in Table 3–3. Both DNA polymerase and RNA polymerase can act simultaneously with the same DNA primer in vitro. Magnesium, rather than manganese, has to be used as

T A B L E 3–3 *Priming efficiencies*

Enzyme	Native DNA	Denatured DNA	Poly dT
RNA polymerase, E. coli	Very active	Less active	Active
DNA polymerase, E. coli or animal	Active	More active	Inactive (E. coli), active (animal)

the required metal ion. Although manganese would stimulate both reactions, it also facilitates the incorporation of ribonucleotides into DNA with the formation of a hybrid type of molecule (see Reference 25). If DNA is required by both enzymes, one might ask why there is no quantitative interference between the two enzymes during the incubation. This is probably because the DNA primer is in excess in the experiment, saturating all available enzyme sites. Alternatively, DNA may be in excess, because it is rapidly replicated by the DNA polymerase.

Apparently both strands of DNA are copied by the RNA polymerase in vitro, since the base ratios of the RNA from single- and from double-stranded ϕX 174 DNA produced by DNA polymerase are complementary in one case and show Watson-Crick pairing in the second. The base ratio A + T/G + C of double-stranded ϕX 174 DNA is 1.31, that of the in vitro RNA product was also 1.31. The in vivo situation will however be different, because it has been shown that RNA made in vivo after T4 infection has unequal ratios of A:U and of G:C.[15] In this case probably only one strand of DNA is being copied.

Nearest-neighbor-frequency experiments similar to those performed on the product of DNA polymerase may also be carried out during the RNA-polymerase reaction and on the RNA product formed. The frequencies agree quite well with those of the primer DNA, indicating that the RNA strands formed in vitro are of opposite polarity, as are those of the DNA primer.

Base analogs substitute as expected from their behavior in the DNA-polymerase reaction, although the rate is usually a little slower. For example, UTP can be replaced by 5-F-UTP (30 per cent as efficient) (Figure 3–10) or by 5-Br-UTP (50 per cent);

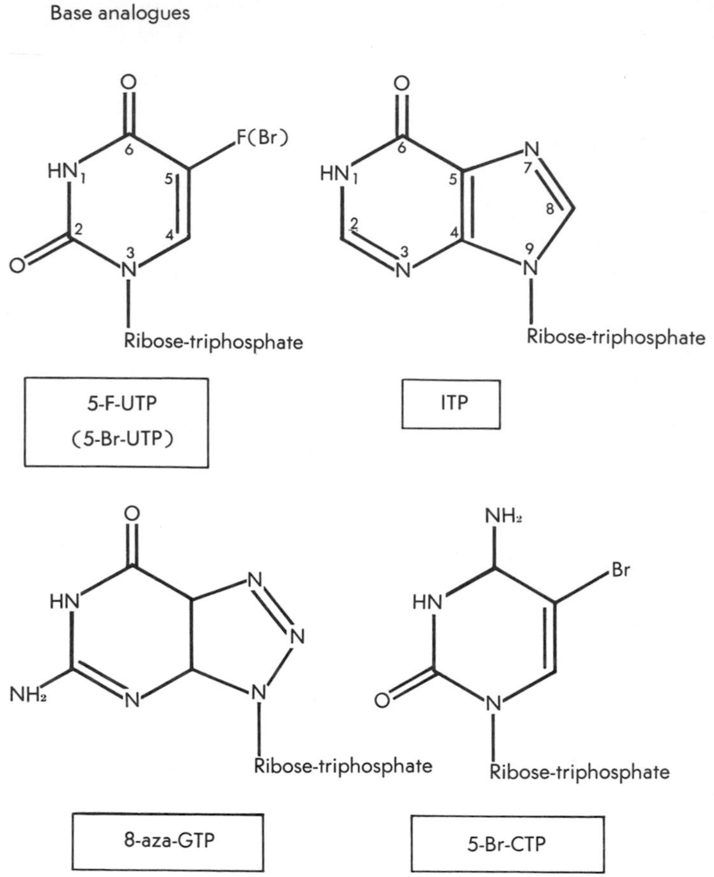

Base analogues

FIGURE 3–10   *The structures of some base analogs of ribonucleoside triphosphates.*

GTP may be replaced by ITP (30 per cent) or 8-aza-GTP (18 per cent); CTP by 5-Br-CTP (90 per cent).

SOLUBLE RNA

The nucleotide sequences of s-RNA are peculiar in that they contain, in addition to the four usual major bases, smaller quantities of the so-called additional nucleotides. Chief among those are pseudo-uridylic acid and ribo-thymidylic acid (Figure

3–11). There are two principal ways in which these might be formed in the s-RNA molecule. If we suppose that s-RNA is also a product of the RNA-polymerase reaction using a DNA template, we guess that the additional nucleotides could be incorporated in the form of their triphosphates by means of the DNA-dependent RNA-polymerase reaction. Alternatively, they might be formed in situ by the conversion of normal uridylic acid already in the nucleotide chain to the isomeric pseudo-uridylic acid (see scheme in Figure 3–12). In the same way other uridylic acid residues already within the chain are known to be

FIGURE 3–11   *The structures of pseudo-uridylic acid and ribothymidylic acid.*

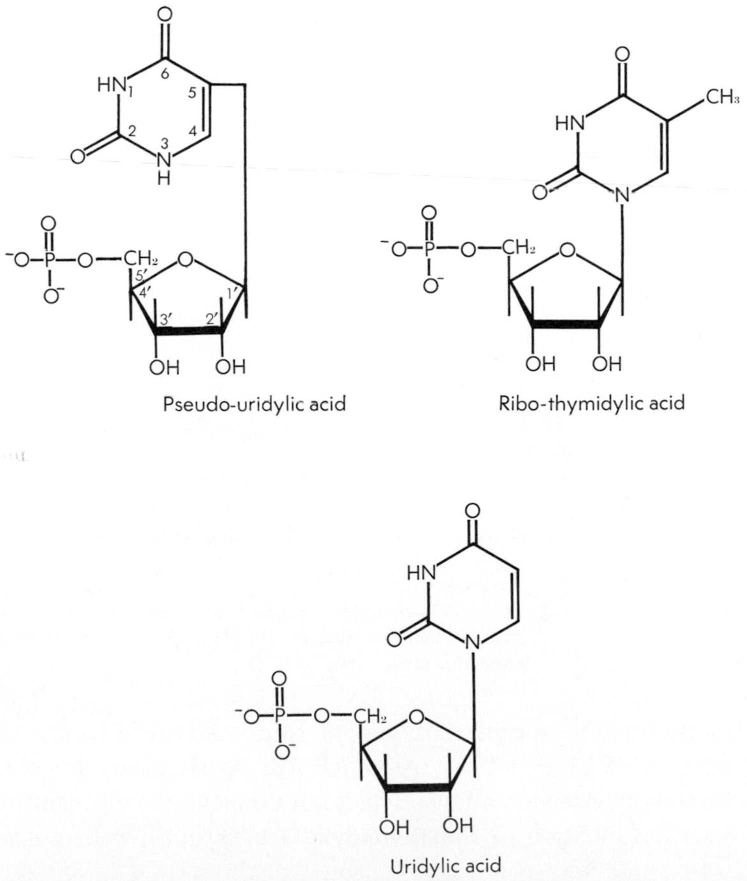

Pseudo-uridylic acid   Ribo-thymidylic acid

Uridylic acid

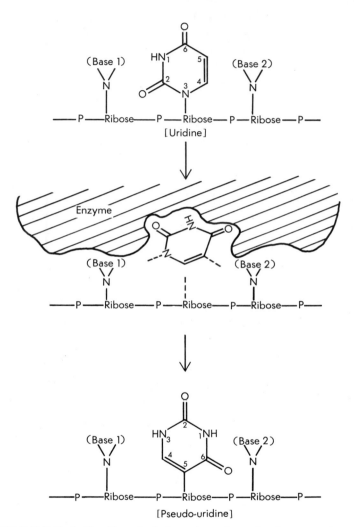

FIGURE 3–12 *Hypothetical reaction scheme for the conversion of a uridylic acid residue in a polynucleotide chain into pseudo-uridylic acid.*

methylated by specific enzymes to form ribo-thymidylic acid residues (Figure 3–13). Although the mechanisms for the formation of pseudo-uridylic acid is not yet clear, the mechanism for the formation of ribo-thymidylic acid is quite well under-

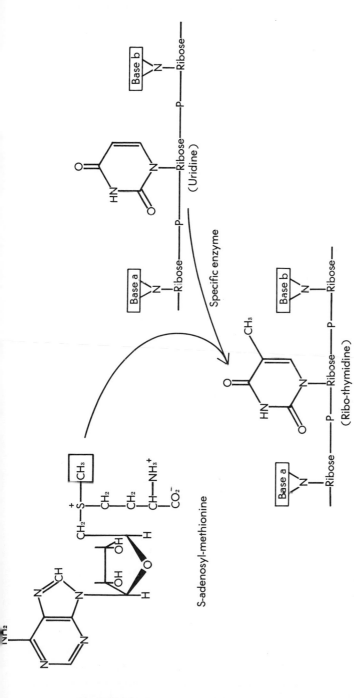

FIGURE 3-13 *Scheme for the enzymatic methylations of a uridylic acid residue in the poly-nucleotide chain to form ribo-thymidylic acid.*

TABLE 3–4 *Incorporation of pseudo-uridylic acid (ψTP) and ribo-thymidylic acid (rTTP) by RNA polymerase*[a]

Nucleotides in incubation	Labeled nucleotide incorporated, mμmoles
GTP, CTP, UTP, AT³²P	2.10
Same, but omit GTP, or CTP, or UTP	0.11–0.14
ψTP, GTP, CTP, AT³²P	2.06
ψT³²P, GTP, CTP, ATP	2.10
Same, but omit GTP, or CTP, or ATP	0.06–0.08
rTT³²P, GTP, CTP, ATP	1.90
Same, but omit GTP, or CTP, or ATP	0.03–0.04

[a] After Reference 25.

stood. This subject will be discussed more extensively when we talk about the structure of s-RNA (Chapter 5).

It was of interest to find out whether the RNA polymerase itself is capable of dealing with the triphosphates of pseudo-uridine and ribo-thymidine directly. As can be seen in the results in Table 3–4, these triphosphates are indeed incorporated, as is the normal UTP analog; the enzyme will accept these isomeric triphosphates equally well. It appears, however, that the pseudo-uridine triphosphate and ribo-thymidine triphosphate do not occur as such in the cell. Therefore, it is more likely that the mechanism for the formation of these isomers is an enzymatic one acting on nucleotide residues already in the polymer. Although the isomeric triphosphates are incorporated quantitatively, it may well be that the nearest-neighbor frequencies are influenced by whether UTP is also present.

It should also be pointed out that each s-RNA molecule ends at its amino acid acceptor end with the sequence . . . pCpCpA. These last three nucleotides are added sequentially by a special "terminal-adding" enzyme system and not by the polymerase. The precursors are CTP and ATP.

ACTINOMYCIN D INHIBITION

The inhibition of RNA polymerase by actinomycin D has been studied extensively. This antibiotic will inhibit both DNA polymerase and DNA-dependent RNA polymerase in vitro, probably by binding to G containing regions of double-stranded

DNA. During partial inhibition, the copying by the enzyme of G- and C-containing sequences in DNA is preferentially inhibited.[13]

RNA polymerase activity is inhibited much more strongly by the antibiotic than is the DNA-polymerase reaction. For example, under given conditions at a concentration of antibiotic of 1×10^{-6} M, RNA polymerase is 90 per cent inhibited, whereas the DNA-polymerase reaction is only 5 per cent inhibited. The RNA-polymerase reaction, which is primed by poly dT or poly d(AT), is not inhibited, indicating also that actinomycin D combines preferentially with regions of DNA that are rich in G. The inhibition is more marked when native DNA is the primer and less marked with denatured DNA. It has also been reported that actinomycin D is not bound well by denatured DNA.

The molecular size of the RNA produced by the RNA-polymerase reaction has a sedimentation constant of between 4 and 7.5 S; its average length is about 300 nucleotides as measured by end-group determination. This is somewhat lower than might have been expected, possibly as a result of the presence of contaminating ribonucleases.

In conclusion we can say that, although both strands of DNA are copied by the in vitro RNA-polymerase reaction, it is likely that only one strand is copied in vivo (see References 11a and 11b). A question that remains unanswered is the problem of whether the RNA polymerase can copy regions of DNA from the middle of the DNA chain or whether it needs to start at one end of the chain. This is of fundamental importance in the whole problem of how the genetic message of the DNA is transcribed into messenger RNA (see discussion by Spiegelman[11]).

It is currently assumed that all types of RNA are produced by a DNA-dependent RNA polymerase that copies nucleotide sequences from definite regions of the DNA molecule. The evidence for this mechanism is by no means watertight as yet, being based largely on the ability of RNA molecules to hybridize, that is, to form hybrid double-stranded molecules by heating and slow cooling with homologous DNA molecules (see Chapter 5). In each of these cases however, the *extent* of complementarity between the DNA and the RNA strands that hybridize is not clear, because this is based on the resistance of such hybrid strands to digestion with pancreatic ribonuclease. The resistance actually observed does not usually exceed 70 to 80 per cent. There remains therefore a small residue of doubt as to whether the r-RNA and the s-RNA are necessarily exact replicas of sections of the DNA molecule, or whether their hybridization is fortuitous. It has also been suggested that r-RNA and s-RNA are formed by an RNA-dependent RNA polymerase by a process of self-replication. However, the arguments in favor of all types of RNA being made on DNA by the DNA-dependent RNA polymerase are greatly strengthened by the finding that actinomycin D, which inhibits this enzyme specifically, shuts off the synthesis of all three types of RNA.

RNA-DEPENDENT RNA POLYMERASE

The existence of this enzyme[18] was expected, owing to the known replication of virus RNA inside infected cells. The enzyme was first demonstrated by Reddi,[19] in 1961, who found that the RNA of tobacco mosaic virus would stimulate the synthesis of RNA in spinach extracts. The enzyme has also been demonstrated in *E. coli*[20] by August et al. and by Weiss, in the same year, in *M. lysodeikticus.*[21] The RNA-dependent RNA polymerase has not yet been purified as carefully as the DNA-dependent enzyme. Nevertheless it has been possible to show by the analysis of nearest-neighbor frequencies that replication of nucleotide sequence is exact. In fact there is still some doubt as to whether DNA- and RNA-dependent polymerases are definitely two separate enzymes.

SITE OF RNA SYNTHESIS IN ANIMAL CELLS

It has been known for some time that nuclear RNA is labeled much more rapidly than cytoplasmic RNA. From this it may be deduced that the DNA-dependent RNA polymerase, which is mainly localized in the nucleus, is primarily responsible for the synthesis of RNA, which eventually reaches the cytoplasm. However, we cannot exclude the possibility that some cytoplasmic synthesis of RNA also occurs. For example, the nucleus

of the extremely large single-celled organism *Acetabularia* may
be removed, and the remainder of the cell is still capable of
synthesizing RNA. In other words, the evidence of exactly
where in the cell RNA is synthesized is still conflicting.
Autoradiographic studies sometimes indicate the chromosome or
the nucleolus as the primary site of RNA synthesis. On the
other hand, the enzyme that adds the terminal nucleotides to
s-RNA is definitely located in the cytoplasm; however this
enzyme system is entirely different from the RNA polymerase.

POLYNUCLEOTIDE PHOSPHORYLASE

The enzyme polynucleotide phosphorylase was discovered by
Grunberg-Manago and Ochoa[22] in 1955 in extracts of *Azoto-
bacter vinelandii* (= A. *agilis*). This enzyme is now available in
highly purified form from a great variety of microorganisms and
it may also exist in pig liver nuclei.[23] Although the name
suggests that the primary activity of the enzyme is a phosphorolytic one, the reverse reaction, which involves the synthesis
of polyribonucleotides, has been studied even more extensively
in vitro.

Although the enzymes from bacteria such as E. *coli*, A. *agilis*,
and M. *lysodeikticus* are similar, species differences can nevertheless be demonstrated in the enzymatic properties of these
preparations. Purification is extensive, being up to 300-fold for
the E. *coli* enzyme. Crude enzyme preparations contain appreciable amounts of nucleic acid, which may in fact play a role in
the initiation of the polymerization reaction by this enzyme.
Progressive purification reduces the amount of nucleic acid
present and reduces the onset of the unprimed polymerization
reaction. The molecular weight of polynucleotide phosphorylase as measured in a sucrose gradient is approximately 230,000.
For the preparation of polyribonucleotides, which has been one
of the most important practical uses of this enzyme, even
partially purified preparations may be used.

The enzyme catalyzes the following reaction:

$$n\text{YPP} \underset{\text{Mg}^{++}}{\overset{\text{polynucleotide phosphorylase}}{\rightleftharpoons}} (\text{YP})_n + n\text{P}_i$$

It should be noted that the enzyme uses ribonucleoside *diphosphates* to synthesize a polyribonucleotide, whereas the RNA polymerase uses the *triphosphates*. Accordingly, polynucleotide phosphorylase liberates inorganic phosphate, whereas the RNA polymerase liberates pyrophosphate. Another point of difference is the fact that no nucleotide-sequence template molecule is required by the phosphorylase, but then the synthesized polyribonucleotide does not have a specific nucleotide sequence either.

The reaction favors synthesis of the polyribonucleotide, provided rather high concentrations (see below) of the nucleotide diphosphates are present. The enzyme can produce homopolymers, in which all the Y groups are the same, or random copolymers from a mixture of two or more different nucleoside diphosphates.

Phosphorolysis, the process for which the enzyme is named, is the above reaction proceeding from right to left; it may be demonstrated in the presence of radioactively labeled inorganic phosphate, which becomes incorporated into nucleoside diphosphate. Phosphate exchange is also catalyzed by this enzyme in the presence of magnesium ions. In contrast to the pyrophosphorolysis catalyzed by the DNA-dependent RNA polymerase mentioned earlier, the phosphate exchange does not require the presence of a priming polynucleotide.

KINETICS

Magnesium ions are required for in vitro activity of the enzyme. Manganous ions (Mn^{++}) do not substitute for Mg^{++}; they inhibit the reaction. The pH optimum is sharp at 8.1 for the A. *agilis* enzyme when measured by the inorganic phosphate exchange reaction. The pH optimum is a broad plateau from 7.5 to 9 for the same enzyme in the polymerization reaction, and for phosphorolysis a broad pH optimum between 8.1 and 10 is found. The kinetics are complex, because of the involvement of nucleoside diphosphate-magnesium complexes as the active form of the substrate. However, for the A. *agilis* enzyme, saturating concentrations for ADP and for IDP (compare formula for ITP in Figure 3–10) are in the range of 0.10 to 0.05 M. This concentration is high by comparison with the concentrations of triphosphates used for the RNA-polymerase enzyme. Moreover, the saturating concentrations for the nucleoside diphosphates depend on the magnesium ion concentration; therefore the enzyme does not appear to follow true Michaelis-Menten kinetics with respect to the diphosphates. Some highly purified enzyme preparations are dependent on the presence of polylysine or other polyamines for activity.

An enzyme preparation that is only partially purified will produce high molecular weight polyribonucleotides from the diphosphates without an initial lag phase. The more purified preparations on the other hand do show such a lag phase, probably a result of the removal of priming quantities of contaminating oligo- or polynucleotides. From the kinetics one would expect that only fairly short chains of polyribonucleotides would be produced, because of the inhibition of the polymerization reaction by the rising concentration of inorganic phosphate produced in the course of the reaction. Actually, rather long chains of polyribonucleotides are made, and this is due to another primed reaction taking over as soon as priming chains of polynucleotide are available. Growth of these priming chains is then the most rapid reaction, so that high molecular weights are obtained.

The polymerized polyribonucleotide products may be precipitated from the reaction mixture with acid or alcohol, with high salt concentrations, or with bases such as streptomycin. The molecular weights of the products range from 30,000 to 2×10^6. The polymers are linear polymers with the usual 3'–5' phosphodiester linkages, exactly like those found in naturally occurring RNA (see, for example, Figure 3–3). The product is sensitive to the usual ribonucleases with the usual specificities and also to digestion by snake venom diesterase, which yields only 5' phosphates.

p.Y.p.Y..........p.Y.p.Y.p.Y

The polymeric product has a 5'-phosphate group at one end and a nucleoside ending at the other end. In all chemical and physical respects except nucleotide sequences, it resembles naturally occurring RNA.

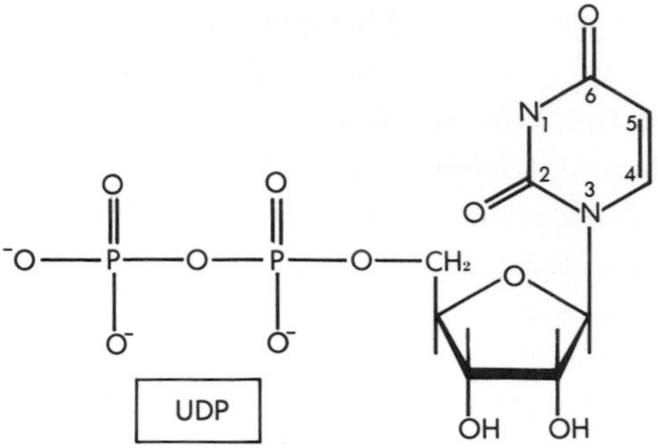

FIGURE 3-14   *The structure of UDP.*

POLYNUCLEOTIDE PHOSPHORYLASE SPECIFICITY

This enzyme is absolutely specific for ribonucleoside diphosphates (for example, in Figure 3-14) and for the presence of two phosphate groups as a 5'-pyrophosphate grouping.   No reaction occurs with either triphosphates or monophosphates.   Some distinction can be shown between the different bases (see Table 3-5), in the sense that some are polymerized more readily than others.   For example, until quite recently, it was difficult to make a homopolymer containing guanine or even a copolymer containing more than a small amount of guanine.   This is

TABLE 3-5   *Substrate specificity for synthesis by polynucleotide phosphorylase[c]*

Active	Inactive
ADP	ppUp
CDP	ppAp
UDP	5,6-Dihydro-UDP[a]
GDP	4-aza-UDP[a]
IDP	β-D-Arabinosyl-UDP[b]
N-Methyl-UDP[a]	Deoxyribo-TDP
2-Thio-UDP[a]	
5-F(Br,Cl,I)-UDP[a]	
Ribo-TDP	
8-aza-GDP[a]	

[a] See formula in Figure 3–14 for placement of substituents.
[b] D-Arabinose takes the place of D-ribose in Figure 3–14.
[c] After Reference 6a.

probably due to the ready formation of guanine-containing polymers into a four-stranded helical configuration that effectively inhibits further action by the polynucleotide phosphorylase. At higher dilutions and at lower pH values and at lower ionic strengths homopolymers containing guanine can be produced.[24]

PRIMING BY OLIGONUCLEOTIDES WITH FREE 3'-OH GROUPS

Such oligonucleotides prime the synthetic reaction and long chains are formed by the addition of new monomer units; that is, the primer chain is covalently incorporated into the product:

pApA + UDP → pApApUpUpUpU   etc.

The action of pancreatic ribonuclease on such a product leads to the formation of uridine from the nucleoside end group together with many residues of free 3'-uridylic acid (Up) and the primer oligonucleotide in the form of the oligonucleotide pApApUp. By such means it can be shown that the primer is covalently linked to the polyribonucleotide product.

Maximum stimulation of the synthetic reaction depends on the length of the primer. For example, maximum stimulation is obtained with the above dinucleotide pApA at a concentration of 2.4 mM, with the corresponding trinucleotide (pApApA) at a concentration of 0.42 mM, and with the tetranucleotide (pApApApA) at 0.17 mM. In these reactions the enzyme elongates existing primer oligonucleotide chains and each primer molecule initiates the formation of one long polymeric product. The reaction mixture does not become as highly viscous as it does in the unprimed reaction; a considerable number of primer molecules are present, leading to a rather large number of growing chains, each of which is not nearly so long as those formed by the very few primer molecules in the unprimed reaction during its lag phase. There is no apparent base specificity for primer in this primed reaction.

PRIMING BY OLIGONUCLEOTIDES WITH 3'-PHOSPHATE GROUPS

These oligonucleotides are usually inhibitory, but they can also overcome the lag phase for the polymerization of UDP or ADP. The primers are not covalently incorporated into the polymeric product, which is highly viscous; the added primer can be recovered quantitatively from the reaction mixture. The detailed mechanism of this kind of primed reaction, however, is not completely understood.

PHYSIOLOGICAL FUNCTION OF POLYNUCLEOTIDE PHOSPHORYLASE

It is hard to see how this enzyme can play a physiological role in the synthesis of specific RNA molecules in vivo, because it seems to polymerize ribonucleotides in a random fashion, at least in vitro. On the other hand, the enzyme must be important, because it is found in large quantities in so many different bacteria and also in other types of cells. There is a direct relationship between the amount of RNA synthesis and the amount of polynucleotide phosphorylase present at certain stages of the growth cycle. There is even a suggestion that this enzyme can be made in the presence of chloramphenicol, which stops the synthesis of most other proteins.

Conceivably, in vivo the enzyme is responsible for the breakdown of RNA by a process of phosphorolysis, but the in vitro rate of phosphorolysis is slow, particularly for s-RNA and r-RNA. As mentioned earlier, this may be due to the existence of secondary structure in solutions (at least in vitro) of these RNA molecules. Perhaps m-RNA is broken down by this enzyme in conformity with the observation that synthetic messengers such as polyU are rapidly broken down in relatively crude bacterial extracts to form 5' nucleotides. This would involve the action of polynucleotide phosphorylase together with another phosphatase-like enzyme to convert the 5'-diphosphates to the 5'-monophosphates.

REFERENCES

1. Volkin, E., and Astrachan, L. (1956), "Phosphorus Incorporation in *Escherichia coli* Ribonucleic Acid after Infection with Bacteriophage T2." *Virology*, **2**, 149.

2. Fresco, J. R., Klotz, L. C., and Richards, E. G. (1963), "A New Spectroscopic Approach to the Determination of Helical Secondary Structure in Ribonucleic Acids." *Cold Spring Harb. Symp. Quant. Biol.*, **28**, 83.

3. Felsenfeld, G., and Cantoni, G. L. (1964), "Use of Thermal Denaturation Studies to Investigate the Base Sequence of Yeast Serine s-RNA." *Proc. Natl. Acad. Sci.*, **51**, 818.

4. Spencer, M., Fuller, W., Wilkins, M. H. F., and Brown, G. L. (1962), "Determination of the Helical Configuration of RNA Molecules by X-ray Diffraction Study of Crystalline Amino Acid Transfer RNA." *Nature*, **194**, 1014.

5. Fresco, J. R., and Alberts, B. M. (1960), "The Accommodation of Non-complementary Bases in Helical Polyribonucleotides and Deoxyribonucleic Acids." *Proc. Natl. Acad. Sci.*, **46**, 311.

6. Spirin, A. (1963), "Some Problems Concerning the Macromolecular Structure of Ribonucleic Acids." *Progr. Nucl. Acid Research*, **I**, 324.

6a. Grunberg-Manago, M. (1963), "Polynucleotide Phosphorylase." *Progr. Nucl. Acid Research*, **1**, 93.

7. Weiss, S. B., and Gladstone, L. (1959), "A Mammalian System for the Incorporation of Cytidine Triphosphate into RNA." *J. Am. Chem. Soc.*, **81**, 4118.

8. Weiss, S. B. (1960), "Enzymatic Incorporation of Ribonucleoside Triphosphates into the Interpolynucleotide Linkages of Ribonucleic Acid." *Proc. Natl. Acad. Sci.*, **46**, 1020.

9. Hurwitz, J., Bresler, A., and Diringer, R. (1960), "The Enzymatic Incorporation of Ribonucleotides in Polyribonucleotides and the Effect of DNA." *Biochim. Biophys. Res. Comm.*, **3**, 15.

10. Furth, J. J., Hurwitz, J., and Anders, M. (1962), "The Role of DNA in RNA Synthesis." *J. Biol. Chem.*, **237**, 2611.

11. Spiegelman, S., and Hayashi, M. (1963), "The Present Status of the Transfer of Genetic Information and Its Control." *Cold Spring Harb. Symp. Quant. Biol.*, **28**, 161.

11a. Hayashi, M., Hayashi, M. N., and Spiegelman, S. (1963), "Restriction of in Vivo Genetic Transcription to one of the Complementary Strands of DNA." *Proc. Natl. Acad. Sci.*, *U.S.*, **50**, 664.

11b. Hayashi, M., Hayashi, M. N., and Spiegelman, S. (1964), "DNA Circularity and Strand Selection in the Generation of Genetic Messages." *Proc. Natl. Acad. Sci., U.S.,* **51,** 351.

12. Hurwitz, J., Furth, J. J., Anders, M. and Evans, A. (1962), "The Role of DNA in RNA Synthesis." *J. Biol. Chem.,* **237,** 3752.

12a. Chamberlin, M., and Berg, P. (1962), "DNA-directed Synthesis of RNA by an Enzyme from *E. coli.*" *Proc. Natl. Acad. Sci., U.S.,* **48,** 81.

13. Hurwitz, J., Evans, A., Babinet, C., and Skalka, A. (1963), "On the Copying of DNA in the RNA Polymerase Reaction." *Cold Spring Harb. Symp. Quant. Biol.,* **28,** 59.

14. Geiduschek, E. P., Nakamoto, T., and Weiss, S. B. (1961). "The Enzymatic Synthesis of RNA: Complementary Interaction with DNA." *Proc. Natl. Acad. Sci.,* **47,** 1405.

15. Bautz, E. K. F., and Hall, B. D. (1962), "The Isolation of T4 Specific RNA on a DNA-Cellulose Column." *Proc. Natl. Acad. Sci.,* **48,** 401.

16. Fleissner, E., and Borek, E. (1962), "A New Enzyme of RNA Synthesis: RNA Methylase." *Proc. Natl. Acad. Sci.,* **48,** 1199.

17. Nirenberg, M. W., Jones, O. W., Leder, P., Clark, B. F. C., Sly. W. S., and Pestka, S. (1963). "On the Coding of Genetic Information." *Cold Spring Harb. Symp. Quant. Biol.,* **28,** 554.

18. Baltimore, D., and Franklin, R. M. (1963), "Properties of the Mengovirus and Poliovirus RNA Polymerases." *Cold Spring Harb. Symp. Quant. Biol.,* **28,** 105.

19. Reddi, K. K. (1961), "Polyribonucleotide Synthetase." *Science,* **133,** 1367.

20. August, J. T., Ortiz, P. J., and Skalka, A. S. (1962), "RNA Dependent Ribonucleotide Incorporation." *Federation Proceedings,* **21,** 371.

21. Nakamoto, T., and Weiss, S. B. (1962), "The Biosynthesis of RNA: Priming by Polyribonucleotides." *Proc. Natl. Acad. Sci.,* **48,** 880.

22. Grunberg-Manago, M., and Ochoa, S. (1955), "Enzymatic Synthesis and Breakdown of Polynucleotides; Polynucleotide Phosphorylase." *J. Am. Chem. Soc.,* **77,** 3165.

23. Hilmoe, R. J., and Heppel, L. A. (1957), "Polynucleotide Phosphorylase in Liver Nuclei." *J. Am. Chem. Soc.,* **79,** 4810.

24. Fresco, J. R., and Su, D. F. (1962), "Polynucleotides." *J. Biol. Chem.,* **237,** PC3305.

25. Kahan, F. M., and Hurwitz, J. (1962), "The Role of DNA in RNA Synthesis, IV. The Incorporation of Pyrimidine and Purine Analogues into RNA." *J. Biol. Chem.,* **237,** 3778.

FOUR §§ SEQUENCE ANALYSIS OF MACROMOLECULES, PARTICULARLY RNA

WE KNOW AT PRESENT OF THREE KINDS OF BIOLOGICALLY IMPORTANT, long-chain macromolecules that carry information in the sequences of their subunits: DNA, RNA, and protein. To understand the role of each of these molecules completely, we have to know their subunit sequences in addition to their over-all configuration. To appreciate the significance of an active site in the case of a protein enzyme, for example, we need to know the amino acids of which it is composed; we also wish to know the amino acid sequence of the rest of the molecule, since that sequence determines the three-dimensional structure of the whole molecule and, therefore, of the active site.

PROTEINS

Amino acid-sequence analysis of protein chains has progressed enormously in the past 20 years. The introduction by Sanger[1] of new chemical techniques for determining the end amino acid in a chain and for handling small peptide fragments enabled him and his colleagues to determine the whole sequence of the protein insulin.[2] This achievement was followed by the determination of the sequence of the enzyme pancreatic ribonuclease by Hirs, Moore, and Stein[3,3a] and their colleagues and by Anfinsen et al.[4] By now a number of other proteins have had their amino acid sequence determined, including various hemoglobins, cytochrome *c*, tobacco mosaic virus protein, chymotrypsin and trypsin, to mention only a few. An experimenter can now reasonably expect to solve the amino acid sequence of a new protein in from three to ten years, given a good supply of pure protein, a peptide chain length below 300, and an immense amount of patience! Unless something quite unexpected turns up, the methods now available should be adequate for any of the usual proteins.

These methods are discussed in more detail in the companion volume in this series *Enzymes: Structure and Function* by Bernhard (New York: Benjamin, in production). The techniques rely primarily on the existence of several pure proteolytic enzymes of high specificity for the particular amino acid in the peptide chain where they will hydrolytically break the chain. The enzymes trypsin, chymotrypsin, elastase, and carboxypeptidase A and B have well-defined specificities, particularly trypsin. The enzyme, pepsin, has, together with other useful enzymes, much less stringent specificity requirements. Equally important, the techniques of partition and ion exchange chromatography, of zone electrophoresis and countercurrent distribution are well developed and enable the investigator to separate the mixtures of such peptide fragments obtained.[5]

In addition, chemical methods for determining the amino acids at each end of a peptide chain are far advanced, as is the chemical stepwise degradation of peptides by which one amino acid at a time is removed and identified. Here we might mention the Edman-Sjöquist technique,[6] which involves the use of phenylisothiocyanate for stepwise degradation. A chemical method that has also proved useful is the specific cleavage at a methionine residue with cyanogen bromide.[7] However, it is most important to realize, and no detriment to the ingenuity of protein chemists, that the sequence analysis of proteins has been so successful, because proteins are composed of some 20 different kinds of amino acid subunits. This fact alone makes for greater selectivity in breaking the chain into fragments and for easier separation, analysis, and identification of such fragments. Many different and unique fragments will usually be obtained, making it easier to deduce a unique over-all sequence.

NUCLEIC ACIDS

The situation in the nucleic acids is very different. Because there are only four different common bases, s-RNA apart, enzymatic degradation yields many rather short fragments with a much lower degree of uniqueness of sequence; in other words, the same short sequences will be obtained from different parts of the nucleic acid chain.

The situation is particularly difficult in DNA, where the hydrolytic enzymes, the deoxyribonucleases, have such broad specificities that very little sequence information can be obtained with them. Only an over-all idea of patterns of nucleotide sequences can be seen. In addition, only enormously long molecules of DNA are available; the most promising one for sequence analysis would be, for example, ϕX 174 DNA, because it presumably has a unique base sequence and consists of only one type of molecule with one sequence. However, there are far too many nucleotide units (some 5500) even in this molecule, so that a sequence analysis will not be possible until there is a major breakthrough in this field.

In a chemical approach which involves heating DNA with diphenylamine and formic acid at 30°C for 17 hr, the DNA is first depurinated and then split at the residual 2-deoxyribose.[8] In this and other ways,[9] sequences containing only pyrimidines are obtained, and these can be isolated and identified. For example, in calf thymus DNA, Burton[8] was able to show the occurrence in small amounts of sequences up to 7 pyrimidine nucleotides long. These "runs" of pyrimidine-neighboring bases are quantitatively characteristic of the particular DNA. Information can also be obtained about purine-neighbor sequences.[10] Together with nearest-neighbor-frequency analysis (see Chapter 2), the sequence information in DNA is still very meager, and we must await a major advance in degradative techniques and in methods for the isolation of homogeneous DNA molecules of manageable size.

RNA is more amenable to current degradative techniques, partly because fairly small molecules (s-RNA, 75 nucleotides) are available; these have more than four kinds of bases (methylated bases, pseudo-uridylic acid, etc.) and they may now be obtained in reasonably homogeneous form.[11] The structural studies of high-molecular-weight RNAs are however still quite embryonic. An exception is the RNA from tobacco mosaic virus, which, though large (MW = 2×10^6), is assumed to be of one molecular species with one unique base sequence. The recent end-group studies (discussed again later in this chapter) by Fraenkel-Conrat[12] and Whitfeld[13] showed the outline structure to be:

Ap...(6000 nucleotides)...p(U or C)pCpCpA

RNA is a long-chain molecule (see Figure 2–2) made up of a repeating backbone of alternating ribose and phosphate residues to which are attached at each ribose one of four types of nitrogenous bases: adenine, guanine, cytosine, and uracil. Whereas the chemical structure of the ribose phosphate backbone does not carry any information (but is of course necessary for the structure of the molecule), the specific sequence of the four bases is believed to be unique and highly significant, for example, in m-RNA carrying the information required to make a particular polypeptide chain. Thus it is of the greatest interest to determine the nucleotide sequences of homogeneous preparations of RNA molecules with informational content. Of course a similar problem exists in the nucleotide sequences of the DNA molecule.

Experimental attack on the nucleotide sequences of RNA has been promising, owing to three structural aspects of the RNA molecule. *First,* by virtue of possessing a 2′ hydroxyl group in the ribose, the molecule is sensitive to attack by mild alkali.

This leads to complete degradation of RNA to mononucleotides and facilitates greatly the analysis of oligonucleotides and of whole RNA. *Second,* the presence of the 2′ hydroxyl group has enabled the development of a useful chemical stepwise degradative procedure[14] from the end of an oligonucleotide having both the 2′- and the 3′-hydroxyl groups free. Such stepwise degradation leads to the liberation of the bases of an oligonucleotide in sequential order and thus gives extremely useful sequence information. *Third,* and most important, the discovery of several highly specific ribonucleases has enabled workers in this field to perform specific degradation of RNA molecules to oligonucleotides. These oligonucleotides have sequences ending in particular and characteristic bases.

A typical section of an RNA molecule, such as the tetranucleotide sequence illustrated in Figure 4–1 may be subjected to a variety of degradative procedures, which we shall describe. The action of dilute hydrochloric acid leads to the formation of free purine bases (adenine and guanine) and to the pyrimidine nucleotides in the form of their 2′ and 3′ phosphates. A mixture of 2′ and 3′ phosphates is obtained because, under the influence of the strong acid, migration of the phosphoryl group occurs from the 3′ position to the 2′ position via a 2′, 3′-cyclic phosphate, and vice versa.

The action of dilute alkali (0.3 M KOH at 37°C for 12 to 16 hr) leads to the complete hydrolysis of every internucleotide linkage in a normal RNA molecule and to the liberation of all the bases in the form of a mixture of 2′ and 3′ nucleotides (see Figure 4 2). Again a mixture of the two isomers is obtained in every case, because the presence of the 2′-hydroxyl group in the ribose leads to the formation of an intermediate cyclic phosphate ester by attack of the ionized 2′-hydroxyl group on the phosphate and cleavage of the phosphate-5′-hydroxyl bond. It is the intermediate formation of this cyclic phosphate that greatly facilitates the alkaline hydrolysis of RNA. Eventually the alkali will cleave the cyclic phosphate, but randomly, producing a mixture of not necessarily equal amounts of the two isomers.

The most highly specific ribonuclease[15] currently available is

also written . . . GpApUpCp . . .

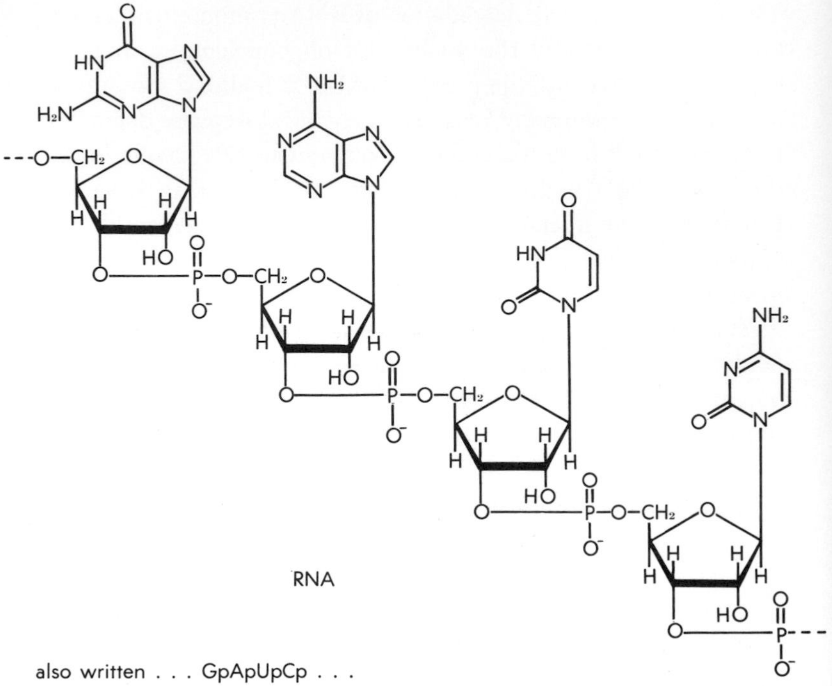

FIGURE 4-1   *The structural formula of a short portion of a typical RNA molecule. Underneath is given a shorthand notation of the same sequence. By convention the linkage G-3'-phosphate-5'-A is written as GpA, and a nucleotide ending with a 3'-linked phosphate group as ...Cp, for example. Similarly, a nucleotide ending with a 5'-linked phosphate is denoted by pA..., for example.*

derived from a mold product known as Takadiastase, and this enzyme is called ribonuclease T_1. The enzyme splits (Fig. 4–3) between the phosphate attached to the 3'-hydroxyl group of a guanylic acid residue and the 5' ribose of whatever nucleotide is next, producing oligonucleotides and mononucleotides ending in 3' phosphates attached to guanylic acid. Ribonuclease T_1 has no specificity with respect to the base attached to this neighboring ribose unit. It is not known whether this ribonuclease has a preference for single- or for double-stranded RNA.

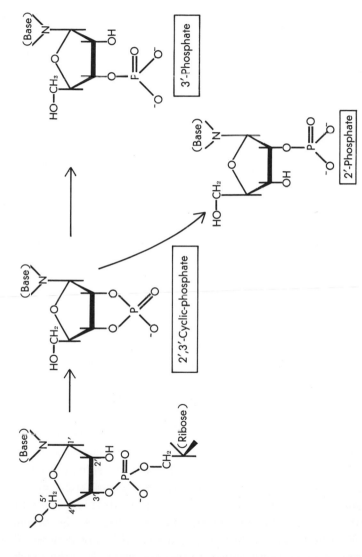

FIGURE 4-2 *The cyclic intermediate in the alkaline hydrolysis of RNA.*

The other specific ribonuclease is pancreatic ribonuclease, which was actually the first ribonuclease to be purified and studied.[16] This enzyme has a specificity for the pyrimidine bases (Figures 4–3 and 4–4), particularly for nucleotides formed by uracil and cytosine. It produces from RNA a mixture of mono- and oligonucleotides ending in a 3'-phosphate group attached to either uracil or cytosine nucleosides. Both these ribonucleases (T_1 and pancreatic) first produce as intermediate an oligonucleotide ending in a 2',3'-cyclic phosphate group, which is then split at a slower rate by the same enzyme to produce the 3' phosphate only. If other pyrimidine nucleotides occur in an RNA molecule (Figure 4–4), such as pseudo-uridylic acid or ribo-thymidylic acid, these are also sensitive to the action of pancreatic ribonuclease and will lead to the formation of oligonucleotides ending in these unusual pyrimi-dine nucleotides, again with a 3'-phosphate group.

There is very definite evidence to indicate that pancreatic ribonuclease acts preferentially on RNA that does not contain double-stranded helices, such helices being more resistant to the action of the enzyme. For example, a double helix of s-RNA stabilized by the addition of magnesium ions[17] is con-siderably less easily hydrolyzed by the enzyme; the inhibition can be reversed by the addition of EDTA, which is known to complex and remove magnesium ions.

Chemical reagents have been developed that will combine specifically with the keto group of uracil and will render such an altered or modified uracil nucleotide grouping insensitive to attack by pancreatic ribonuclease. Thus an increase in the specificity of pancreatic ribonuclease may be achieved. Such reagents are, for example, the substituted carbodiimide devel-oped by Gilham,[18] which forms an adduct with uracil. The reagent can be removed by raising the pH to 10.5.

An oligonucleotide produced by the action of one of the ribonucleases may be further degraded by phosphomonoes-terases such as the alkaline phosphatase[19] of E. coli. This enzyme has no action on internucleotide linkages, but it will remove efficiently terminal phosphate groups producing oligonucleotides with a free 2'- and 3'-hydroxyl group, and also with a free 5'-hydroxyl group at the other end of the oligonucleotide:

pGpCpApAp → GpCpApA + 2 phosphates

Dephosphorylated oligonucleotides are essential as starting materials for the application of the *chemical stepwise degradative* procedure (Figure 4–7) referred to earlier.[14] Dephosphorylated oligonucleotides are also easily attacked by the so-called *phosphodiesterases*. For example, snake venom phosphodiesterase will *sequentially* degrade an oligonucleotide irrespective of the base sequence, starting at the end carrying the free 2'- and 3'-hydroxyl groups. Step by step the enzyme removes each nucleotide in the form of a 5'-nucleotide monophosphate. The terminal base is therefore liberated as a nucleoside, as shown in Figure 4–5. This enzyme is not only extremely useful for the complete degradation of an oligonucleotide to 5'-nucleotides, but its action also serves as a useful end-group method, since the terminal nucleotide is liberated in the form of a nucleoside and may be identified and characterized as such.

It has been reported that, in certain types of s-RNA, an occasional ribose unit will carry a methyl group on its 2'-hydroxyl group. Such a methylated ribose can no longer form the intermediate cyclic phosphate; the internucleotide linkage involved is therefore resistant to hydrolysis by mild alkali. Because the snake venom phosphodiesterase does not form a cyclic phosphate as an intermediate in the hydrolysis of internucleotide linkages, this enzyme is capable of degrading such an alkali-resistant bond, enabling the identification of methoxyribose nucleotides. It may, in addition, be possible at some stage in the future to utilize this enzyme for following the sequential release of mononucleotides and therefore for determining the sequence of nucleotide bases in an oligonucleotide or even a polynucleotide. The enzyme has recently been used by Fraenkel-Conrat[12] in an analysis of the RNA from tobacco mosaic virus. By very careful work with radioactively labeled tobacco mosaic virus RNA, Fraenkel-Conrat was able to remove with snake

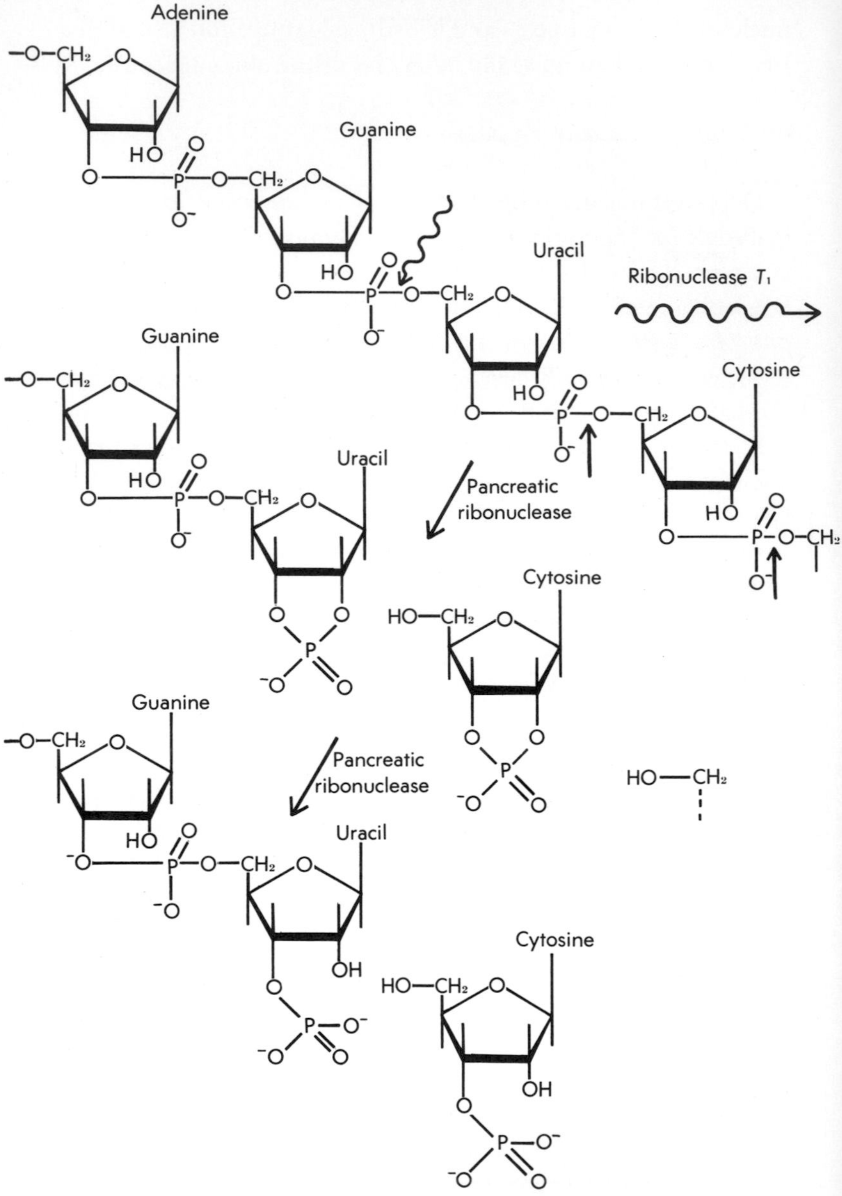

FIGURE 4–3 *Scheme for the degradation of a tetranucleotide in RNA by pancreatic ribonuclease and by ribonuclease*

T_1. In the "shorthand" reaction scheme the symbol for a 2',3'-cyclic phosphate is an exclamation point(!).

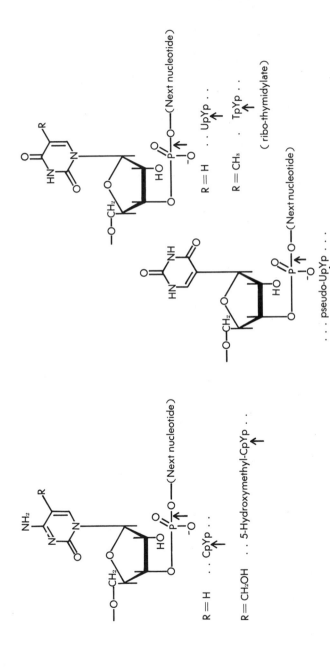

FIGURE 4-4(a) *The specificity of pancreatic ribonuclease. The symbol Yp stands for any nucleotide. Note that 5-hydroxymethyl-Cp, and pseudo-Up are rare bases, found primarily in s-RNA.*

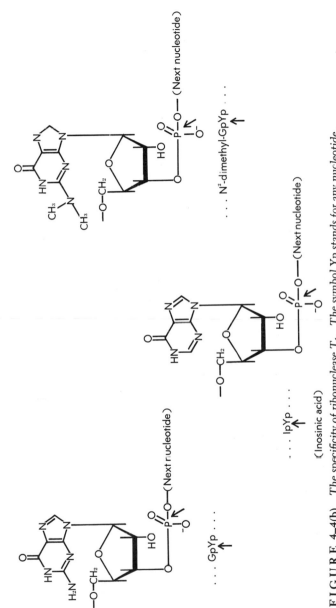

FIGURE 4-4(b) *The specificity of ribonuclease* T₁. *The symbol Yp stands for any nucleotide. Note that N²-dimethyl-Gp and Ip are rarely occuring bases, found primarily in s-RNA. Cleavage next to N²-dimethyl-Gp is slow and apparently does not proceed beyond the 2′,3′-cyclic phosphate* (...N²-dimethyl-G!).

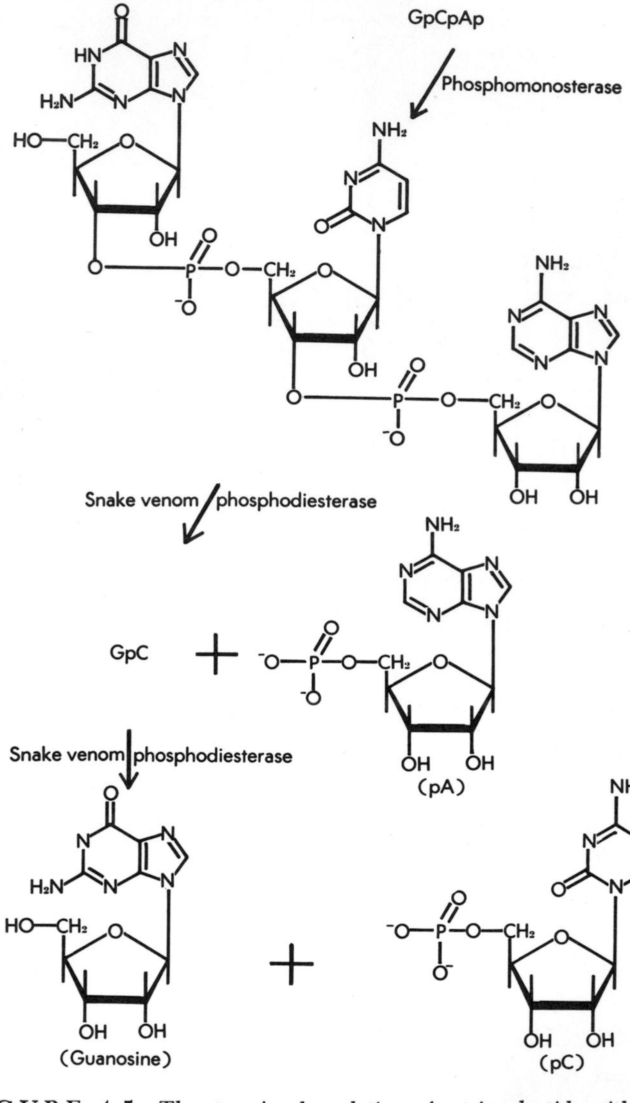

FIGURE 4-5 *The stepwise degradation of a trinucleotide with snake venom phosphodiesterase to produce 5'-mononucleotides (pA, pC) and the first base in the form of its nucleoside (guanosine). If a 3'-phosphate group is originally present, this has to be removed, because it inhibits the phosphodiesterase.*

venom diesterase first one and then two and possibly even three nucleotides from the 2′,3′-hydroxy end of this RNA. By this means he was able to establish the terminal sequence as being . . . CpCpA. He was able to show that an RNA preparation from which the terminal adenosine had been removed by means of the venom diesterase was still infective on tobacco leaves and was able to cause the formation of apparently completely normal virus particles with normal RNA molecules inside them. In other words, although the RNA put into the infected tobacco cell was deficient in its terminal nucleotide, the progeny RNA was intact and did have the terminal adenosine in place. There is at present no satisfactory explanation for this intriguing observation.

The other enzyme that is capable of sequential degradation and has been used in the study of oligonucleotides, is a *spleen phosphodiesterase*. This enzyme attacks an oligonucleotide sequentially from the end carrying a free 5′-hydroxy group, i.e., the end opposite the end attacked by snake venom diesterase. Spleen phosphodiesterase produces nucleotides ending with 3′-phosphate groups without the intermediate formation of any cyclic phosphates. The terminal nucleotide (originally at the end with free 2′,3′-OH groups) is liberated as a nucleoside and may be identified and used for end-group determination. It should be added that spleen phosphodiesterase is inhibited if the 5′-hydroxyl group carries a phosphate, and that snake venom phosphodiesterase is inhibited if the 3′-hydroxyl group of the oligonucleotide carries a phosphate grouping.

Clearly, by means of the information obtained through all these methods, the nucleotide sequence of an oligonucleotide may in principle be determined (Figure 4–6). However, the length of an oligonucleotide that could be so analyzed cannot be too great, because with only four different bases available to form the sequence, repeat sequences will be so frequent as to introduce many ambiguities into the ordering of fragments obtained by different degradative procedures.

The *chemical stepwise degradation* of RNA (Whitfeld[14]) applies only to an oligonucleotide with free 2′- and 3′-hydroxyl groups at the end. Oxidation with periodate cleaves this

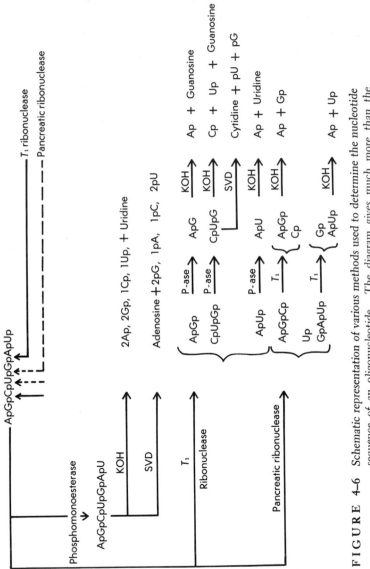

FIGURE 4-6 *Schematic representation of various methods used to determine the nucleotide sequence of an oligonucleotide. The diagram gives much more than the minimum information required to define the sequence. SVD = snake venom diesterase; P-ase = phosphomonoesterase; KOH = total alkaline hydrolysis to 2'- or 3'-mononucleotides.*

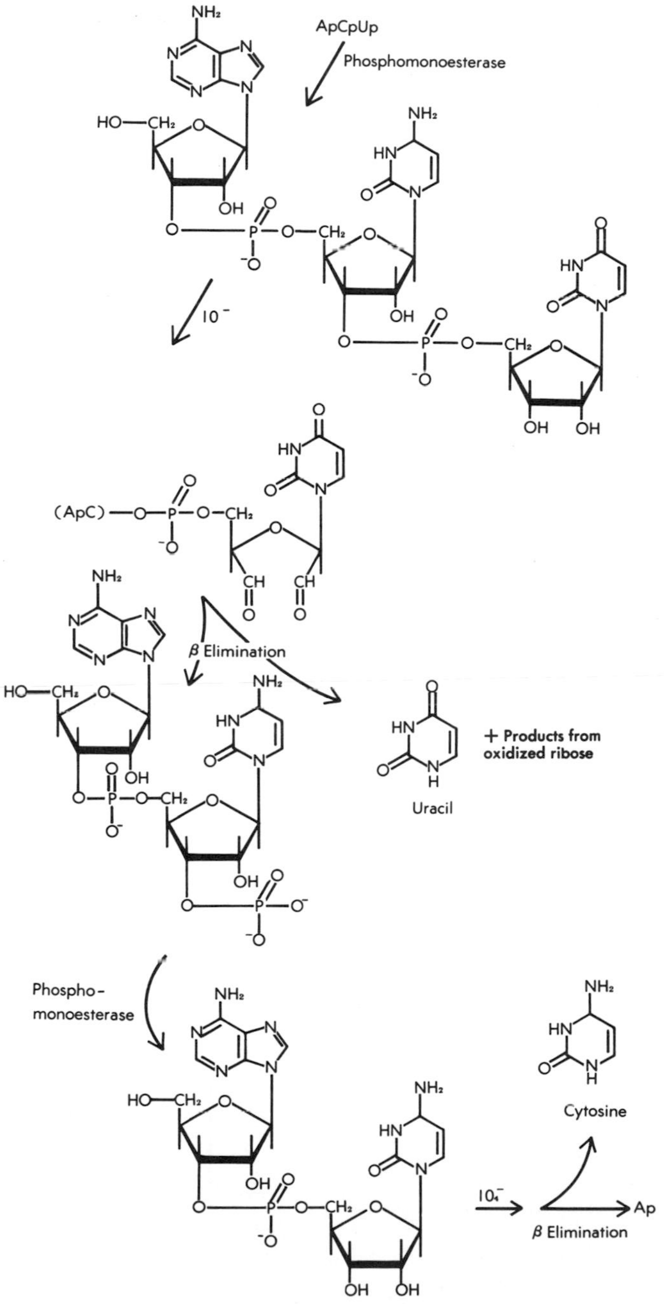

FIGURE 4–7 *Stepwise degradation of an oligonucleotide with two cycles of the Whitfeld periodate method.*

cis-glycol with the formation of a dialdehyde (Figure 4–7). At pH 10 or at pH 7 in the presence of a primary amine such as cyclohexylamine, this dialdehyde undergoes β-elimination with the liberation of the terminal base as a free base and the liberation of the degraded ribose unit. The rest of the oligonucleotide is one unit shorter, but it has a terminal 3′ phosphate attached to it. This phosphate has to be removed with phosphomonoesterase before the next treatment of the new terminal grouping with periodate. A repetition of these two steps, periodate oxidation and phosphatase action, can in principle lead to the sequential liberation of all the bases of the original oligonucleotide. In practice this has not been carried out beyond three or four steps, but the method holds great promise of being useful in the future.

Finally, mention should be made of a chemical modification that can be introduced into RNA molecules and oligonucleotides. By reaction with hydroxylamine, Zillig and his colleagues[20] have shown that at pH 6 cytosine is the only base attacked to any great extent. Two molecules of hydroxylamine add to the cytosine ring with a considerable change in spectrum. Treatment of *E. coli* r-RNA at pH 6 yielded material from which no cytidylic acid was liberated by hydrolysis with pancreatic ribonuclease. However, alkaline hydrolysis showed no decrease in cytidylic acid content, probably because the original addition of hydroxylamine at the 4,5 double bond is reversible in strong alkali. Reaction of the RNA at pH 10 gave a product yielding oligonucleotides with pancreatic ribonuclease, but no uridylic acid. At pH 10 hydroxylamine will attack uracil, leading to the removal of uracil from the RNA as a cyclic derivative and leaving on the ribose unit hydroxylamine in the form of ribose oxime. The ribose-oxime "nucleotide" is now no longer sensitive to hydrolysis by pancreatic ribonuclease, and this enzyme will produce, from such a modified RNA, oligonucleotides ending primarily in cytidylic acid. At pH 10, however, there is still a slight amount of attack on cytosine also, so that the specificity of the reaction is not quite absolute. Some time in the future such chemical modifications will be used for enhancing the specificity of pancreatic ribonuclease, thus leading to longer oligonucleotides and more sequence information.

REFERENCES

1. Sanger, F. (1949), *Cold Spring Harb. Symp. Quant. Biol.*, **14**, 153.

2. Sanger, F., Tuppy, H., Thompson, E. O. P., and others, summarized in detail in Harris, J. I., and Ingram, V. M., "Methods of Sequence Analysis in Proteins," *Analytical Methods in Protein Chemistry*, eds. Alexander, P., and Block, R. J., Pergamon Press, New York, 1960, Vol. **II**.

3. Hirs, W., Moore, S., and Stein, W. H. (also Anfinsen, C. B., *et al.*), summarized in detail in Harris, J. I., and Ingram, V. M., "Methods of Sequence Analysis in Proteins," *Analytical Methods in Protein Chemistry*, eds. Alexander, P., and Block, R. J., Pergamon Press, New York, 1960, Vol. **II**.

3a. Smyth, D. G., Stein, W. H. and Moore, S. (1963), "The Sequence of Amino Acid Residues in Bovine Pancreatic Ribonuclease: Revisions and Confirmations." *J. Biol. Chem.*, **238**, 227.

4. Discussed in Anfinsen, C. B. (1959), "The Molecular Basis of Evolution." Wiley, New York.

5. Bailey, J. L. (1962), "Techniques in Protein Chemistry." Elsevier, New York.

6. Edman, P. (1950), "Method for Determination of the Amino Acid Sequence in Peptides." *Acta Chem. Scand.*, **4**, 277 and 283; Eriksson, S., and Sjöquist, J. (1960), "Quantitative Determination of N-Terminal Amino Acids in some Serum Proteins." *Biochim. Biophys. Acta*, **45**, 290; Harris, J. I., and Roos, P. (1959), "The Structure of β-Melanocyte-Stimulating Hormone from Pig Pituitary Glands." *Biochem. J.*, **71**, 434.

7. Gross, E., and Witkop, B. (1961), "Selective Cleavage of the Methionyl Peptide Bonds in Ribonuclease with Cyanogen Bromide." *J. Am. Chem. Soc.*, **83**, 1510.

8. Burton, K., Lunt, M. R., Petersen, G. B., and Siebke, J. C. (1963), "Studies of Nucleotide Sequences in DNA." *Cold Spring Harb. Symp. Quant. Biol.*, **28**, 27.

9. Spencer, J. H., and Chargaff, E. (1963), "Studies on the Nucleotide Arrangement in DNAs. Parts V and VI." *Biochim. Biophys. Acta*, **68**, 9 and 18.

10. Tamm, C., Hodes, M. E., and Chargaff, E. (1952), "The Formation of Apurinic Acid from DNA of Calf Thymus." *J. Biol. Chem*, **195**, 49.

11. Apgar, J., Holley, R. W., and Merrill, S. H. (1962), "Purification of the Alanine-, Valine-, Histidine- and Tyrosine-acceptor RNAs from Yeast." *J. Biol. Chem.*, **237**, 796.

12. Singer, B., and Fraenkel-Conrat, H. (1963), "Studies of Nucleotide Sequences in TMV-RNA." *Biochim. Biophys. Acta*, **72**, 534.

13. Whitfeld, P. R. quoted in Reference 12.

14. Whitfeld, P. R. (1954), "A Method for the Determination of Nucleotide Sequence in Polyribonucleotides." *Biochem. J.*, **58**, 390.

15. Takahashi, K. (1962), "The Structure and Function of Ribonuclease T_1, Part II." *J. Biochem.* (Japan), **51**, 95.

16. See review on pages 558–575 in Schmidt, G. (1955), "Nucleases and Enzymes attacking Nucleic Acid Components" in *The Nucleic Acids, Vol. I*, eds. Chargaff, E., and Davidson, J. N., Academic Press, New York, 1955.

17. Nishimura, S., and Novelli, G. D. (1963), "Resistance of sRNA to Ribonucleases in the Presence of Magnesium Ions." *Biochem. Biophys. Res. Comm.*, **11**, 161; Litt, M., and Ingram, V. M. (1964), "Chemical Studies on Amino Acid Acceptor RNAs, Part II." *Biochemistry*, **3**, 560.

18. Gilham, P. T. (1962), "An Addition Reaction Specific for Uridine and Guanosine Nucleotides and its Application to the Modification of Ribonuclease Action." *J. Am. Chem. Soc.*, **84**, 687.

19. Heppel, L. A., Harkness, D. R., and Hilmoe, R. J. (1962), "A Study of the Substrate Specificity and other Properties of the Alkaline Phosphatase of *Escherichia coli*." *J. Biol. Chem.*, **237**, 841.

20. Verwoerd, D. W., Kohlhage, H., and Zillig, W. (1961), "Specific Partial Hydrolysis of Nucleic Acids in Nucleotide Sequence Studies." *Nature*, **192**, 1038.

FIVE §§ PROTEIN SYNTHESIS

AMINO ACID ACTIVATION
AND THE ROLE OF s-RNA

FOR EACH AMINO ACID THERE IS A SPECIFIC ACTIVATING ENZYME whose function it is to activate the carboxyl group of that amino acid (reviewed by Berg[1]). ATP is required for the reaction, as may be seen in the equation of Figure 5–1; as a result amino acyl-AMP is formed and inorganic pyrophosphate is released. The amino acyl-AMP is not liberated into solution, but remains bound to the activating enzyme. The reaction is reversible, because in the presence of radioactive pyrophosphate, incorporation of the radioactivity into ATP may be observed. In fact, it is possible to test for the presence of the activating enzyme or to estimate the enzymatic activity by measuring the rate of incorporation of radioactive inorganic pyrophosphate into ATP.

The amino acyl-AMP:enzyme complex reacts with amino-acid-specific s-RNA molecules to form amino acyl-s-RNA as illustrated in Figure 5–1. The enzyme is liberated to be used again and AMP is also formed. For each amino acid there

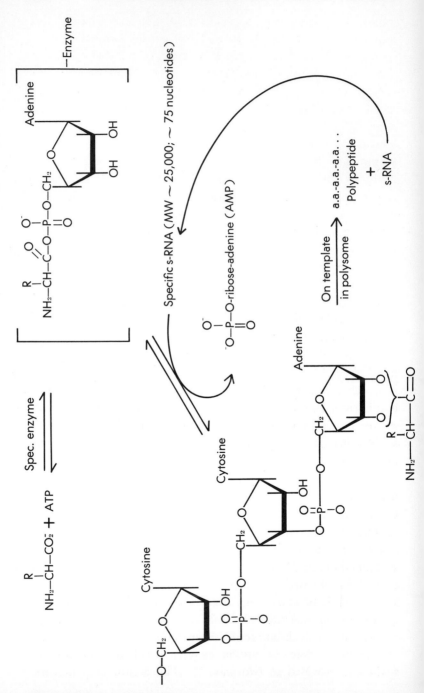

FIGURE 5–1   *The activation of an amino acid and its attachment to s-RNA.*

appears to be at least one specific s-RNA molecule present. The amino acid is attached by its carboxyl group, forming an ester linkage to either the 2'- or the 3'-hydroxyl group of the ribose in the terminal adenosine group of the s-RNA molecule.[2,3] It is not at all clear yet in which form, 2' or 3', the amino acyl-s-RNA is first made or in which form it is utilized, although a report has appeared placing the amino acyl group on the 3'-hydroxyl group.[4] However, recent work[5] has shown that the amino acyl group interchanges between these two possible positions with great rapidity; for example, one of the slowest, valyl-s-RNA, shows acyl migration 2'↔3' with a half-life under normal physiological conditions of much less than 1 sec. Such an amino acyl-s-RNA molecule is also subject to hydrolysis under physiological conditions, but this process proceeds very much less rapidly than does acyl migration. Nevertheless, hydrolysis is sufficiently rapid so that it is not possible to charge an s-RNA preparation in vitro completely with amino acids; instead a steady-state concentration is reached. This consideration may account for the failure of many experimenters to achieve 100 per cent conversion of s-RNA into amino acyl-s-RNA. On the other hand, it is possible to show saturation, not at the 100 per cent level but at some lower level. Alternatively, we note that the equilibrium constant for valyl- and threonyl-s-RNA formation ranges between 0.3 and 0.6, indicating that the amino acyl-s-RNA linkage has the same high-energy character as the parent amino acyl-AMP compound.

In the presence of ATP and of an excess of activating enzyme, a preparation of unfractionated s-RNA may be saturated to a definite level with increasing amounts of an amino acid. Further additions of this amino acid do not increase the amount of label attached to the s-RNA. On the other hand, if now a second amino acid is added (Table 5–1), it will be taken up and attached to its specific s-RNA molecules in the preparation; and so on. It is, of course, necessary for this experiment that all activating enzymes (Table 5–2) are present, as well as all types of amino acid specific s-RNA molecules.

The proof that the amino acid is attached covalently to s-RNA is provided in two ways.[2,3] The action of pancreatic

TABLE 5-1   *Separate sites for linking amino acids to acceptor RNA[a]*

Experiment	Radioactive Amino acid added	Incorporation into amino acyl s-RNA, counts/min.
1	Leucine	3759
	Valine	1646
	Methionine	468
	Mixture of above	5832
	Calculated sum	5873
2	Valine	947
	Leucine	1038
	Valine, then leucine	2006
	Calculated sum	1985
3	Valine	947
	Methionine	448
	Valine, then methionine	1434
	Calculated sum	1395

[a] From Reference 6.

ribonuclease upon a radioactively labeled amino acyl-s-RNA will degrade the s-RNA with the liberation of the terminal adenosine moiety to which the radioactive amino acid is still attached (see Figure 5–1).   This amino acyl-adenosine compound may be isolated by its characteristic behavior in electrophoresis or in chromatography.   Its structure can be proved by further degradation to adenosine and the amino acid.   All the other nucleotides of the s-RNA chain appear in the hydrolysate in the form of the 3′ mononucleotides or oligonucleotides ending in 3′-phosphates.

A second way in which the attachment of the amino acid to the s-RNA may be shown is by the action of potassium periodate on amino acyl-s-RNA and on free s-RNA.   In the latter case, the action of the periodate is to split oxidatively the carbon-carbon bond between the 2′- and 3′-hydroxyl groups in the ribose of the terminal adenosine, which are free in uncharged s-RNA (Figure 5–1).   s-RNA molecules that are combined with the amino acid via an ester linkage at the 2′ or 3′ hydroxyl are protected from the attack of periodate. The following experiment has been carried out[3]: s-RNA was enzymatically labeled with radioactive methionine. The methionyl-s-RNA preparation was purified and treated with periodate. After destroying the excess reagent, the methionine group was removed by hydrolysis at pH 10. The resulting s-RNA could not be labeled enzymatically by any amino acid except methionine. This shows that the terminal adenosine group of methionine-specific s-RNA was protected against the attack by the reagent, whereas the other s-RNA molecules specific for other amino acids were not so protected and therefore had their reactive end group destroyed.

T A B L E 5–2 *Specificity of enzyme preparations for amino acyl-adenylate and amino acyl-s-RNA formation*[a]

Enzyme specific for	Amino acid tested	Amino acyl-AMP formation[b]	Amino acyl-s-RNA formation[b]
Leucine	Leucine	358	3.2
	Valine	13.2	0.18
	Methionine	8.0	< 0.01
	Isoleucine	< 3.0	< 0.01
Valine	Valine	560	25
	Leucine	< 0.5	< 0.01
	Isoleucine	< 4.0	< 0.01
	Methionine	2.0	< 0.01
Isoleucine	Isoleucine	768	3.3
	Leucine	31	0.07
	Valine	416	< 0.03
	Methionine	41	0.07
Methionine (*E. coli* enzyme)	Methionine	356	3.5
	Leucine	4.0	< 0.01
	Valine	< 3.0	< 0.01
	Isoleucine	< 3.0	< 0.01
Methionine (yeast enzyme)	Methionine	44	0.016
	Leucine	< 0.4	< 0.001
	Valine	< 0.4	< 0.001
	Phenylalanine	< 0.4	< 0.001

[a] From Reference 6.
[b] In μmoles/mg enzyme protein/hr.

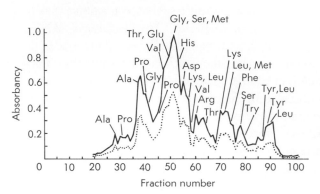

FIGURE 5-2　*The distribution pattern obtained by countercurrent distribution for 970 transfers of E. coli B s-RNA ———————, absorbancy at 260 mμ; ...., absorbancy at 280 mμ. Peak fractions containing the various amino acid acceptor activities are indicated by the arrows. (After Reference 8.)*

STRUCTURE OF s-RNA

Preparations of s-RNA as ordinarily prepared from a microorganism, from mammalian liver, or from rabbit reticulocytes have approximately the same molecular weight (25,000) and a single nucleotide chain, which is of the order of 75 to 80 nucleotides long. At one end of the molecule is a free 5′ phosphate grouping attached to a terminal guanylic acid residue. At the other end of the chain, where the amino acid is attached, the nucleotide sequence always ends in . . . CpCpA, as illustrated in Figure 5–1. It is believed that the nucleotide sequences in the rest of the molecule differ in the different amino acid-specific s-RNA molecules.

A preparation of s-RNA will normally contain a mixture of all the commonly occurring amino acid-specific s-RNAs. They may be separated best by Holley's countercurrent-distribution method,[7] which after two or three cycles can yield very highly purified s-RNA preparations that are specific for alanine, valine, and tyrosine. For some of the amino acids,[8] as illustrated in Figure 5–2, such as leucine, more than one leucine-specific fraction is obtained in this fractionation procedure.[1] It is

possible that the four different fractions of leucine-specific
s-RNA which are observed correspond to different triplet code-
words[9] for the same amino acid, as is implied in the concept of
degeneracy in coding.   On the other hand, it is also possible
that different fractions for leucine-s-RNA are obtained, owing
to chemical degradation or to a combination of leucine s-RNA
with different, or different amounts of, metal ions.   It remains
to be seen whether these different fractions of s-RNA specific
for the same amino acid really differ in their nucleotide sequence, and therefore possibly in their response to degenerate
coding triplets, or whether they are simply artifacts of the
method of isolation or of degradation (see also p. 150).

In solution s-RNA shows hyperchromicity (Figures 5–3 and
5–4), which supports the idea of considerable base pairing in the
molecule.[10,11]   Because this hyperchromicity on heating is completely and rapidly reversible, it has been assumed that the native
molecule at physiological temperature is formed from a single
nucleotide chain bent back upon itself.   The agreement between
the observed physical and chemical (end-group) molecular
weight also supports this idea.   The T_m of s-RNA is low, of the
order of 58°C in 0.1 M NaCl at pH 6.7.   In such a model it is
clear that there is at least one region of the nucleotide chain
where the chain bends back on itself (Figure 5–5) leaving one
or more loops.   Possibly it is the part of the molecule with exposed nucleotide bases which recognizes the nucleotide se-

FIGURE 5–3   *Changes in absorbancy of s-RNA in different solvents
as a function of temperature.   [After A Tissières, J.
Mol. Biol., 1, 368 (1959).]*

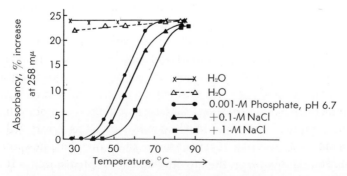

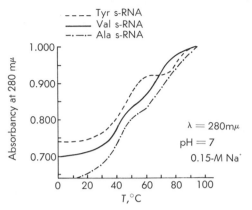

FIGURE 5-4   *Changes in absorbancy on heating solutions of purified yeast alanine, valine, and tyrosine-specific s-RNAs. The solvent is 0.15 M Na⁺ (phosphate), pH 7.0. (After Reference 12.)*

quence of the m-RNA when the s-RNA aligns itself on the m-RNA template. Cantoni[13] postulated that it is this loop in the structure of the s-RNA molecule that contains the base sequence complementary to the coding triplet of the m-RNA; he has called this the *nodoc*, because it is complementary to the *codon*, the current term for the coding unit.

We can recognize four special sites on the s-RNA molecule: *first*, the amino acid attachment site, which is . . . CpCpA and which appears to be the same for all types of s-RNA; *second*, there must be a specific site that recognizes the specific amino acid-activating enzyme. This particular site varies between different types of s-RNA and is specific for a given amino acid. We have no idea at the moment of where this site might be; conceivably it is next to the . . . CpCpA site of amino acid attachment. The *third* important site on the s-RNA molecule is the nodoc or coding-recognition site, which is of course also specific for a particular type of s-RNA molecule, and specific for one of the amino acids. It seems unlikely that any of these sites should be formed by the ribose-phosphate backbone in a portion of the molecule that is DNA-like in structure. It is more likely that these sites are at the unpaired nucleotide bases in the bends or loops of the s-RNA structure where the bases are exposed.   It is not until the complete nucleotide sequence of one or several specific s-RNA molecules are available that we can attempt to build models showing the secondary structure of such a molecule; we can then begin to see the characteristics of the different "active" sites.

It will also be necessary for an s-RNA molecule to interact with the ribosomes, so that we might speak of a *fourth* region on the s-RNA molecule, the ribosome recognition site (see also page 123).   This last site may be necessary, because an s-RNA trinucleotide sequence attached by base pairing to a triplet on the messenger RNA is thermodynamically not stable enough

F I G U R E 5–5   *Two possible models for s-RNA configuration.   The amino acid-attachment site is indicated.*

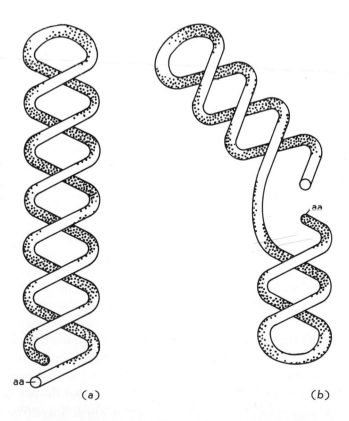

(a)   (b)

to ensure a sufficiently long time of positioning of the amino acyl-s-RNA on the template.

In this connection we should also mention that s-RNA is peculiar in that it contains the so-called additional bases. Chief among these is pseudo-uridylic acid, which is the 5-ribosyl isomer of uridylic acid (see Figure 3–11). Inosinic acid also occurs, although rarely; it presumably has base-pairing properties similar to guanylic acid. Then there are a number of methylated nucleotide bases: the various methylated guanines, methylated uracil, which is thymine, occurring as a ribonucleotide; methylated adenines, and methylated cytosines. Some of these methylated derivatives undoubtedly cannot take part in base pairing,[14] because the methyl groups take the place of the hydrogens necessary for hydrogen bond formation. They would necessarily form loops or unpaired regions of nucleotide sequence. Possibly these additional bases form part of one or more of the "active" sites of the s-RNA molecule.

It is believed that the nucleotide sequence of s-RNA is formed by DNA-dependent RNA polymerase transcribing some portion of the DNA molecule[15] in the nucleus. This process cannot account for the complete structure of s-RNA, not even the complete *primary* structure of s-RNA. The terminal . . . CpCpA end of each s-RNA molecule is formed by a specific enzyme or enzymes which reversibly attach the CMP portion of CTP (twice) and the AMP portion of ATP (once) to the end of an s-RNA chain (Figure 5–6). It seems as if the RNA polymerase makes a nucleotide chain without the last three nucleotides and that these are then attached in their correct sequence by the terminal-adding enzyme or enzymes using CTP and ATP. These same enzymes will release the terminal nucleotides on incubation with excess inorganic pyrophosphate.

The alignment of amino acyl-s-RNA molecules on the m-RNA template is illustrated in Figure 5–7, which also shows how the amino acids are thought to link together to form peptide bonds in the finished polypeptide chain. It should be pointed out that we do not know the polarity (parallel or antiparallel) of the nucleotide chain forming the s-RNA-coding site with respect to the polarity of m-RNA. It is however clear that the polarities of messenger RNA and of the DNA from which it is copied are

F I G U R E 5–6 *The addition of terminal CMP and AMP residues to
s-RNA by the terminal adding enzyme.*

likely to be opposite (see Chapter 3). However, the direction in
which the peptide chain grows in relation to the polarity of the
messenger RNA is now known to be from the 5′ end, i.e. from
left to right in Figure 4–1.

REQUIREMENTS FOR PROTEIN SYNTHESIS

In Table 5–3 are listed the ingredients that must be present in a
cell-free incubation mixture for the synthesis of a finished soluble
protein. The ribosomes themselves are not active unless they
are combined with messenger RNA in the presence of mag-

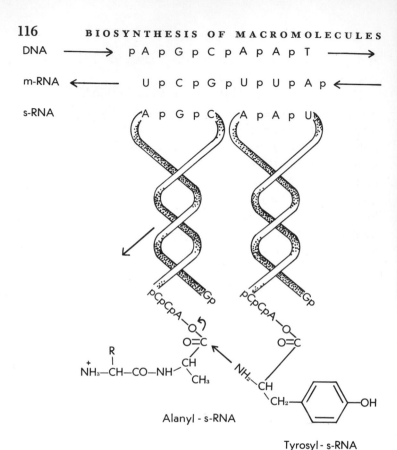

DNA $\longrightarrow$ p A p G p C p A p A p T $\longrightarrow$

m-RNA $\longleftarrow$ U p C p G p U p U p A p $\longleftarrow$

s-RNA

Alanyl - s-RNA

Tyrosyl - s-RNA

FIGURE 5–7   *The alignment of amino acyl-s-RNA on the template and the condensing of two amino acyl groups to form a peptide bond. Note the release of one of the s-RNA molecules. The arrows indicate the polarities of the DNA and the m-RNA chains.*

nesium ions. Magnesium ions are required in order to assure the stability of the ribosomes and their attachment to m-RNA. The concept[16-21] of a heavy ribosome or polysome involves the idea of an assembly of a number of ribosomes along the m-RNA molecule. For example, in hemoglobin biosynthesis there is evidence[17-21] to suggest that, on the average, the polysome unit which synthesizes one or the other of the hemoglobin peptide chains (approximately 150 amino acids) contains some five ribosomes per m-RNA. The evidence for the polysomal unit and the hypothesis concerning their mode of action will be discussed later in this chapter.

The function of the GTP is not at all understood,[22,23] but it is necessary to maintain this compound at the triphosphate level. This would suggest that GTP is involved in some energy-yielding process. It has even been postulated that it is required in order to permit the movement of ribosomes along the m-RNA in the polysome unit. However, all we really know about it is that it must be added to the cell-free incubation mixture for biosynthesis to occur, particularly if we are looking for finished, soluble peptide chains rather than merely the incorporation of labeled amino acids into precipitable peptide material. Evidence is accumulating[22,23] that two soluble enzyme fractions from the so-called supernatant fraction of cell extracts are required for a complete system of protein synthesis. Such fractions remain in the supernatant after ribosomes and polysomes are spun down from cell extracts. The enzymes have been purified by column chromatography to a considerable extent, and they have been separated into two fractions.[22,23] Probably one of these enzymes is necessary for the release of soluble hemoglobin from polysomes making this protein.

The need for an SH compound in the incubation mixture is related to the necessity of maintaining those enzymes active that require a free SH group for their full activity. For the synthesis of a complex protein such as hemoglobin, which in

T A B L E   5–3   *Requirements of protein synthesis (cell-free)*

Ribosomes (ribosomal protein and r-RNA)	
m-RNA	Polysomes
Mg^{++}	
Amino acids	
ATP	
Activating enzymes	a.a. s-RNA
s-RNA	
GTP	
Condensing enzyme	
Releasing enzyme	
SH compound, e.g., mercaptoethanol	

addition to the peptide chain contains the heme groups, it is also necessary to provide a source of such prosthetic groups in the incubation mixture. In most preparations the actual amount of protein made is so minute that sufficient heme prosthetic group is in fact always present.

STRUCTURE OF RIBOSOMES

Ribosomes are nucleoprotein particles composed of a basic protein or proteins and ribosomal RNA (See chapter 3). Single ribosomes may be prepared from cell extracts by differential centrifugation in the presence of magnesium. The ribosomes proper sediment with a sedimentation constant of 78 to 80 S, after the larger debris (nuclei and mitochondria) have come down. Polysomes can only be obtained after very gentle lysis of cells, and they are best harvested in a sucrose-density gradient (see later).

Single ribosomes may also be isolated from cell extracts, after removal of larger particles, by precipitation at pH 5 and by chromatography on ion exchange columns. In E. coli the ribosomes[24] contain 60 per cent protein by weight and 40 per cent RNA; their stability depends on the magnesium concentration. The different ribosome subunits found in bacterial extracts are illustrated in Figure 5–8; these types are isolated from extracts of cells ground with alumina in which, through the rough grinding procedure, ribosomal aggregates, the polysomes, are broken to single ribosomes. In a fairly high magnesium concentration (1mM) 70 S and 100 S ribosomes are seen with molecular weights of 2.8 and 5.9×10^6, respectively. On lowering the magnesium concentration to 0.1 mM however, these ribosomes disaggregate forming a mixture of 30 S and 50 S ribosomes with molecular weights of 0.85 and 1.8×10^6, respectively (Figure 5–8). The disaggregation is reversible and, when the magnesium ion concentration is restored to 1 mM, we again observe the formation of 70 S particles by aggregation of 30 S and 50 S particles; eventually the 100 S particles reform.

Extraction of separated 30 S and 50 S ribosome preparations with phenol yield r-RNA. The 30 S ribosome particle gives rise

to an r-RNA with a molecular weight of 550,000 and a sedimentation constant of 16. The larger 50 S particle on the other
hand gives rise to r-RNA with a molecular weight of 1.15×10^6
and a sedimentation constant of 23 S, or to two equivalents of
16 S r-RNA.

Beyond these physical measurements the study of the structure of ribosomal particles has not progressed very far. As yet we
can assign no definite function to the r-RNA, other than a
structural function, and no definite function to the ribosomal
protein. We know that preparations of bacterial ribosomes
contain a few enzymes, such as a ribonuclease that does not
become active until the ribosomes dissociate in low magnesium
concentrations. However, it now seems likely that these enzymes are merely adsorbed when the cells are lysed and are not
properly a part of the ribosome.

FIGURE 5–8   The dissociation and association reactions of E. coli
ribosomes. Note also the types of r-RNA that can be
extracted with phenol. (After Reference 24.)

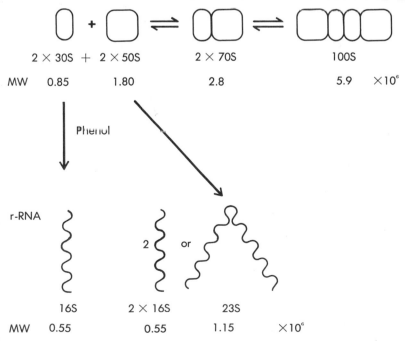

CODING SPECIFICITY OF s-RNA

A beautiful experiment was performed by Lipmann and von Ehrenstein[25] in 1961, who showed that s-RNA from one species may be used to synthesize a protein typical of a different species. In the rabbit reticulocyte, the immature red cell, virtually the only protein synthesized is rabbit hemoglobin. This cell is equipped with active ribosomes in the polysome configuration. In a cell-free system, von Ehrenstein and Lipmann added to purified rabbit ribosomes and polysomes, that is, containing the m-RNA for rabbit hemoblobin, the following additional factors: GTP, a supernatant enzyme fraction, and s-RNA from *E. coli*, which had been previously charged with amino acids using *E. coli* activating enzymes. This amino acyl-s-RNA from *E. coli* was freed from protein and contained all the amino acids required for the synthesis of hemoglobin, of which, however, only leucine was radioactive with ^{14}C. In this cell-free system hemoglobin was synthesized. About 66 per cent of the radioactivity of the added ^{14}C-leucine-s-RNA was transferred to protein (Figure 5–9); some 70 per cent of this 66 per cent was eventually found in soluble hemoglobin. The experiment represents a rather efficient transfer of radioactive amino

FIGURE 5–9   *Time curve of* ^{14}*C-leucine transfer from E. coli s-RNA to hemoglobin, measured as total acid precipitable protein. (After Reference 25.)*

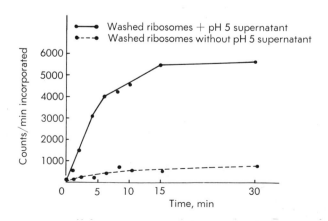

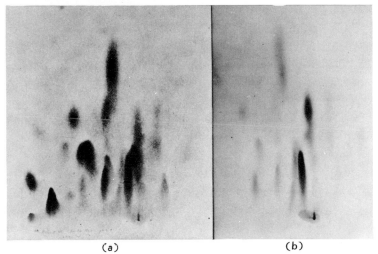

(a)   (b)

FIGURE 5–10   (a) Ninhydrin stain of the fingerprint of a tryptic
digest of soluble rabbit hemoglobin produced in the
experiment of Figure 5–9.   (b) Radioautogram of the
same fingerprint.   (After Reference 25.)

acid into soluble protein by the usual standards of such a
system.

Next, the radioactive "new" rabbit hemoglobin was mixed
with some unlabeled rabbit hemoglobin as carrier; it was heat
denatured and digested with trypsin. The resultant mixture of
tryptic peptides was separated by fingerprinting,[26] a two-dimen-
sional combination of paper electrophoresis and paper chromatography. Subsequently this fingerprint was developed with
ninhydrin to reveal the positions of the tryptic peptides from
the carrier rabbit hemoglobin and also exposed to an X-ray
film to locate the tryptic peptides of the newly synthesized
radioactive hemoglobin. It was clear that the two patterns
(Figure 5–10) were superimposable and that the radioactive-
leucine-containing peptides corresponded to tryptic peptides
from the carrier hemoglobin. This experiment proved that, in
the presence of rabbit m-RNA in rabbit ribosomes and polysomes and E. coli s-RNA, the amino acids were inserted into
their correct places in the peptide chain. In other words, the
information for making the protein was to be found in the
polysome fraction and presumably in the m-RNA of that

fraction. The second conclusion from this important experiment is that the coding sites of the bacterial s-RNA and the site for recognizing ribosomes are identical with the coding sites and ribosome-recognition sites of the homologous rabbit reticulocyte s-RNA, which would normally have been used. This is evidence in favor of the universality of the genetic code.

Once the amino acid has been attached to its specific s-RNA, the future fate of that amino acid is decided by the coding properties of its s-RNA adaptor. That this is so was first shown by some ingenious experiments of Chapeville et al.[27] They took *E. coli* s-RNA and charged it with radioactive ^{14}C-cysteine. Presumably cysteine is now linked to cysteine-specific s-RNA. Through reduction with Raney nickel, they were able to remove the sulfur from the cysteinyl-s-RNA compound and replace it by hydrogen without breaking the linkage between the amino acid and the s-RNA [Eq. (5–1)]. As

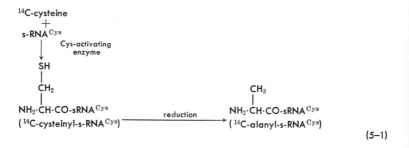

$$(5-1)$$

a result of this reduction, cysteine is converted to alanine so that we now have ^{14}C-alanyl-s-RNA^{cys}. Using a cell-free system based on the experiments of Nierenberg and Ochoa (see later in this chapter), Chapeville and his co-workers were able to show that the ^{14}C-alanine was now incorporated by synthetic polyribonucleotides that contained only U and G and had the triplets required for the incorporation of cysteine. This UG copolymer did not stimulate the incorporation of ^{14}C-alanine, however, when this was attached in the usual way to s-RNA^{ala}, i.e., s-RNA specific for alanine. Furthermore, the ^{14}C-alanyl-s-RNA^{cys} was not incorporated by polyribonucleotides that did have the coding properties for alanine (attached to alanine-specific s-RNA). This experiment shows that the amino acid goes where the s-RNA directs.

In an extension of this experiment, von Ehrenstein et al.[28] were able to direct the incorporation of this chemically modified ^{14}C-alanyl-s-RNA[cys] into peptides from newly synthesized soluble hemoglobin. They asked the question whether the ^{14}C-alanine bound to an adaptor s-RNA molecule specific for cysteine would be found in tryptic peptides normally containing alanine or in peptides normally containing cysteine of the newly synthesized hemoglobin. The result is shown in Table 5–4. The only peptide containing radioactivity is one normally containing cysteine and no alanine. Conversely, those other peptides that normally contain alanine but no cysteine have not incorporated any radioactivity. The radioactivity found in peptide number 13 can be accounted for mostly in the form of alanine. The necessary control experiments were also carried out and showed that ^{14}C-cysteinyl-s-RNA[cys] was also incorporated only into peptide number 13. On the other hand, ^{14}C-alanyl-s-RNA[ala] was not incorporated into peptide 13, but was incorporated into most of the other alanine-containing peptides. This experiment confirms that the placement of a given amino acid on the template is directed by the specificity of the s-RNA adaptor.

The stabilization of the s-RNA on the coding site cannot be due entirely to interaction of a triplet on the m-RNA with a triplet on the s-RNA molecule. It has been shown[29] that the T_m for a thymine-containing trinucleotide attached to polyadenylic acid is $-12°C$. The corresponding figure for an octanucleotide is $-3°C$ and for a dodecanucleotide, $12°C$. Although the hydrogen bonds formed by the base pair GC are stronger, it is likely that attachment of s-RNA to the m-RNA by triplets alone is not sufficient to allow peptide-bond formation to occur. Presumably then there is also some additional nonspecific binding of s-RNA to the ribosomes of such a nature that the amino acyl-s-RNA is firmly held, but that the discharged s-RNA is less firmly held and easily released from the ribosomes.

TABLE 5-4

Peptide number[a]	Number of residues		^{14}C-Ala-s-RNA[cys] incubation, cpm	^{14}C-Cys-s-RNA[cys] incubation, cpm	^{14}C-Ala-s-RNA[ala] incubation, cpm
	Alanine	Cysteine			
4	2	0	0	0	0(?)
10	3	0	0	0	9.1
13	0	1	10.2 (largely ^{14}C-alanine)	13.1 (all ^{14}C-cysteine)	0
15	3	0	0	0	15.3

[a] Arbitrary numbers.

MESSENGER-RNA FORMATION

The early cytochemical evidence indicated a connection between RNA and protein synthesis.[30,31] The idea of a messenger RNA—a template for protein synthesis distinct from the bulk RNA of the ribosomes—goes back to an observation by Hershey[32]: following phage infection of a bacterium, net synthesis of RNA stopped, but a small RNA fraction turned over rapidly. The name and the concept of "messenger RNA" were developed much later by Jacob and Monod[33] for their interpretation of the mechanism of enzyme induction and repression in bacteria (see historical synopsis of m-RNA by Lipmann[34]).

The most influential early evidence for the existence of an RNA fraction having the properties of m-RNA was obtained in 1956 by Volkin and Astrachan.[35] After infection of a bacterium with the bacteriophage, the synthesis of normal bacterial RNA and proteins ceases, but after a short lag the synthesis of bacteriophage-specific proteins begins. During that lag period and before the synthesis of new protein can begin, some RNA is rapidly synthesized; this is not ribosomal RNA, but presumably the new messenger RNA directed by the infecting bacteriophage DNA and required for the synthesis of bacteriophage proteins. Volkin and Astrachan showed that this new RNA has a base composition resembling somewhat that of the T2 DNA but unlike that of the host E. coli DNA. The new RNA also did not resemble r-RNA in its base composition. Probably this was the first demonstration of the formation of m-RNA.

One of the clearest demonstrations of the formation of messenger RNA was the experiment of Brenner, Jacob, and Meselson.[36] They grew bacteria in a medium containing the heavy isotopes of carbon and nitrogen, that is to say ^{13}C and ^{15}N. At the time of infection of the bacteria with T4 bacteriophage, a *pulse* of radioactive phosphate (^{32}P) was given and at the same time the bacteria were transferred to a medium containing the normal light isotopes of carbon and nitrogen (^{12}C and ^{14}N); therefore, all new cell components made after phage infection were made with a light isotope. After a few minutes the cells were broken open, carrier cell extract was added and the extract was put in an ultracentrifuge into a gradient of cesium chloride for the analysis of the different components. In such a density gradient during ultracentrifugation, the ribosomes will occupy characteristic positions according to their molecular weight (i.e., 50 S, 70 S, etc.) and according to whether they are composed of heavy carbon and nitrogen or light carbon and nitrogen. In this way it was possible to distinguish ribosomes made before phage infection (heavy) from new ribosomes made after phage infection (light). In addition, the new phage-specific RNA, the new m-RNA, was characterized by being radioactive with ^{32}P. Fractions were obtained from such a gradient experiment and analyzed for UV-absorbing material, that is to say for the bulk (light) r-RNA, and for radioactivity derived from the ^{32}P-labeled new m-RNA.

From the position of the ^{32}P-labeled new messenger RNA in the gradient it was possible to decide whether this new m-RNA was associated with the old (heavy) ribosomes formed before infection or with new (light) ribosomes formed after infection. The results showed quite clearly that *the newly synthesized m-RNA formed after phage infection is associated with the old ribosomes.* This finding is in agreement with the general concept that m-RNA is formed on DNA and then becomes associated with pre-existing ribosomes to form the active polysome complex. In a further experiment, it was shown that radioactive sulfate was incorporated into the old ribosomes that had been made before infection. Radioactive sulfate would be incorporated as the result of protein synthesis in the form of the amino acids methionine and cysteine. It is therefore the pre-existing ribosomes together with the newly formed messenger RNA that are active in protein synthesis.

Spiegelman[37] also found that after infection of *E. coli* with bacteriophage T2, rapidly labeled RNA (m-RNA containing ^{32}P) is formed. This may be prepared together with the pre-existing unlabeled RNA by extraction with phenol. In electrophoresis a new faster-moving fraction of RNA, containing the radioactivity, moves ahead of the unlabeled bulk RNA. It was concluded that this was evidence for the formation of a different type of RNA as the result of phage infection, although it is not at all clear why such a newly formed RNA should differ in its electrophoretic mobility. More convincing are his experiments with such labeled RNA in a gradient of sucrose in the ultracentrifuge. This gradient separates RNA molecules according to their size, and they are characterized by their sedimentation constant. In this experiment Spiegelman found that the bulk of the RNA that had no radioactive label was to be found in the two major peaks characteristic of r-RNA which had sedimentation constants of 18 S and 25 S. On the other hand, that RNA which is made very rapidly after phage infection could be detected only by its radioactivity; it sedimented as a heterogeneous collection of molecules with widely different sedimentation constants, but showing a peak at a sedimentation constant of 8 S (Figure 5–11). This result indicated that after phage infection,

FIGURE 5–11 *Sedimentation in a sucrose density gradient of ^{32}P-labeled whole RNA from E. coli. (a) RNA from T2-phage infected cells, given ^{32}P between 5 and 7 min after infection. (b) RNA from control cells given a 2-min pulse of ^{32}P. (See Reference 15.)*

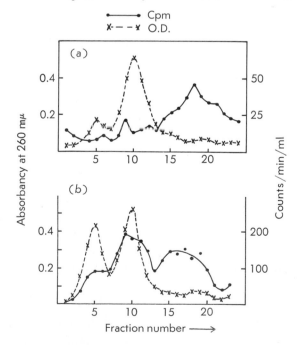

a type of RNA is made that differs in its physical properties from ribosomal RNA. Also, the rapidly labeled phage-specific RNA formed DNA-RNA hybrids, but only with phage DNA on heating and slow cooling, indicating that the RNA contained base sequences complementary to phage DNA. A short pulse (^{32}P) experiment with uninfected cells showed that they also formed this rapidly synthesized, smaller RNA in addition to r-RNA.

In 1961 Gros, Watson, and their colleagues[38,39] demonstrated quite clearly the formation of m-RNA in *uninfected* bacteria. They exposed cultures of *E. coli*, which had been starved of uracil, to a 30-sec supply of ^{14}C-uracil at 28°C, followed by varying times of exposure to ^{12}C-uracil; then they looked for the appearance of this RNA-specific label in the components of the cell extracts. Again the method of analysis is that of a sucrose-gradient ultracentrifugation, which separates molecules such as ribosomes and RNA according to their sedimentation constants, that is, according to their size. The bacterial cells, after the pulse and a varying time in cold ^{12}C-uracil, were harvested in a medium containing unlabeled uracil. Sedimentation in the sucrose gradient gave the pictures shown in Figure 5–12. Fractions of the gradient were analyzed for total RNA by ultraviolet-light absorption and for radioactivity, that is, for newly formed RNA. The ultraviolet-absorption curve shows the characteristic sedimentation pattern to be expected from a normal bacterial cell, with s-RNA (the smallest molecule) at the top of the gradient and two sizes of ribosomes sedimenting at 30 S and 50 S. Radioactivity measurements on the other hand show a rapidly labeled peak in a different region between s-RNA and the 30 S ribosome peak (Figure 5–12a); this then is the newly formed, or messenger, RNA. It should be noted that the peak is trailing toward the higher sedimentation constants, indicating that here again a heterogeneous collection of m-RNA molecules of different lengths is formed.

In the second part of the experiment (Figures 5–12b and c) the bacteria that had been exposed to the short pulse of ^{14}C-uracil were incubated with unlabeled uracil long enough (6

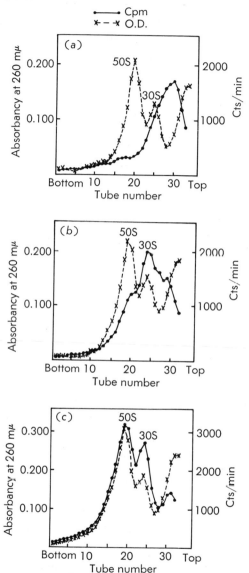

FIGURE 5–12 *Sedimentation in sucrose gradient of ribosomes and RNA made in uninfected E. coli cells with a pulse of ^{14}C-uracil. All extracts made in 10^{-4} M Mg. (a) = Sedimentation after only a 2-min chase with ^{12}C-uracil. (b) = Sedimentation after a 6-min chase. (c) = Sedimentation after a 20-min chase (After Reference 39.)*

or 20 min) for the m-RNA fraction to decay. This constitutes a "chase" experiment, in which the radioactivity is "chased" from a metabolically unstable form into a more stable molecule. The measurement of ultraviolet-absorption shows s-RNA and two peaks of ribosomes at 30 S and 50 S. However, the radioactivity pattern this time is different; especially after the longer chase (20 min with ^{12}C-uracil), it follows the contours of the 30 S and 50 S ribosomes, indicating that the radioactive-uracil counts previously present in the lighter m-RNA peak have now been incorporated into the 30 S and 50 S ribosomes, presumably in the form of ribosomal RNA. The radioactive uracil of m-RNA has been chased into ribosomal RNA. This is an indication not only that m-RNA is formed rapidly during such a short-pulse experiment, but also that it is degraded again rapidly into r-RNA. Only a little of the radioactivity originally in messenger RNA has appeared in soluble RNA.

The instability of the m-RNA is more characteristic of the bacterial system than of some mammalian systems. For example, the reticulocyte has an m-RNA that is stable over a considerable period of time.[40] Such reticulocytes synthesize hardly any m-RNA and indeed they have no, or very little, DNA left in them, because their nuclei have disintegrated. It is therefore not surprising that such a cell is no longer capable of making messenger RNA and no formation of messenger RNA has been detected in them. On the other hand, reticulocytes do synthesize a protein and therefore contain presumably a stable m-RNA.

In B. subtilis, Levinthal et al.[41] have shown that, although the m-RNA is unstable, it nevertheless persists sufficiently long to allow it to be used approximately 15 times for the synthesis of the corresponding proteins before it is degraded and before its components are merged with the mononucleotide pool of the cell. Figure 5–13 illustrates the relationship between m-RNA, r-RNA, and the nucleotide pool. Messenger RNA is continuously made from the components of the nucleotide pool and it decays again with a half-life of approximately 2 min in B. subtilis. Ribosomal RNA on the other hand is made considerably more slowly from the pool, but nucleotides built into

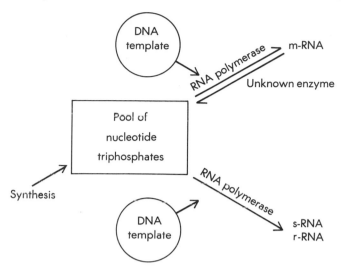

FIGURE 5–13 *Model for the flow of RNA precursors into various forms of RNA in the bacterial cell.*

r-RNA are trapped into a stable molecule and are not returned to the pool. At least this is the view of these workers. This ability on the part of the bacterium to make rapidly a relatively unstable m-RNA gives it much more flexibility to adjust its production of particular proteins and enzymes to changes in environment. Changes in bacterial physiology as the result of enzyme induction would not have been nearly as effective if the m-RNA were not turning over rapidly. Presumably a mammalian cell does not require such great flexibility, and its messenger RNA appears to be much more stable.

It is interesting to note that RNA polymerase together with DNA primer will stimulate the incorporation of amino acids into insoluble protein material in a cell-free system. Presumably the DNA-dependent RNA polymerase produces an additional quantity of RNA of the messenger type, which is active in protein synthesis. This represents a *stimulation* of amino acid incorporation over and above that produced by the originally present m-RNA in the cell-free preparation. The stimulation is inhibited by the addition of actinomycin D, which is further indication that the antibiotic acts at the level of DNA. Although, as was shown in Chapter 3, various analog triphosphates can replace their normal analogs in the in vitro RNA-polymerase reaction, the products made with the aid of such analog triphosphates do not stimulate the incorporation of amino acids. An exception is the analog 5-fluoro-UTP, which replaces UTP both in the polymerase reaction and in the stimulation of protein synthesis. This last observation is valid for the incorporation of the amino acids tyrosine, lysine, isoleucine, and valine.

STRUCTURE OF POLYRIBOSOMES (POLYSOMES)

It was observed[16,42] that the ribosome fractions most active in protein synthesis in *E. coli* were those with a sedimentation constant higher than 70 S. It seemed then that certain classes of heavy ribosomes had some additional component and that they were perhaps the primary site of protein synthesis, with the smaller ribosomes being degradation products of the larger aggregates.

The most striking demonstration of the existence of polysomes came from the examination of the molecular size of the active ribosomes that synthesize hemoglobin in rabbit reticulocytes.[17-20] When the cells are broken by drastic methods, such as severe osmotic shock, or freezing and thawing, or grinding, ultracentrifugation in a sucrose gradient shows mainly ribosomes with a sedimentation constant of 76 S. These correspond to a molecular weight of approximately 4×10^6 and are called "single ribosomes" or monoribosomes. When the reticulocytes are incubated with radioactive amino acids before lysis and then submitted to this drastic treatment, radioactivity is associated with the 76 S particles or monoribosomes. Of course, there is also radioactivity in the soluble hemoglobin, which has a very much lower sedimentation constant at approximately 4 S. These same monoribosomes when purified may also be used to incorporate radioactive amino acids into protein, but the amount of soluble hemoglobin that can be made by them is very small indeed.

If, on the other hand, the reticulocytes after incubation with radioactive amino acids are lysed very gently by lowering the ionic strength, the sedimentation pattern in the sucrose gradient looks very different, as illustrated in Figure 5–14. It is seen that under these conditions a peak of heavier ribosomes is obtained in addition to the 76 S peak of monoribosomes; the heavier peak has a sedimentation constant of approximately 170 S. What is even more important is that the radioactivity due to the amino acids, which presumably resides in newly formed polypeptide chains, is associated almost exclusively with this heavier ribosome peak. In addition there is the peak of radioactivity at the top of the gradient, corresponding to 4 S, which is derived from the soluble hemoglobin formed before lysis. The active heavy ribosomes have been named *polysomes* and, from their sedimentation constant, may be calculated to contain on the average five 76 S particles each.

Taking fractions from such a gradient around the heavy ribosome peak and examining the particles in an electron microscope, Warner, Rich, and Hall[17] were able to show that clusters of ribosomal particles predominated in this heavy peak, whereas the 76 S peak from the sucrose gradient contained almost exclusively single particles. The most common number

FIGURE 5–14   *Sedimentation in a sucrose gradient of an extract of rabbit reticulocytes which had been incubated at 37°C for 45 sec with mixed ^{14}C-amino acids. For details see Reference 19. The arrows labeled 4, 5, and 6 represent the sedimenting positions of ribosomal tetramers, pentamers, and hexamers with their respective calculated distribution patterns, as indicated.*

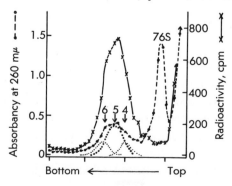

of single ribosomes per polysome was five, with fewer clusters of four and six and very few clusters of three and seven ribosome particles (Figure 5–14). Preparations of polysomes stained with uranyl acetate for RNA show very thin threads between the ribosome particles on the polysome (Figure 5–15). It is possible that these thin threads correspond to the messenger RNA on which the five single ribosome particles are aligned.

More recently, the existence of such polysome aggregates has been demonstrated in other mammalian cells,[21] especially in HeLa cells[43] in tissue culture, the polysomes of which are very much longer, containing perhaps some 40 ribosomes. Probably these correspond to very long m-RNA molecules containing more than one polypeptide chain-forming unit. In agreement with this idea, at various stages of growth, such HeLa polysomes sometimes show an uneven distribution of ribosomes along their length as if various regions of this long m-RNA are read at different speeds or with different frequency.

The proposed mode of action of the polysome and protein synthesis is illustrated in Figure 5–16. Single ribosomes are supposed to move along the length of the m-RNA synthesizing a polypeptide chain as they go along. When they come to the end of the messenger RNA, that is, the end of the polysome, they fall off and release the newly formed peptide chain. It is also possible that the peptide chain is released before the ribosome leaves the polysome unit. As one ribosome leaves at one end of the m-RNA, a new empty ribosome is supposed to attach itself at the other end to begin its travel along the template. Some variants on this scheme have been suggested in the case when the final protein is an aggregate of a number of poly-peptide chains; perhaps the ribosome that is ready to leave the m-RNA with its fully grown peptide chain hands this chain on to the penultimate ribosome, so that the complete peptide chain can dimerize with the next one in line, which is almost complete. Eventually, then, a dimer would be released into solution, such as might be the case in the formation of hemoglobin. In a more complex arrangement, any number of subunits can aggregate in this fashion (see also Reference 9, Chapter 6).

Although the above constitutes a plausible scheme for the

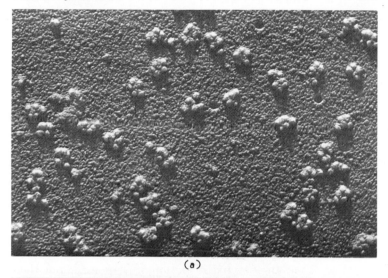

(a)

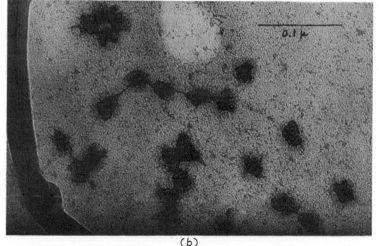

(b)

FIGURE 5–15 *Electron microphotographs of polysomes from rabbit*
reticulocytes, obtained as in Figure 5–14. (a) *shad-*
owed preparation, (b) *preparation stained with uranyl*
acetate to reveal RNA. (*Courtesy of Dr. A. Rich.*)

synthesis of a protein on ribosome aggregates, it cannot as yet be
taken as fully proved. In particular the idea that the ribosomes
and the polysome are held together by m-RNA is still partly
conjectural, although this is certainly the easiest way of explain-

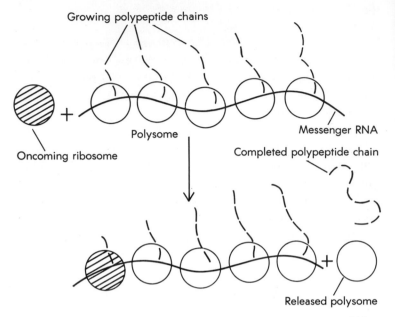

FIGURE 5–16   *A schematic model of polysome function.*   (*After Reference 19.*)

ing the experimental results.   The scheme demands that the ribosomes should move along the messenger RNA strand, and one of several remaining questions is the origin of the energy required for such movement.

ASSEMBLY OF A PEPTIDE CHAIN

Since so much is known about the structure of the hemoglobin peptide chains and since the intact immature red cell is a good synthetic system, the main product of which is the single protein hemoglobin, rabbit reticulocytes have become popular for the study of protein synthesis.   Dintzis[44,45] has answered the question of whether a peptide chain grows in a linear fashion from one end to the other, or whether it might not grow from the middle outward, or in several places at the same time.   For his studies Dintzis used rabbit reticulocytes from animals made anemic by the injection of phenylhydrazine.   Figure 5–17 shows the theoretical model that Dintzis uses as his scheme for the synthesis of soluble hemoglobin.

As we have seen, protein synthesis occurs in the ribosomes, or more particularly in the polyribosome particles in the cell. In the case of the reticulocyte, these ribosomes and polysomes are free and are not attached to an endoplasmic reticulum, as they are in other mammalian cells such as the liver cells (see Figure 1–2). If we look at a cell and ask: What is the state of the hemoglobin peptide chains in the average ribosome, the model will show that there is a distribution of unfinished (and unlabeled) peptide chains of varying lengths, as indicated at the top of Figure 5–17 at time t_1. Some chains will hardly have begun to grow, others will be almost finished, and there will be still others of intermediate length. If at that time one gives a short pulse of radioactive amino acid, for example ³H-leucine, to

FIGURE 5–17 *Model of sequential peptide chain growth.* (*From Reference 44.*)

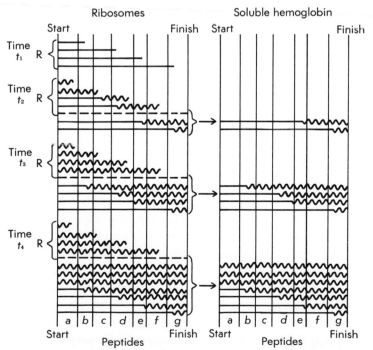

such a cell, each peptide chain will grow a small length of radioactive peptide chain during that pulse as shown at time t_2 in the figure. The length of the pulse at time t_2 is short compared to the time it takes to make the whole chain. After such a short time interval only a few of the peptide chains will be complete enough to be released, and we shall therefore find among the soluble hemoglobin molecules some peptide chains, which have that portion of the chain labeled that was synthesized last.

If we have a means of separating and examining different portions of the peptide chain of the soluble hemoglobin, and if we can locate the radioactivity in such portions of the peptide chain, we can deduce which part of the chain is synthesized last. If the length of time of the exposure to radioactive leucine is increased, each peptide chain will grow more, as shown at time t_3 in the figure. More and more label will appear in the finished peptide chains of the soluble hemoglobin until at time t_4 and at longer times, label will be distributed more or less evenly throughout the length of the peptide chain.

Dintzis studied the soluble hemoglobin released by the ribosomes after pulse experiments with tritiated leucine for various lengths of time. He used trypsin to split the peptide chains into a definite number of small peptides, labeled *a* to *g* in Figure 5–17; these fragments were separated and characterized by paper chromatography and paper electrophoresis. The number that is really required in these experiments is the specific activity of leucine in each of the individual peptide fragments *a* to *g*. However, this number is technically difficult to determine when working with small amounts of protein and relatively low levels of radioactivity, because the yield of each peptide fragment is variable from experiment to experiment and also differs from peptide to peptide. An internal standard is desirable, corresponding to the portions of peptide chain made before the pulse began. Radioactivity resulting from the pulse could then be compared to that standard. At the end of each experiment Dintzis added carrier hemoglobin, which was uniformly labeled with radioactive ^{14}C-leucine from a long incubation of reticulocytes with that amino acid. The pulse experiment itself was performed with ^{3}H-leucine. At the end of the pulse and after the cells were opened, Dintzis added his uniformly labeled ^{14}C-leucine hemoglobin and digested the mixture with trypsin. In each isolated peptide he was then able to determine the ratio of ^{3}H to ^{14}C and, since the latter label was uniform for each peptide, this ratio gave him a measure of the specific activity of tritium label in each peptide. In fact, before the trypsin digestion, Dintzis isolated the α and β peptide chains on a carboxymethylcellulose column and then digested each chain separately.

The kind of data he obtained are reproduced in Figure 5–18, where the α and the β peptide chains are shown separately. The relative amount of tritium is the measure of label in each peptide acquired during the pulse experiment. The peptide numbers given in Figure 5–18a are quite arbitrary, but Dintzis found that he could arrange his data as more or less straight lines by putting these peptides in a sequence of increasing relative tritium radioactivity. This in itself has no significance, because any series of increasing numbers can be arranged in such a sequence. The important thing is that, at the next stage, he and Naughton were able to correlate the time order of the labeled peptides with the space order of these peptides in the peptide chain.[45] At an incubation time of 4 min at 15°C only the four peptides near the carboxyl end of the chain received significant amounts of radioactivity, indicating that that end of the chain is made last. On the other hand, 7 min was evidently long enough to complete a whole peptide chain and at 16 min more than one chain was made; in other words a new round of synthesis had begun. Dintzis' experiments were done at 15°C to slow down sufficiently the rate of synthesis so that early enough samples could be withdrawn. At this temperature he found that the over-all rate of synthesis is approximately one-fourth the rate of 37°C. From this it would appear that one peptide chain is made in about 7 min at 15°C or 1.5 min at 37°C.

The fact that an approximately linear plot is obtained in the α-chain experiments, that for short pulses only the peptides on the right-hand side of the figure are labeled, and that at

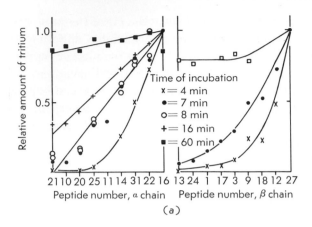

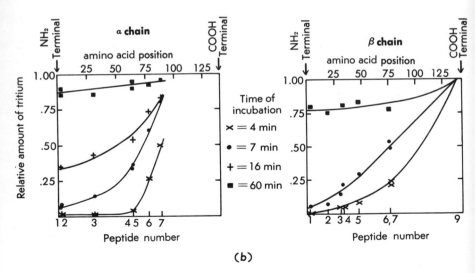

FIGURE 5–18   (a) *Distribution of* ³H*-leucine among tryptic peptides of soluble rabbit hemoglobin after various times of incubation at 15°C. The points at 7 min are the average of six experiments.* (From Reference 44.) (b) *Distribution of* ³H*-leucine among tryptic peptides of soluble rabbit hemoglobin. The data of Figure 5–18a replotted to indicate the true chemical position of each point in the* α*- or* β*-peptide chain.* (Dintzis and Knopf, *Informational Macromolecules,* Academic Press, New York, 1963.)

increasing pulse times the slope of the plot becomes almost zero, agrees with the model proposed by Dintzis and illustrated in Figure 5–17. The experiments show, within the limits of the techniques employed, that the chain grows linearly from one end to the other and that the amino acids are added sequentially. However, since only leucine was used in these experiments, we cannot be sure what happens in the peptide chain sequences between the individual leucine residues. The possibility cannot be ruled out that, at certain points in the chain, groups of amino acids are added, although this possibility seems remote.

Dintzis[44] also showed that the "hottest" amino acid in the α chain (in his peptide number 16) is in fact at the C-terminus of the chain. He digested pulse-labeled chains with carboxypeptidases A and B, which liberated arginine and other residues from the C-terminus of that chain and thereby removed his peptide 16 from its usual position on the fingerprint. The corresponding experiment with the β chain was not quite so successful. Nevertheless, the α-chain experiment indicated that the C-terminal peptide is the last one to be made in the synthesis of at least the α chain and that the growth of the chain therefore begins at the N-terminus and then proceeds along the chain. More recently, Dintzis and Naughton[45] have compared the amino acid compositions of the tryptic peptides of the rabbit hemoglobin that was used in these experiments with a known composition of the tryptic peptides of the human α and β chains. There is a striking degree of similarity between these two sets of peptides; this similarity enabled them to assign a provisional order for their labeled peptides by assuming a high degree of homology between rabbit hemoglobin and human hemoglobin. The idea that a peptide chain grows linearly from the N-terminus is strengthened, because their purely empirical sequence of peptide numbers in Figure 5–18a was in fact confirmed in every single instance by their new determination of peptide sequence from the analysis of the tryptic peptides.

The over-all conclusion that the peptide chain grows linearly from the N-terminus was previously reported by Bishop, Leahy, and Schweet[46] for hemoglobin synthesis and by Yoshida and Tobita[47] for bacterial amylase. More recently Anfinsen and

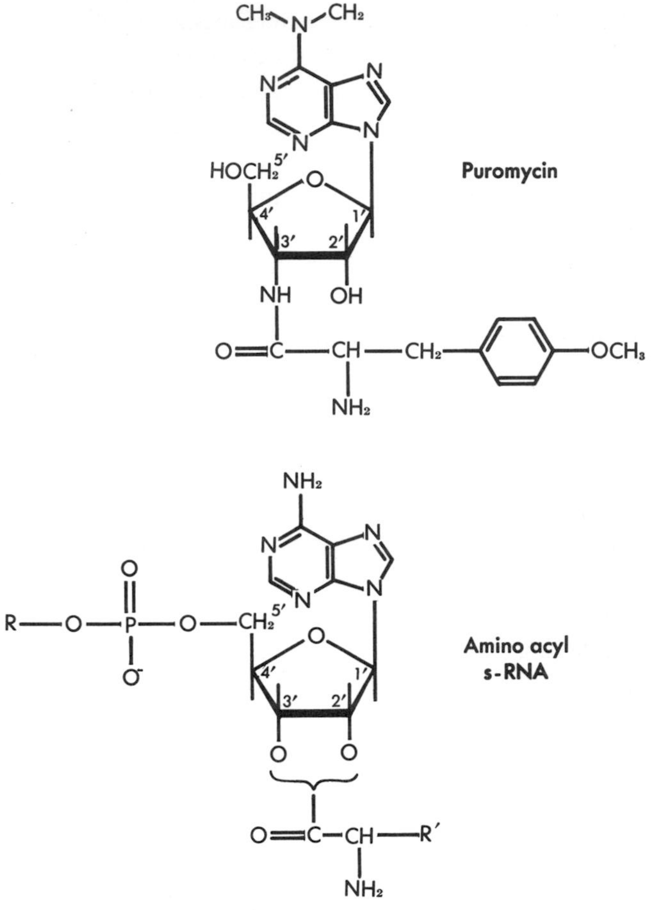

FIGURE 5-19   The structure of puromycin and of the amino acyl-
adenosine terminal of sRNA (R is the continuing
sRNA chain and R' is the side chain of an amino
acid).

Canfield,[48] working with chicken lysozyme, have obtained data
similar to those of Dintzis.   The lysozyme data are most
convincing, because they combine the results of pulse-label
experiments with the accurately known positions in the peptide
chain of the radioactive amino acids used.   We now have,
therefore, a reasonably clear picture of this fundamental aspect
of protein synthesis.

Although the assembly of a peptide chain is apparently linear, it is not necessarily at a uniform rate along the length of the peptide chain. When the results of the pulse-label experiments in the α- and β-peptide chains of rabbit hemoglobin in Figure 5–18a are replotted (Figure 5–18b) using the accurate geographic positions of the various leucine residues, the curvature in the 7-min line of the β chain almost completely disappears, but there is now a pronounced concavity in the 7-min plot for the α chain. Taking it at face value, this implies that the rate of assembly along the α peptide chain of hemoglobin is not uniform, with a rate-controlling step or steps somewhere near the middle of the peptide chain.

PUROMYCIN

The antibiotic puromycin has a chemical structure resembling that of amino acyl-sRNA, as was first noted by Yarmolinsky and de la Haba in 1959.[48a] The formula is shown in Figure 5–19, and it will be seen that the most obvious differences between puromycin and RNA-amino acid arise because the adenine moiety carries two methyl groups on its amino nitrogen and the tyrosyl residue, which forms the amino acid residue, is also methylated in its phenolic oxygen group. Perhaps most important is the fact that, instead of an ordinary ribose group, the molecule contains an amino sugar. In other words, the amino acyl grouping is not attached by an ester linkage as in amino acyl-sRNA, but rather by an amide grouping.

Although the precise mode of action of puromycin is not known, the substance appears to inhibit protein synthesis at a late stage, for in the protein synthesizing system which uses amino acyl-sRNA and ribosomes, compounds containing the amino acids originally attached to sRNA appear in an alcohol-soluble fraction of the incubation mixture. The formation of these soluble products is dependent upon puromycin and all the components needed for protein synthesis and it is inhibited by chloramphenicol.[48b] It is suggested that these alcohol-soluble materials are peptides or fragments of incomplete peptide chains released from the ribosome by puromycin.

It has also been found that in reticulocytes the antibiotic puromycin promotes the rapid nonenzymatic release of soluble protein from the ribosomes (polyribosomes). In particular the studies with C^{14}-labeled puromycin[48e] showed that the antibiotic was covalently bound to the soluble polypeptide released from the ribosomes in reticulocytes. Apparently, one residue of puromycin was bound to the released polypeptide for each N-terminal valine, that is, one for each polypetide chain. It was suggested that puromycin may substitute for an amino acyl-sRNA unit in binding to the peptidyl-RNA of the completed portion of the peptide chain, thus becoming itself the C-terminal residue of the peptide chain. Because puromycin, however, would have no s-RNA chain to bond the peptide to the ribosome, such a substitution would interrupt the further extension of the peptide chain and result in separation of the incomplete peptide chain from the ribosome.

The problem of puromycin action has been approached in another way: by determining the structural requirements both for inhibition of protein synthesis and for release of incomplete peptide chains. Both the 2′-puromycin isomer and the 5′-puromycin isomer (analogs of the structures in Figure 5–19) are completely inactive.[48d]

The effectiveness of several amino acid analogs of puromycin was also tested. Only those compounds having an aromatic amino acid have much activity, although the leucine analog is slightly active in the usual incorporation system. Also, the optical activity of the amino acid is important because, for example, the D-phenylalanyl analog has little or no activity compared to the L isomer. The analogs containing glycine, leucine, and even tryptophane are completely or almost completely inactive. The failure of most of the compounds with nonaromatic amino acids to inhibit protein synthesis is somewhat surprising, if puromycin really acts as an analog of amino acyl-sRNA. These differences, however, could reflect a tighter binding to an active site by compounds that contain an aromatic sidechain. The rather precise requirements for inhibition both in the position of the sidechain of puromycin and in its configuration suggest that puromycin acts by specific binding to an enzyme

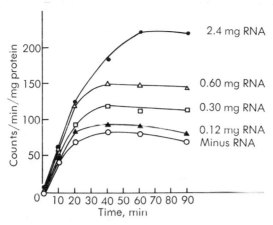

FIGURE 5–20 Dependence of ^{14}C-valine incorporation into insoluble
peptides upon ribosomal RNA in the cell-free system
derived from E. coli. (See Reference 49.)

site or perhaps by specific binding to the ribosomes.   Another
attractive possibility is that puromycin inhibits the peptide polymerase component required for complete protein synthesis.

POLYRIBONUCLEOTIDES AND THE GENETIC CODE

In 1961, Nirenberg and Matthaei[49] made the brilliant discovery
that synthetic polyribonucleotides can stimulate the incorporation of amino acids into peptide-like material in a cell-free
system derived from E. coli. Their incubation mixture consisted of washed ribosomes from E. coli, s-RNA, all the amino
acids commonly occurring in proteins (at least one of which was
radioactively labeled), GTP, ATP, and mercaptoethanol.   In
addition a supernatant fraction containing the amino acid-
activating enzymes and the condensing enzyme (see Table 5–3)
were required, although in their system they only measured
incorporation of amino acids into insoluble peptide-like material.   After preincubation to allow endogenous messenger RNA
to decay, they found (Figure 5–20) that the addition of
homologous or heterologous bulk RNA stimulated the incorporation of amino acids considerably, provided a sufficient quantity
of s-RNA was present.   This reconstituted system also showed

that the *stimulation* of amino acid incorporation resulting from the addition of RNA was not sensitive to DNase, whereas the original endogenous incorporation activity was sensitive, because it destroyed the DNA template needed to replenish the supply of m-RNA.

Next they made the exciting observation that polyU, a high-molecular-weight polyribonucleotide containing only U, also stimulated amino acid incorporation (Figure 5–21), but only that of phenylalanine. The product was presumably poly-phenylalanine in peptide form. Actually small amounts of leucine were also incorporated; the reason for this is still not entirely clear, although it now appears that with increasing Mg^{++} concentration, an increasing proportion of leucine is incorpo-rated. Nirenberg showed that the incorporation of phenylal-anine required phenylalanyl-s-RNA as a necessary intermediate and in that respect resembled protein synthesis. From this result, and assuming the validity of a triplet code, Nirenberg and Matthaei deduced that the code for phenylalanine at the

F I G U R E   5–21   *Stimulation of incorporation of* [14]*C-phenylalanine by polyuridylic acid in the cell-free system derived from E. coli. ○ = without polyuridylic acid; △ = with polyuridylic acid. (After Reference 49.)*

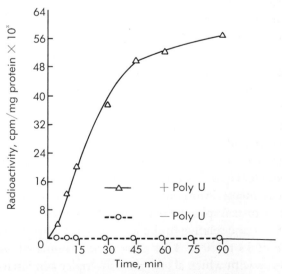

m-RNA level is UUU. Although their early characterization of the product as a polypeptide of phenylalanine left something to be desired, recent experiments[50-52] on the incorporation of phenylalanine and other amino acids in this system clearly showed the formation of labeled peptides. It can also be shown that polyU added to single ribosomes of E. coli will form aggregates that are similar to the expected polysomes with a high sedimentation constant and have the ability to incorporate radioactive phenylalanine into insoluble polyphenylalanine.

Similar experiments have also been carried out in a number of mammalian systems principally derived from reticulocytes and from mammalian tumor cells,[53] and in these it seems also that polyU will stimulate specifically the incorporation of phenylalanine into peptide material, together with a variable proportion of leucine.

A high proportion of the polyU added is actually degraded to mononucleotides. For this reason the stoichiometry of the reaction between polyU and single ribosomes is not easy to determine. It is also not entirely clear whether polyU will act as a messenger by combining only with empty single ribosomes or whether it can displace pre-existing m-RNA.

Through the use of synthetic copolymers (produced by polynucleotide phosphorylase) containing different proportions of two or more bases, the incorporation of amino acids other than phenylalanine has been investigated in the laboratories of Nirenberg[50] and of Ochoa.[51] One such experiment is illustrated in Table 5-5. For each copolymer a large number of different incubations are performed, each containing all the commonly occurring amino acids but with only one of them radioactive, a different one in each incubation. In this way and for each polyribonucleotide, the stimulation of incorporation of a particular amino acid by the addition of a polyribonucleotide may be measured. In Table 5-5 this stimulation is expressed *relative* to *the stimulation of incorporation of phenylalanine* by the same polymer. For example, the polymer UA stimulates the incorporation of tyrosine relative to the incorporation of phenylalanine as a ratio of 13 to 100. This ratio is then compared with the probabilities with which all the possible triplet combinations of

TABLE 5–5   *Code experiment*[a]

Amino acid	UA	UG	Code letters
Base ratio	U = 0.87 A = 0.13	U = 0.76 G = 0.24	
Probability of triplet relative to UUU = 100	UUU 100 (UUA) 13 (UAA) 2.2 AAA 0.3	UUU 100 (UUG) 32 (UGG) 10.6 GGG 3.4	
Phe	100	100	UUU
Arg	0	1.1	
Ala	1.9	0	
Ser	0.4	3.2	
Pro	0	0	
Tyr	13	0	(UUA)
Isoleu	12	1.0	(UUA)
Val	0.6	37	(UUG)
Leu	4.9	36	(UUG) also UUC
Cys-SH	4.9	35	(UUG)
Try	1.1	14	(UGG)
Gly	4.7	12	(UGG)
Met	0.6	0	
Glu	1.5	0	

[a] From Reference 54.

bases may occur in the polyribonucleotide. It is a basic assumption in this argument that the polyribonucleotide is very long and has a random sequence of bases. Simple probability arguments allow one to calculate the frequency of the triplet UUA relative to the triplet UUU, which is put at a frequency of 100, and so on for the other possible triplets. The probability of finding such a triplet is then compared with the ratio of incorporation stimulation of the polymer for a given amino acid.

In the example quoted, the tyrosine incorporation approaches the frequency with which the triplet UUA occurs in the polymer. For this reason the code letters UUA are assigned to tyrosine and for the same reason the code letters UUA are also assigned to isoleucine. None of the other amino acids tried are stimulated sufficiently by this particular polyribonucleotide, nor do they give reliable incorporation figures. These low incorporations are therefore ignored for the purpose of assigning code letters.

The fact that the same code letters are assigned to both tyrosine and isoleucine shows that this kind of argument cannot determine the sequence of bases within the code word. These are presumably different for the tyrosine and the isoleucine (for example UUA and UAU, or some other order). Similarly for the UG-containing polyribonucleotide, which is the second example in Table 5–5, the code letters for valine, leucine, and cysteine and for tryptophan and glycine may be deduced. In this way code letters have now been assigned for all the commonly occurring amino acids and a selection is given in Table 5–6.

Very recently, Nirenberg and Leder (International Congress of Biochemistry, New York, 1964)[56] showed that trinucleotides of known sequence will direct the specific attachment of partic-

T A B L E 5–6 *Summary of RNA code letters*

Amino acid	RNA code letters[a]			
Alanine	CCG	UCG[b]	ACG[b]	
Arginine	CGC	AGA	UGC[b]	CGA[b]
Asparagine	ACA	AUA	ACU[b]	
Aspartic acid	GUA	GCA[b]	GAA[b]	
Cysteine	UUG			
Glutamic acid	GAA	GAU[b]	GAC[b]	
Glutamine	AAC	AGA	AGU[b]	
Glycine	UGG	AGG	CGG	
Histidine	ACC	ACU[b]		
Isoleucine	UAU	UAA		
Leucine	UUG	UUC	UCC	UUA
Lysine	AAA	AAU		
Methionine	UGA			
Phenylalanine	UUU	CUU		
Proline	CCC	CCU	CCA	CCG[b]
Serine	UCU	UCC	UCG[b]	ACG
Threonine	CAC	CAA		
Tryptophan	GGU			
Tyrosine	AUU			
Valine	UGU	UGA[b]		

[a] Arbitrary nucleotide sequence. (From Reference 50.)
[b] Probable.

ular amino acyl-s-RNA molecules to ribosomes. For example, the trinucleotide GpUpU allowed attachment of valyl-s-RNA, but not of others. Furthermore, the trinucleotides UpGpU and UpUpG were not effective. Through this experiment it seems that the *sequence* of the coding triplet for valine is: —GUU, an exciting and important advance in our understanding of protein synthesis.

Although all the early experiments required polyribonucleotides containing a lot of uridylic acid in order to obtain demonstrable amino acid incorporation into insoluble polypeptides, this is now thought to be due to the fact that the technique used for measuring incorporation consisted of precipitation of peptide material with trichloracetic acid. For the precipitation to be effective, the peptide has to be quite insoluble; this is facilitated by the incorporation of large amounts of phenylalanine during the incubation; therefore polyribonucleotides with a rather high proportion of uridylic acid were used so that the code letters UUU should appear with reasonable frequency in the polyribonucleotide. It should be remembered that, even when we are testing for, say, the incorporation of ^{14}C-tyrosine, all the other amino acids including phenylalanine are present in nonradioactive form. More recently[50,51] it was found that, through the use of additional precipitating agents such as tungstic acid, other polyribonucleotides could be used that contain no uridylic acid at all (Figure 5–22). For example poly-A incorporated the amino acid lysine very efficiently. For this reason the table of code words now also contains words with no U in them.

It will be seen from the table of code letters that some amino acids have more than one group of code letters assigned to them. This is the so-called degeneracy of coding.[55] It means that stimulation of incorporation of those particular amino acids occurred with more than one polyribonucleotide. Using the argument as before (frequency of amino acid incorporation and frequency of occurrence of triplets), one is forced to conclude that an amino acid (e.g., leucine) is coded for by more than one grouping of code letters. The degeneracy of coding implies that

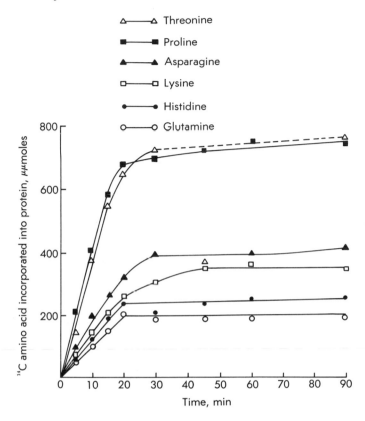

FIGURE 5-22 The rate of ^{14}C-amino acid incorporation in the E. coli cell-free system into protein, directed by a polyribonucleotide containing A and C only in the proportion 47:53. Incubations were stopped at the times indicated by the addition of 3.0 ml of 10 per cent TCA at 3°. The samples were heated at 90° for 20 min to hydrolyze the precipitated amino acyl-s-RNA, chilled, and then filtered through Millipore filters and washed with 5 per cent TCA at 3°. Radioactivity measurements were performed in a thin-window gas-flow counter with a counting efficiency of 23 per cent. Each point represents the μμmoles of ^{14}C-amino acid incorporated into protein due to the addition of poly AC.

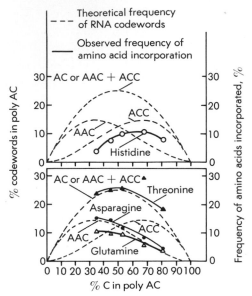

FIGURE 5-23   *Comparison of the incorporation data for ^{14}C-histidine, ^{14}C-threonine, ^{14}C-asparagine, and ^{14}C-glutamine with the theoretical frequencies of doublet and triplet code letters in various poly-AC polyribonucleotide preparations. The solid lines represent the experimentally determined incorporation data. The dotted lines represent the theoretical frequencies of RNA code letters (see Reference 50). The frequency of amino acids incorporated is expressed for each amino acid as the per cent of all amino acids incorporated by a polymer of a certain AC composition.*

an m-RNA template is made to provide for the insertion of leucine into the peptide chain by more than one triplet of bases. Correspondingly, we would expect the existence of more than one leucine-specific s-RNA molecule among the mixture of s-RNA molecules. It has been shown by countercurrent distribution methods[7,8] that s-RNA will yield more than one fraction capable of incorporating the amino acid leucine. Furthermore, Berg[1] has shown that at least two different nucleotide sequences may be found in leucine-specific s-RNA. Both results would tend to substantiate the idea of degeneracy in coding and provide a molecular basis for it. On the other hand, the relation between the different leucine s-RNAs and different polyribo-nucleotides with different coding properties is not at all clear at the moment. For now, we should regard the whole question of degeneracy in coding as unsettled and in a state of flux.

The concept of coding degeneracy is also required to explain some of the nitrous acid mutants of tobacco mosaic virus protein (see Chapter 6). However, several assumptions are involved in the interpretation of these mutants anyway, so that other explanations can also be made.

The over-all conclusions from this description of various aspects of protein synthesis is that the main outlines of the mechanism are fairly clear, but that there are many unsolved problems: for example, the degeneracy in coding, the requirement for GTP, the nature and function of the releasing and condensing enzymes, the precise relationship between structure and function of the s-RNA molecule, the mode of action of polysomes, and the properties of the m-RNA template that determine the beginning and the end of a peptide chain assembly, to mention only a few. No doubt the next few years will bring answers to some of these problems and perhaps some surprises.

REFERENCES

1. Berg, P. (1961) "Specificity in Protein Synthesis." *Ann. Rev. Biochem.*, **30**, 293.

2. Zachau, H. G., Acs, G., and Lipmann, F. (1958), "Isolation of Adenosine Amino Acid Esters from a Ribonuclease Digest of Soluble Liver Ribonucleic Acid." *Proc. Natl. Acad. Sci.*, **44**, 885.

3. Preiss, J., Berg, P., Offengand, E. J., Bergmann, F. H., and Dieckmann, M. (1959), "The Chemical Nature of the RNA-Amino Acid Compound Formed by Amino Acid Activating Enzymes." *Proc. Natl. Acad. Sci.*, **45**, 319.

4. Sonnenbichler, J., Feldmann, H., and Zachau, H. G. (1963), "Identifizierung der Amino-acyl-sRNA als 3'-Ester des terminalen Adenosins." *Zeitschrift Physiol. Chemie*, **334**, 283; Feldmann, H., and Zachau, H. G. (1964), "Chemical Evidence for the 3'-Linkage of Amino Acids to sRNA." *Biochem. Biophys. Res. Comm.*, **15**, 13.

5. McLaughlin, C. S., and Ingram, V. M. (1964), "Aminoacyl Position in Aminoacyl sRNA." *Science,* **145,** 942.

6. Berg, P., Bergmann, F. H., Ofengand, E. J., and Dieckmann, M. (1961), "The Enzymic Synthesis of Amino Acyl Derivatives of Ribonucleic Acid. I. The Mechanism of Leucyl-, Valyl-, Isoleucyl-, and Methionyl-Ribonucleic Acid Formation." *J. Biol. Chem.,* **236,** 1726.

7. Apgar, J., Holley, R. W., and Merrill, S. H. (1962), "Purification of the Alanine-, Valine-, Histidine-, and Tyrosine-acceptor Ribonucleic Acids from Yeast." *J. Biol. Chem,* **237,** 798.

8. Goldstein, J., Bennett, T. P., and Craig, L. C. (1964), "Countercurrent Distribution Studies of *E. coli* B sRNA." *Proc. Natl. Acad. Sci.,* **51,** 120.

9. Weisblum, B., Benzer, S., and Holley, R. W. (1962), "A Physical Basis for Degeneracy in the Amino Acid Code." *Proc. Natl. Acad. Sci.,* **48,** 1449.

10. Spencer, M., Fuller, W., Wilkins, M. H. F., and Brown, G. L. (1962), "Determination of the Helical Configuration of RNA Molecules by X-ray Diffraction Study of Crystalline Amino Acid Transfer RNA." *Nature,* **194,** 1014.

11. Spencer, M. (1963), "X-ray Diffraction Studies of the Secondary Structure of RNA." *Cold Spring Harb. Symp. Quant. Biol.,* **28,** 77.

12. Fresco, J. R., Klotz, L. C., and Richards, E. G. (1963), "A New Spectroscopic Approach to the Determination of Helical Secondary Structure in Ribonuclic Acids." *Cold Spring Harb. Symp. Quant. Biol.,* **28,** 83.

13. Cantoni, G. L., Ishikura, H., Richards, H. H., and Tanaka, K. (1963), "Studies on Soluble Ribonucleic Acid." *Cold Spring Harb. Symp. Quant. Biol.,* **28,** 123.

14. Ingram, V. M., and Sjöquist, J. A. (1963), "Studies on the Structure of Purified Alanine and Valine Transfer RNA from Yeast." *Cold Spring Harb. Symp. Quant. Biol.,* **28,** 133.

15. Spiegelman, S., and Hayashi, M. (1963), "The Present Status of the Transfer of Genetic Information and Its Control." *Cold Spring Harb. Symp. Quant. Biol.,* **28,** 161.

16. Risebrough, R. W., Tissières, A., and Watson, J. D. (1962), "Messenger-RNA Attachment to Active Ribosomes." *Proc. Natl. Acad. Sci.,* **48,** 430.

17. Warner, J. R., Rich, A., and Hall, C. E. (1962), "Electron Miscroscope Studies of Ribosomal Clusters Synthesizing Hemoglobin." *Science,* **138,** 1399.

18. Marks, P. A., Burka, E. R., and Schlessinger, D. (1962), "Protein Synthesis in Erythroid Cells, I. Reticulocyte Ribosomes Active in Stimulating Amino Acid Incorporation." *Proc. Natl. Acad. Sci.*, **48**, 2163.

19. Warner, J. R., Knopf, P. M., and Rich, A. (1963), "A Multiple Ribosomal Structure in Protein Synthesis." *Proc. Natl. Acad. Sci.*, **49**, 122.

20. Gierer, A. (1963), "Function of Aggregated Reticulocyte Ribosomes in Protein Synthesis." *J. Mol. Biol.*, **6**, 148.

21. Wettstein, F. O., Staehelin, T., and Noll, H. (1963), "Ribosomal Aggregate Engaged in Protein Synthesis: Characterization of the Ergosome." *Nature*, **197**, 430.

22. Hardesty, B., Arlinghaus, R., Shaeffer, J., and Schweet, R. (1963), "Hemoglobin and Polyphenylalanine Synthesis with Reticulocyte Ribosomes." *Cold Spring Harb. Symp. Quant. Biol.* **28**, 215.

23. Nakamoto, T., Conway, T. W., Allende, J. E., Spyrides, G. J., and Lipmann, F. (1963), "Formation of Peptide Bonds—I." *Cold Spring Harb. Symp. Quant. Biol.*, **28**, 227.

24. Watson, J. D. (1963), "Involvement of RNA in the Synthesis of Protein." *Science*, **140**, 17.

25. von Ehrenstein, G., and Lipmann, F. (1961), "Experiments on Hemoglobin Biosynthesis." *Proc. Natl. Acad. Sci.*, **47**, 941.

26. Ingram, V. M. (1958), "Abnormal Human Haemoglobins—I." *Biochim. Biophys. Acta*, **28**, 539.

27. Chapeville, F., Lipmann, F., von Ehrenstein, G., Weisblum, B., Ray, W. J., Jr., and Benzer, S. (1962), "On the Role of Soluble RNA in Coding for Amino Acids." *Proc. Natl. Acad. Sci.*, **48**, 1086.

28. von Ehrenstein, G., Weisblum, B., and Benzer, S. (1963), "The Function of sRNA as Amino Acid Adaptor in the Synthesis of Hemoglobin." *Proc. Natl. Acad. Sci.*, **49**, 669.

29. Lipsett, M. N., Heppel, L. A., and Bradley, D. F. (1961), "Complex Formation between Oligonucleotides and Polymers." *J. Biol. Chem.*, **236**, 857.

30. Caspersson, Torbjoern O. (1950), *Cell Growth and Cell Function*. W. W. Norton, New York.

31. Brachet, J. (1955), "The Nucleic Acids," eds. E. Chargaff and J. N. Davidson, Vol. **II**, page 476, Academic Press, New York.

32. Hershey, A. D. (1953), "Nucleic Acid Economy in Bacteria Infected with Bacteriophage T2." *J. Gen. Physiol.*, **37**, 1.

33. Jacob, F., and Monod, J. (1961), "Genetic Regulatory Mechanisms in the Synthesis of Proteins." *J. Mol. Biol.*, **3**, 318.

34. Lipmann, F. (1963), "Messenger Ribonucleic Acid." *Progr. Nucl. Acid Research*, **I**, 135.

35. Volkin, E., and Astrachan, L. (1956), "Phosphorus Incorporation in *Escherichia coli* RNA after Infection with Bacteriophage T2." *Virology*, **2**, 149.

36. Brenner, S., Jacob, F., and Meselson, M. (1961), "An Unstable Intermediate Carrying Information from Genes to Ribosomes for Protein Synthesis." *Nature*, **190**, 576.

37. Spiegelman, S. (1961), "The Relation of Informational RNA to DNA." *Cold Spring Harb. Symp. Quant. Biol.*, **26**, 75.

38. Gros, F., Hiatt, H., Gilbert, W., Kurland, C. G., Risebrough, R. W., and Watson, J. D. (1961), "Unstable RNA Revealed by Pulse Labelling of *Escherichia coli*." *Nature*, **190**, 581.

39. Gros, F., Gilbert, W., Hiatt, H. H., Attardi, G., Spahr, P. F., and Watson, J. D. (1961), "Molecular and Biological Characterization of Messenger RNA." *Cold Spring Harb. Symp. Quant. Biol.*, **26**, 111.

40. Marks, P. A., Burka, E. R., Rifkind, R., and Danon, D. (1963), "Polyribosomes Active in Reticulocyte Protein Synthesis." *Cold Spring Harb. Symp. Quant. Biol.*, **28**, 223.

41. Levinthal, C., Fan, D. P., Higa, A., and Zimmerman, R. A. (1963), "The Decay and Protection of Messenger RNA in Bacteria." *Cold Spring Harb. Symp. Quant. Biol.*, **28**, 183.

42. Tissières, A., Schlessinger, D., and Gros, F. (1960), "Amino Acid Incorporation into Proteins by *Escherichia coli* Ribosomes." *Proc. Natl. Acad. Sci.*, **46**, 1450.

43. Penman, S., Scherrer, K., Becker, Y., and Darnell, J. E. (1963), "Polyribosomes in Normal and Poliovirus-Infected Hela Cells and Their Relationship to Messenger-RNA." *Proc. Natl. Acad. Sci.*, **49**, 654.

44. Dintzis, H. M. (1961), "Assembly of the Peptide Chains of Hemoglobin." *Proc. Natl. Acad. Sci.*, **47**, 247.

45. Naughton, M. A. and Dintzis, H. M. (1962), "Sequential Biosynthesis of the Peptide Chains of Hemoglobin." *Proc. Natl. Acad. Sci.*, **48**, 1822.

46. Bishop, J., Leahy, J., and Schweet, R. (1960), "Formation of the Peptide Chain of Hemoglobin." *Proc. Natl. Acad. Sci.* **46**, 1030.

47. Yoshida, A., and Tobita, T. (1960), "Studies on the Mechanism of Protein Synthesis." *Biochim. Biophys. Acta.*, **37**, 513.

48. Canfield, R. E. and Anfinsen, C. B. (1963), "Nonuniform Labeling of Egg White Lysozyme." *Biochemistry*, **2**, 1073.

48a. Yarmolinsky, M. B. and de la Haba, G. L. (1959) *Proc. Natl. Acad. Sci. U.S.*, **45**, 1721.

48b. Nathans, D., v. Ehrenstein, G., Monro, R., and Lipmann, F. (1962) *Federation Proc.*, **21**, 127.

48c. Allen, D. W., and Zamecnik, P. C. (1962) *Biochim. Biophys. Acta*, **55**, 865.

48d. Nathans, D., Allende, J. E., Conway, T. W., Spyrides, G. J., and Lipmann, F. (1963), "Informational Macromolecules," eds. Vogel, H. J., Bryson, V., and Lampen, J. O. (Academic Press, New York).

49. Nirenberg, M. W., and Matthaei, J. H. (1961), "The Dependence of Cell-Free Protein Synthesis in *E. coli* upon Naturally Occurring or Synthetic Polyribonucleotides." *Proc. Natl. Acad. Sci.*, **47**, 1588.

50. Nirenberg, M. W., Jones, O. W., Leder, P., Clark, B. F. C., Sly, W. S., and Pestka, S. (1963), "On the Coding of Genetic Information." *Cold Spring Harb. Symp. Quant. Biol.*, **28**, 549.

51. Speyer, J. F., Lengyel, P., Basilio, C. Wahba, A. J., Gardner, R. S., and Ochoa, S. (1963), "Synthetic Polynucleotides and the Amino Acid Code." *Cold Spring Harb. Symp. Quant. Biol.*, **28**, 559.

52. Bretscher, M. S. (1963), "The Chemical Nature of the sRNA-polypeptide Complex." *J. Mol. Biol.*, **7**, 446.

53. Weinstein, I. B. (1963), "Comparative Studies on the Genetic Code." *Cold Spring Harb. Symp. Quant. Biol.*, **28**, 579.

54. Matthaei, J. H., Jones, O. W., Martin, R. G., and Nirenberg, M. W. (1962), "Characteristics and Composition of RNA Coding Units." *Proc. Natl. Acad. Sci, U.S.*, **48**, 666.

55. Crick, F. H. C. (1963), "The Recent Excitement in the Coding Problem." *Progr. Nucl. Acid Research*, **I**, 163.

56. Leder, P., and Nirenberg, M. W. (1964), "RNA Code words and Protein Synthesis, II. Nucleotide Sequence of a Valine RNA Code word." *Proc. Natl. Acad. Sci., U.S.*, **52**, 420.

SIX §§ GENETIC CONTROL
OF PRIMARY
PROTEIN STRUCTURE

HUMAN HEMOGLOBINS

THE CHEMICAL EFFECT OF A MUTATION ON THE STRUCTURE OF A
particular protein can be clearly illustrated and was first demonstrated in the case of the abnormal human hemoglobins.[1] Of
course in this instance we can say nothing about the actual alteration in DNA structure. All that we know is that an inherited defect in hemoglobin structure is passed on in a simple
Mendelian fashion as a single gene, and therefore we assume
that there is, or has been, an alteration in that structural gene on
the DNA which controls the particular hemoglobin peptide
chain.

There are two adult human hemoglobins, hemoglobin A and
hemoglobin A_2, accounting, respectively, for 90 and 2½ per cent
of total hemoglobin. The rest is largely the so-called hemoglobin A_3, a derivative of hemoglobin A in old red cells. Chemically
these hemoglobins are made up of four peptide chains, such that
hemoglobin A may be written $a_2\beta_2$ and hemoglobin A_2 as $a_2\delta_2$

(reviewed in Reference 2). The four peptide chains of hemo-globin A are of two different kinds, two α chains and two β chains, and their amino acid sequence is controlled by two structural genes, an α gene and a β gene. Of course, since humans are diploid organisms, each individual has maternal and paternal α and β genes. The hemoglobin A_2 contains the same α-peptide chains controlled by the same structural genes. The other half of the hemoglobin A_2 molecule, however, is made up of δ-peptide chains[3] of somewhat different amino acid sequence from the β-peptide chains and controlled by separate δ structural genes. Again we have one maternal and one paternal δ structural gene. Mutations in the α structural gene affect both hemoglobin A and hemoglobin A_2, mutations in the β structural gene only hemoglobin A, and mutations in the δ structural gene only hemoglobin A_2 (reviewed in Reference 4).

In people who suffer from sickle-cell anemia, as Pauling and Itano[5] showed in 1949, an electrophoretically different form of hemoglobin exists. Such patients, instead of having normal hemoglobin A, have a hemoglobin in their red cells which has a slower electrophoretic mobility and therefore has fewer net negative charges in the hemoglobin molecule. Pauling and Itano postulated that this was an instance of a *molecular disease*, in which the clinical condition of sickle-cell anemia is due to the presence of a chemically altered protein molecule. In the same year (1949), Neel[6] showed that this disease was inherited in a simple Mendelian fashion and that the homozygotes for sickle-cell anemia produced only the abnormal hemoglobin. The parents of such an individual would be heterozygous for sickle-cell anemia and would not show the clinical manifestations of this disease. It was also demonstrated by Pauling and Itano that the heterozygotes produced two types of hemoglobin, hemoglobin A and hemoglobin S (the abnormal sickle-cell hemoglobin), in amounts that were not quite equal but were in the proportion of 60 per cent of the normal hemoglobin and 30 to 40 per cent of the abnormal hemoglobin. This is consistent with the view that such individuals carry one normal and one abnormal allele for hemoglobin and that both alleles were expressed in their corresponding protein products.

It is the function of hemoglobin to transport oxygen into the tissues. An individual who is homozygous for sickle-cell anemia is sick, because the hemoglobin S in his red cells leads to the formation of paracrystalline aggregates inside the cell under conditions where the oxygen tension is low, as in the tissues.[7,8] The cells become distorted, assume the so-called sickle shape and are destroyed by the spleen. Hence a severe hemolytic anemia results with other side effects, such as the blocking of capillary circulation as a result of the bizarre shape of the sickled red cells. This is then truly a molecular disease.

Later it was shown[1,2] that the chemical abnormality of this hemoglobin-S resides in the replacement of a glutamic acid residue by valine as the sixth amino acid from the N-terminus of the β-peptide chains (Figure 6–1). We see here the chemical effect of this particular mutation on the amino acid sequence of the β chain of hemoglobin. We deduce that, at the genetic level, the abnormality is found only in the β structural gene, that the homozygote has two such abnormal genes, and that the heterozygote has one abnormal and one normal β structural gene. There is no evidence of any abnormality in either the α or the δ chains in a person with sickle-cell anemia and hence in

FIGURE 6–1   *Amino acid sequences at the N-terminus of the β-peptide chains of the abnormal human hemoglobins A, S, C, and $G_{San\ Jos\acute{e}}$. The arrows point to the peptide bonds broken by the proteolytic enzyme trypsin.*

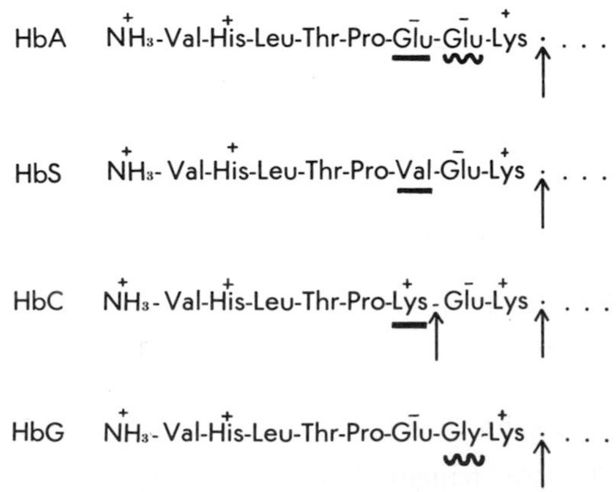

the α or δ structural genes. In a heterozygous individual, only two kinds of major hemoglobin components are found, namely, hemoglobin A in which both β chains are normal and hemoglobin S in which both β chains are abnormal.

$$HbA = \alpha_2^A \beta_2^A \qquad HbS = \alpha_2^A \beta_2^{6,val}$$

The truly hybrid molecule with one normal and one abnormal β-peptide chain per molecule has never been observed and cannot be made as yet in vitro. Perhaps it is a property of the assembly process in the synthesis of hemoglobin that the products of a particular m-RNA dimerize[9] to form, for example, a β_2 subunit before the final assembly of these subunits into the finished hemoglobin molecule (see Chapter 5, page 134). The same is true of the assembly of the α-peptide chains and of the assembly of the δ-peptide chains. Mutants are known of the α and δ locus and many other mutants are known of the β locus, so that altogether we have over 20 mutations to study (see Figures 6–2 and 6–3); in every case, even in the heterozygous condition, no hybrid hemoglobin molecules are formed. Another possibility is that in solution a rapid equilibrium exists between the various hemoglobin subunits and that the method of characterization, electrophoresis, favors the disproportionation of the hybrid into the two different homogeneous forms.

$$2\,\alpha_2^A \beta^A \beta^S \rightleftharpoons \alpha_2^A \beta_2^A + \alpha_2^A \beta_2^S$$

A mutation such as the sickle-cell mutation, where a single amino acid is replaced, is considered to be a point mutation. In bacterial genetics a point mutation is one that can be observed to revert to the normal wild-type situation. Clearly this cannot be observed in the human genetic system, such as the one we have just been talking about, because an event, which is as rare as this reversion would be, is a priori difficult to find in a human population and because a revertant would be indistinguishable from all the other normal individuals. The hemoglobin S amino acid exchange and the others found in the abnormal human hemoglobins (Figure 6–2) have been explained[10] on the basis of single nucleotide base changes in the coding triplets that are now

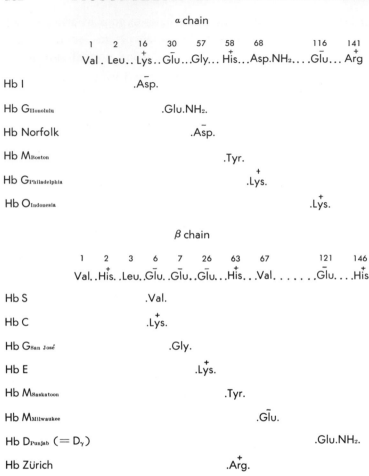

FIGURE 6–2 *Diagrammatic summary of the abnormal human hemo-globins. (See discussion and bibliography in Reference 2.)*

known for the particular amino acids concerned in the abnormalities (Figure 6–4).

Hemoglobin C is another abnormal hemoglobin where the same sixth amino acid from the N-terminus in the β-peptide chain is replaced by the amino acid lysine[11] (see Figure 6–1). In this case the abnormality leads only to a mild anemia, and the solubility of the abnormal hemoglobin is not lower when deoxygenated. Figure 6–2 gives a partial list of the amino acid replacements known in abnormal human hemoglobins in the α- and β-peptide chains. It serves to illustrate the point that amino acid exchanges are possible in many different parts of the α- and β-peptide chains and that amino acids of different types can exchange. The data are too sparse to enable one to talk meaningfully about the frequency of mutations in the particular regions of the structural gene. It should be noted, however, that in the β structural gene there are three positions for which two mutants are known.

As well as illustrating the effect of what are probably point mutations, which result in amino acid exchanges in the peptide chain, we can illustrate another type of genetic abnormality in the abnormal human hemoglobins. This is the so-called hemoglobin Lepore of which two instances have been described in Boston[12] and in Dutch Indonesia.[13] In the case of hemoglobin

FIGURE 6–3   Diagram showing the location of the abnormalities of human hemoglobin in the idealized structure of the molecule (compare with Figure 6–2). N marks the NH$_2$-terminus of each peptide chain.

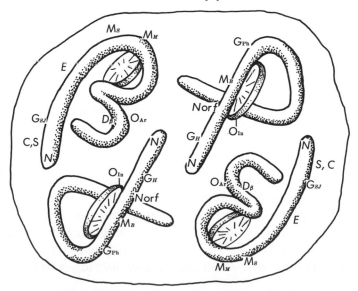

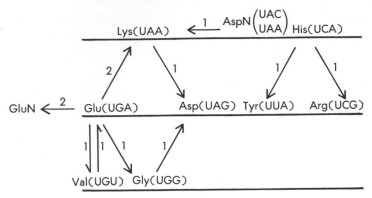

FIGURE 6–4   *The amino acid replacements in the human hemoglobins compared with the changes in triplet code letters.
The numbers show the number of different occurrences.*

Lepore from Boston, Gerald has suggested that the abnormality
of this hemoglobin might be such that a peptide chain exists that
is a hybrid chain having partly β- and partly δ-peptide chain
character.   The chemical analysis by Baglioni[14] confirmed and
extended this suggestion.   He showed that hemoglobin Lepore is
composed of two α chains, which are apparently normal, and two
"non-α" peptide chains in which the portion near the N-
terminus is δ chain in character and in which the portion near
the carboxyl terminus is β chain in character.   It was already
known from the work of Stretton[15] that β- and δ-peptide chains
are similar in length (see legend for Figure 6–5) and that they
differ from each other by the substitution of only eight amino
acids in the positions indicated.   By analyzing the tryptic
peptides obtainable from the non-α peptide chain of hemoglobin
Lepore_{Boston}, Baglioni was able to assign δ- and β-like character
to those tryptic peptides that carried one or more of the eight
substitutions.   In this way he could assign δ-like character from
amino acid number 1 to number 50 in the peptide chain and
β-like character from position number 116 to the end.   It was
not possible to assign peptides in between to either δ- or
β-chain character, because there is no chemical difference
to distinguish them in that region of the peptide chain.   Baglioni
postulated that such a hybrid peptide chain (Figure 6–5) must

arise from a hybrid structural gene that has perhaps arisen by a process of unequal crossing over (Figure 6–6). Such an event, although rare, seems to have happened at least twice (for Lepore$_{Boston}$ and Lepore$_{Hollandia}$) and perhaps more frequently, and may be facilitated by the close similarity between β- and δ-peptide chains. It is possible that this similarity is also expressed in a corresponding similarity between the β and δ structural genes, thus making a mispairing during meiosis a little more likely. It is also known that the β and δ structural loci are genetically linked, although we do not know how closely. However, if they are close together, this makes the possibility of an unequal crossing-over event such as the one leading to hemoglobin Lepore more likely.

The amino acid changes found in the abnormal human

FIGURE 6–5   *Schematic representation of the hemoglobin Le-pore$_{Boston}$ gene and the corresponding ("non-α") pep-tide chain. The shaded portion is δ-chain-like in amino acid sequence and the black portion is β-like. In between, the empty region shows those portions of the peptide chain where β and δ are indistinguishable. The numbers denote peptides obtained by digestion with trypsin. (From Reference 14.)*

Note: Both β and δ chains are 146 amino acids in length; δ differs[3] (and Stretton, unpublished) by the following amino acid changes, counting from the N-terminus:—#9 (β serine → δ threonine), #12 (β thre-onine → δ asparagine), #22 (β glutamic acid → δ ala-nine), #50 (β threonine → δ serine), #116 (β histi-dine → δ arginine), #117 (β histidine → δ asparagine), #125 (β proline → δ histidine), #126 (β valine → δ methionine).

Lepore$_{Boston}$

Gene ---   δ   β

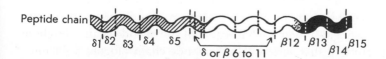

Peptide chain δ1 δ2 δ3 δ4   δ5   δ or β 6 to 11   β12 β13 β14 β15

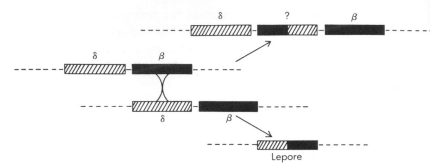

FIGURE 6–6   *The postulated unequal crossing over between a β and a δ structural gene leading to the formation of the Lepore gene (after Reference 14). The unequal crossing over is supposed to have occurred perhaps by breaking and rejoining of the respective DNA molecules. The genotype containing the structural gene β/δ (upper line of drawing) has not yet been seen.*

hemoglobins are illustrated in Figure 6–2. Correlating the type of amino acid exchange with the alteration in the currently accepted code words for these amino acids (Figure 6–4) shows us that the amino acid replacements may be explained on the basis of single base changes in these code words. Although this is the simplest explanation, we have no means of confirming it in the hemoglobin system. In particular, we do not know how many mutational events separate the substitution for a given amino acid. For example, the replacement of glutamic acid by valine in sickle-cell hemoglobin may have been the result of more than one mutational event of which the intermediate forms are no longer available. Nevertheless, with this reservation in mind and also remembering that we are assuming the triplet code, it is suggestive that the amino acid exchanges can be explained in such a simple manner.

MUTATIONS IN THE ''A PROTEIN'' OF E. COLI TRYPTOPHAN SYNTHETASE

Through the elegant work of Yanofsky and his colleagues,[16] we now have very good examples of the chemical effect of mutation on the structure of a protein in a bacterial system where detailed genetic analysis of the structural gene is also possible. In *E. coli*, the enzyme system for the synthesis of the amino acid trypto-phane from indole or indole-glycerol phosphate and serine is composed of two different proteins, the so-called A protein and the B protein. Yanofsky was able to isolate the A protein and to obtain UV-induced mutants that were defective in this particu-lar protein, thus producing an inactive enzyme. In a consider-able number of cases he was able to pinpoint the amino acid exchange which had taken place. Two mutants (A23 and A46), which are illustrated in Figure 6–7, affect the same amino acid (glycine) in the peptide chain of the A protein. The two mutants exchange the glycine in the peptide for either glutamic acid (A46) or arginine (A23), leading in either case to enzymati-cally inactive protein.

The whole A protein has 280 amino acid residues in a single peptide chain. The length of the structural gene controlling its amino acid sequence is 2.5 recombination units long, measured as per cent recombination (see Glossary). Between the two mutants that affect the same amino acid, Henning and Yanof-sky[17] were able to show that recombination occurred with a frequency of 0.004 per cent. This was the first example of genetic recombination occurring within the same amino acid

FIGURE 6–7 *Some mutants and revertants occurring in a peptide of the A protein of E. coli tryptophan synthetase. All the proteins are functional except A23 (Arg) and A46 (Glu). PR = partially active revertant; FR = fully ac-tive revertant. (After Reference 16.)*

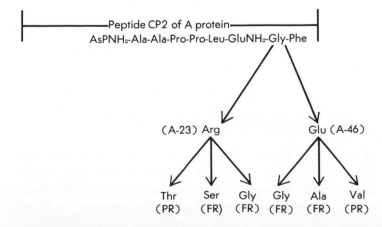

coding unit, the same triplet. It shows very clearly that the coding unit for a single amino acid is itself divisible, as demanded by the concept of a triplet of bases that are coding for such an amino acid.

Spontaneous revertants of these two mutations (Figure 6–7) were found to produce active enzymes,[16] although their A protein did not necessarily have the wild-type amino acid sequence. As can be seen from Figures 6–8 and 6–9, the place originally occupied by glycine may again be filled by glycine, when the reversion of the mutation leads back to the original coding triplet. Other revertants have alanine or serine in place of glycine, and such proteins are also fully active. This is probably because the side chains of alanine and serine, like glycine, are very small. On the other hand, the revertant that carries valine instead of the original wild-type glycine is only partially active enzymatically, presumably because the much larger side chain of the valine residue precludes exact folding of the peptide chain. It is important to note that all the amino acid replacements in this system, illustrated in Figure 6–7, agree with the concept of the triplet code; they may all be explained by the replacement of a single base within the triplet leading to a new code for a new

FIGURE 6–8   Summary of amino acid replacements in the A protein of E. coli tryptophan synthetase occurring at the glycine residue of the peptide CP2, also described in Figure 6–7. The numbers indicate how often each replacement was demonstrated. (After Reference 16.)

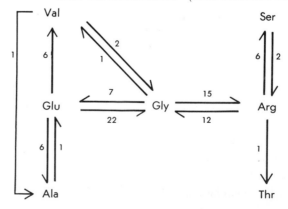

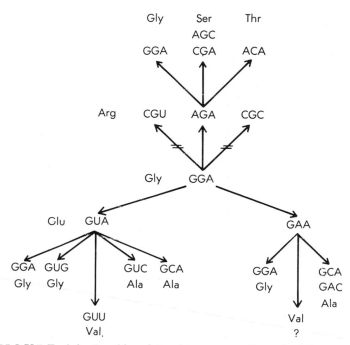

FIGURE 6–9 *Possible relationships among the code letters corresponding to the amino acids in Figure 6–8, starting with the letters GGA for glycine. According to the idea of degeneracy in coding, more than one triplet of code letters can code for an amino acid. Other schemes are possible,[16] beginning with UGG or CGG as code letters for glycine. For each mutational step, those triplets are used that need only a single base change. Only one of the two glutamic acid triplets shown (GUA) gives a known valine triplet by a single base change. ⧧ means that more than a single nucleotide change is required. (After Reference 16.)*

amino acid[16] (Figure 6–9).   As in the case of the human hemoglobins, this fact in itself does not prove that these mutations are indeed due to single base changes, but this is the simplest explanation.   In the case of the *E. coli* protein, however, we are in a much better position to assume that the observed amino acid exchanges are the result of single mutational events.

Recently, Yanofsky and his colleagues[18] studied 16 mutants

TABLE 6–1 *RNA coding letters*

Gly	UGC, AGG, CGG
Glu	AUG, AAG
Ala	CUG, CAG, CCG
Val	UUG
Arg	GUC, GCC, GAA
Ser	CUU, UCC, ACG
Thr	UCA, ACA, CGC, CCA

with alterations in a segment of the A protein. Various point mutations on the genetic map could be placed in order on that map by measuring the frequency of recombination between them and in relation to mutations further away on the gene. The linear order of these point mutants corresponded with the linear order of amino acid substitutions in the peptide chain: the gene structure and the protein structure are colinear. Their results also showed that genetic recombination frequencies are representative of the distances between amino acid residues in the corresponding protein.

Sarabhai, Stretton, Brenner, and Bolle[19] have shown colinearity of gene and peptide structure by an analysis of the enzymatically obtained fragments of the head protein of bacteriophage T4 in certain mutants. They were able to define chemically eight segments of the peptide chain that were found to be in the same order as the corresponding segments on the genetic map.

NITROUS ACID MUTANTS OF TOBACCO MOSAIC VIRUS[20]

In the case of tobacco mosaic virus (Figure 6–10) the genetic element is RNA, not DNA. It is not yet clear whether, upon infection of a tobacco cell by this virus, the infecting RNA acts as m-RNA so that its genetic message is directly translated into amino acid sequences, or whether it acts like DNA and has to be transcribed first into m-RNA. In either case the nucleotide sequence of the RNA is assumed to determine the amino acid sequence of the coat protein of this virus. It should be mentioned that the protein, which constitutes 96 per cent by

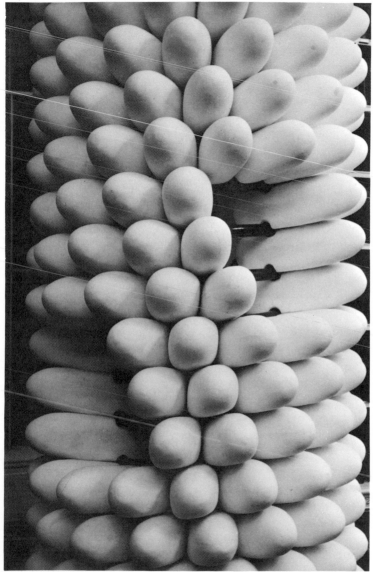

FIGURE 6–10 Model of the molecular structure of tobacco mosaic virus. Only a portion of the long rod-like particle, whose actual dimensions are 150 × 3000 Angstroms, is shown. The inner black coil is the RNA (6400 nucleotides long in the intact molecule); surrounding it are the protein subunits that make up the coat of this protein. Each protein has a single peptide chain of 158 amino acids. (Courtesy of Dr. D. L. D. Caspar and Dr. A. Klug.)

weight of the whole virus, is composed of many identical
subunits, each of which has a chain length of 158 amino acids.
The complete sequence of this protein (Figure 6–12) has been
established through the efforts of Anderer and Schramm,[21] of
Wittmann,[22] and of Fraenkel-Conrat and his colleagues.[23]

It was shown that high concentrations of nitrous acid at pH 5
acted on RNA to deaminate cytosine to form uracil and also
adenine to form hypoxanthine (Figure 6–11), the nucleotide of
which is known as inosinic acid.   As far as base-pairing properties are concerned, inosinic acid behaves like guanylic acid, so
that the deamination of adenine may be considered to lead to its
replacement by guanine.   The case of deamination of guanine
(presumably to xanthine) is not so clear.   Although guanine is
altered in free tobacco mosaic virus RNA (TMV-RNA), it is
not attacked by nitrous acid in the intact virus.   The chemistry
of the guanine alteration in free RNA is not fully understood,

FIGURE 6–11   *Base changes in RNA produced by nitrous acid. Note
that hypoxanthine can hydrogen bond rather like gua-
nine and therefore form a base pair with cytosine.*

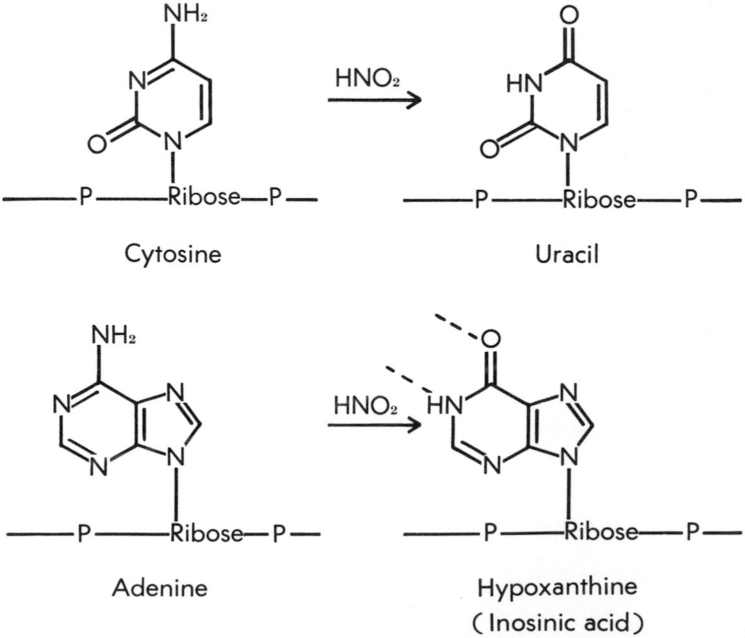

Cytosine   Uracil

Adenine   Hypoxanthine
                                       (Inosinic acid)

Acetyl-Ser—Tyr—Ileu—Thr—Thr—Pro—Ser-GluN—Phe—Val—Phe—Leu—Ser—Ser—Ala—Try—Ala—Asp—Pro
1   2   3   4   5   6   7   8   9   10   11   12   13   14   15   16   17   18   19   20

Ileu—Glu—Leu—Ileu-AspN-Leu-Cys—Thr-AspN-Ala-Leu-Gly-AspN-Phe-GluN-Thr-GluN-GluN-Ala—Arg┬Thr—Val
21   22   23   24   25   26   27   28   29   30   31   32   33   34   35   36   37   38   39   40 41ᵀ 42   43

GluN-Val—Arg┬GluN-Phe-Ser-GluN-Val—Try-Lys-Pro-Ser—Pro-GluN-Val—Thr—Val—Arg┬Phe—Pro—Ser—Asp
44   45   46ᵀ 47   48   49   50   51   52   53   54   55   56   57   58   59   60 61ᵀ 62   63   64   65   66

Phe—Lys—Val—Tyr—Arg┬Tyr-AspN-Ala-Val-Leu-Asp-Pro-Leu—Val—Thr—Ala—Leu—Leu—Gly—Ala—Phe—Asp—Thr
67   68   69   70 71ᵀ 72   73   74   75   76   77   78   79   80   81   82   83   84   85   86   87   88   89

Arg┬AspN-Arg┬Ileu-Ileu-Glu-Val—Glu-GluN-Ala-AspN-Pro—Thr—Thr—Ala—Glu—Thr—Leu—Asp—Ala—Thr—Arg┬
90ᵀ 91   92ᵀ 93   94   95   96   97   98   99   100 101 102 103 104 105 106 107 108 109 110 111 112ᵀ

Arg —Val—Asp—Asp—Ala—Thr—Val—Ala—Ileu—Arg┬Ser-Ala—Asp—Ileu-AspN-Leu-AspN-Leu—Val—Glu—Leu—Ileu—Arg┬Gly
113 114 115 116 117 118 119 120 121 122ᵀ 123 124 125 126 127 128 129 130 131 132 133 134 135ᵀ

Thr—Gly—Ser—Tyr-AspN-Arg┬Ser—Ser-Phe—Glu—Ser—Ser—Gly—Leu—Val—Try—Thr—Ser—Gly—Pro—Ala—Thr
136 137 138 139 140 141ᵀ 142 143 144 145 146 147 148 149 150 151 152 153 154 155 156 157 158

FIGURE 6-12 *The amino acid sequence of the common wild type of tobacco mosaic virus protein. T indicates the points of cleavage by trypsin used for the analysis. The protein is unusual in having its N-terminal group acetylated. (After Reference 20.)*

173

only some of the bases being converted to xanthine; other products are suspected. More than half the nitrous acid mutants were obtained from the treatment of whole virus, so that it is reasonable to assume that most, if not all, mutants are due to either $A \rightarrow I (= G)$ or $C \rightarrow U$.

Under conditions of nitrous acid treatment where most virus particles are inactivated, a high proportion of the survivors are now mutant virus particles. The survival rate was usually only about 10^{-2} to 10^{-4} of normal. Using these survivors to infect the leaves of tobacco plants, mutant colonies of virus may be formed on these leaves and recognized by their abnormal morphology. Other mutants are recognized by their different behavior toward certain species of tobacco plants. About 70 per cent of the new mutants (Table 6–2) that were formed as a result of approximately three to four "hits" by nitrous acid on the RNA showed no chemical difference in the virus protein, in spite of the fact that mutant morphology of the virus infection was caused by a mutant. The remaining mutants did show amino acid exchanges in the virus protein, carrying one or two amino acid substitutions in the peptide chain. The conclusion from these results is that about two-thirds of the genetic material (the TMV-RNA) has a function other than that of coding for the virus coat protein. Perhaps some new enzymes have to be made in the infected host cell or perhaps some as yet undefined function is involved.

TABLE 6–2   *Distribution of the TMV mutants completely investigated*[a]

No. of amino acid exchanges in coat protein	No. of nitrous acid mutants	Spontaneous mutants
0	88	8
1	31	5
2	6	2
3	0	1
>3	0	0
Total	125	16

[a] After Reference 20.

For all nitrous acid and spontaneous mutants investigated, the exchange of single amino acids always occurs *without* changes in the neighboring amino acids. This finding provides strong evidence for the hypothesis that the genetic code is nonoverlapping. Only very special kinds of overlapping codes are still compatible with the results.

These amino acid substitutions are scattered throughout the chain (Figure 6–13). It is possible that all such exchanges are point mutations derived from the action of nitrous acid on a base or bases within the particular coding triplets. Since the supposed chemical mechanism for the action of this mutagen permits precise predictions about what kind of base change has occurred, it is interesting to compare the observed amino acid exchanges with the alterations in the triplet code words. Such a comparison is made in Figure 6–14, where it may be seen that, among the amino acid exchanges illustrated, six out of eleven are in agreement with the proposed chemical mechanism and the proposed code words. The remaining five call for mutational alterations in the code words which cannot be explained on the basis of a change from $C \rightarrow U$ or $A \rightarrow G$. It is possible, that the assignment of the code letters for these particular amino acids is not correct, or that the disagreeing mutants are in fact spontaneous mutants with an unknown origin. The fact that even half the amino acid exchanges are explainable on the basis of the chemical mechanism and of the code letters shown does give one some confidence in the general correctness of the scheme for the genetic control of the amino acid sequences of a protein such as

FIGURE 6–13 *Distribution of the amino acid differences along the tobacco mosaic virus protein chain. Most were obtained with nitrous acid, the rest are spontaneous. Vertical lines of double height indicate that two different amino acid replacements were found at that point. (After Reference 20.)*

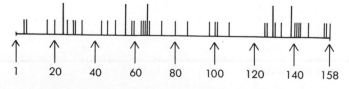

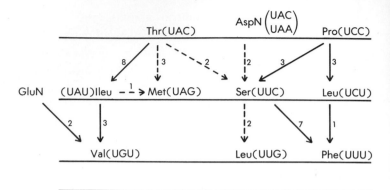

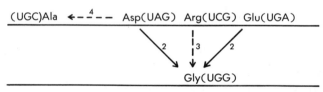

FIGURE 6-14   *The amino acid replacements observed in TMV protein after nitrous acid treatment. The usual triplets (Tables 5–6 and 6–1) are used, but not necessarily the same sequence of code letters. Solid arrows show agreement with the changes in code letters expected from the nitrous acid treatment, dotted arrows show disagreement. The numbers show the number of occurrences. It is assumed that the virus RNA also acts as messenger RNA for making TMV protein. (After Reference 20.)*

this one.   Furthermore, the results imply that the TMV-RNA acts itself as a messenger RNA, since the predicted coding changes in the nitrous acid mutants are those expected for the template, not its complementary nucleotide sequence.

REFERENCES

1. Ingram, V. M. (1957), "Gene Mutations in Human Haemoglobin: The Chemical Difference Between Normal and Sickle Cell Haemoglobin." *Nature*, **180**, 326.

2. Ingram, V. M. (1963), *The Hemoglobins in Genetics and Evolution*, Columbia University Press, New York.

3. Ingram, V. M., and Stretton, A. O. W. (1961), "Human Haemoglobin A₂: Chemistry, Genetics, and Evolution." *Nature*, 190, 1079.

4. Baglioni, C. (1963), Chapter in *Molecular Genetics I* (ed. Taylor, J. H.). Academic Press, New York.

5. Pauling, L., Itano, H. A., Singer, S. J., and Wells, I. C. (1949), "Sickle Cell Anemia, A Molecular Disease." *Science*, 110, 543.

6. Neel, J. V. (1949), "The Inheritance of Sickle Cell Anemia." *Science*, 110, 64.

7. Perutz, M. F., and Mitchison, J. M. (1950), "State of Haemoglobin in Sickle-Cell Anemia." *Nature*, 166, 677.

8. Harris, J. W. (1950), *Proc. Soc. Exptl. Biol. & Med.*, 75, 197.

9. Kiho, Y., and Rich, A. (1964), "Induced Enzyme Formed on Bacterial Polyribosomes." *Proc. Natl. Acad. Sci.*, 51, 111.

10. Smith, E. L. (1962), "Nucleotide Base Coding and Amino Acid Replacements in Proteins, II." *Proc. Natl. Acad. Sci.*, 48, 859.

11. Hunt, J. A., and Ingram, V. M. (1958), "Allelomorphism and the Chemical Differences of the Human Haemoglobins A, S, C." *Nature*, 181, 1062.

12. Gerald, P. S., and Diamond, L. K. (1958). *Blood*, 13, 835.

13. Barnabas, J., and Muller, C. J. (1962), "Haemoglobin Lepore_Hollandia." *Nature*, 194, 931.

14. Baglioni, C. (1962), "The Fusion of Two Peptide Chains in Hemoglobin Lepore and Its Interpretation as a Genetic Deletion." *Proc. Natl. Acad. Sci.*, 48, 1880.

15. Ingram, V. M., and Stretton, A. O. W. (1962), "Human Haemoglobin A₂. Parts I and II." *Biochim. Biophys. Acta.*, 62, 456; 63, 20.

16. Yanofsky, C. (1963), "Amino Acid Replacements Associated with Mutation and Recombination in the A Gene and Their Relationship to In Vitro Coding Data." *Cold Spring Harb. Symp. Quant. Biol.* 28, 581.

17. Henning, U., and Yanofsky, C. (1962), "Amino Acid Replacements Associated with Reversion and Recombination Within the A Gene." *Proc. Natl. Acad. Sci.*, 48, 1497.

18. Yanofsky, C., Carlton, B. C., Guest, J. R., Helinski, D. R. and Henning, U. (1964), "On the Colinearity of Gene Structure and Protein Structure." *Proc. Natl. Acad. Sci.*, 51, 266.

19. Sarabhai, A. S., Stretton, A. O. W., Brenner, S., and Bolle, A. (1964), "Colinearity of the Gene with the Polypeptide Chain." *Nature*, **201**, 13.

20. Wittmann, H. G., and Wittmann-Liebold, B. (1963), "Tobacco Mosaic Virus Mutants and the Genetic Coding Problem." *Cold Spring Harb. Symp. Quant. Biol.*, **28**, 589.

21. Anderer, F. A., Uhlig, H., Weber, E., and Schramm, G. (1960), "Primary Structure of the Protein of Tobacco Mosaic Virus." *Nature*, **186**, 923.

22. Wittmann, H. G. (1960), "Comparison of the Tryptic Peptides of Chemically Induced and Spontaneous Mutants of Tobacco Mosaic Virus." *Virology*, **12**, 609.

23. Tsugita, A., Gish, D. T., Young, J., Fraenkel-Conrat, H., Knight, C. A., and Stanley, W. M. (1960), "The Complete Amino Acid Sequence of the Protein of Tobacco Mosaic Virus." *Proc. Natl. Acad. Sci. U.S.*, **46**, 1463.

SEVEN $\int\int$ POLYSACCHARIDES

WE SHALL NEXT DISCUSS THE BIOSYNTHESIS OF SOME POLYSAC-
charides, because they form a group of macromolecules considerably different from the nucleic acids and the proteins.
Although they are also long-chain polymers made from simple
monomeric units, they are for the most part not ordered into
information-carrying sequences nor are they of definite chain
length. This is because the polysaccharides are either a con-
venient way for the cell to store sugar molecules, as in starch
or glycogen, in which case simple homopolymers are adequate,
or because polysaccharides are used as structural materials,
as in cellulose, which is also a homopolymer. In molecules
such as these, sequence information is not important. On
the other hand, in the polysaccharides that form part of the
immunologically specific cell antigens several kinds of carbohydrate monomers are arranged in specific, although repeating,
sequences. However, it seems likely that these sequences are
the result of the action of a series of specific synthetic enzymes
and that the polysaccharide chain is *not made by the assembly of*

subunits on a template. The same is of course true for the homopolymers starch and glycogen, and perhaps also for cellulose. In this important respect the synthesis of polysaccharide chains differs from the synthesis of the specific sequences in nucleic acid and protein polypeptide chains, which require assembly on a template. However, an exception exists in the synthesis of polyribonucleotides with random sequences by the enzyme polynucleotide phosphorylase, which does not use a template; but then this is strictly an in vitro reaction.

It is important to notice that the biosynthesis of all long-chain macromolecules requires the individual subunits to be in an *activated form.* For nucleic acid synthesis, this form is the nucleoside triphosphate (= nucleotide-pyrophosphate); in the biosynthesis of proteins the activated form is the amino acyl-s-RNA intermediate. For putting together long chains of

FIGURE 7–1 *Different ways of representing* D-*glucose.*

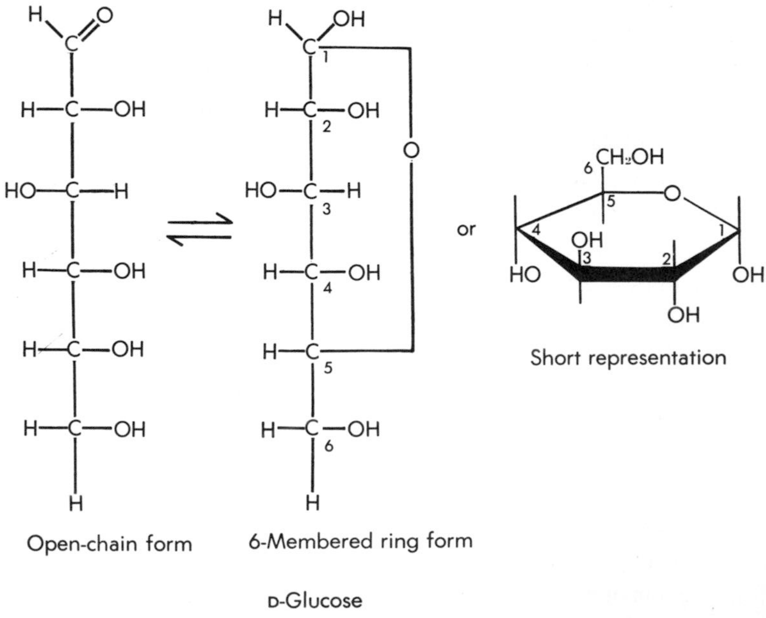
Open-chain form
6-Membered ring form
or
Short representation
D-Glucose

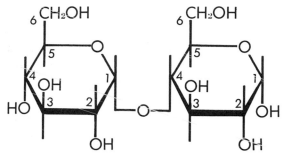

FIGURE 7–2 *The structure of maltose in the α-D form. Note the α-D-(1 → 4) linkage between the two D-glucose units.*

polysaccharides, such as glycogen, the monomer unit, glucose, is in the activated form of UDP-glucose (Figure 7–12).

The polysaccharides are long-chain high-molecular-weight polymers composed of simple sugar (monosaccharide) units. The polymers are linear and they may or may not be branched. A few are cyclic and some may contain units that are derivatives of the simple sugars, as the sulfated and acetylated amino sugars in the chondroitin sulfate of connective tissue (Figure 7–4). The polysaccharides with which we shall deal in this chapter are those whose biosynthesis is best understood: glycogen, starch, and cellulose, which are polymers composed entirely of glucose units. For a discussion of the chemistry of the mono-saccharides, the reader is referred to a general text, for example, Chapter 15 of Karlson, *Introduction to Modern Biochemistry* (New York: Academic Press, 1963); in this chapter we shall give only a few illustrative examples.

The polysaccharides may be divided into two main functional classes: one group serves as structural materials, i.e., cellulose; another group serves as storage materials for monosaccharides, for example, starch, which stores glucose in plants, and glycogen, which stores glucose in animal cells. Starch is composed of two kinds of molecules, called *amylose* (Figure 7–6) and *amylopec-tin* (Figure 7–3). Both are composed entirely of glucose mole-cules linked into very long chains, the difference between them being mainly one of arrangement of these chains. Whereas amylose has simple long chains of glucose linked in an

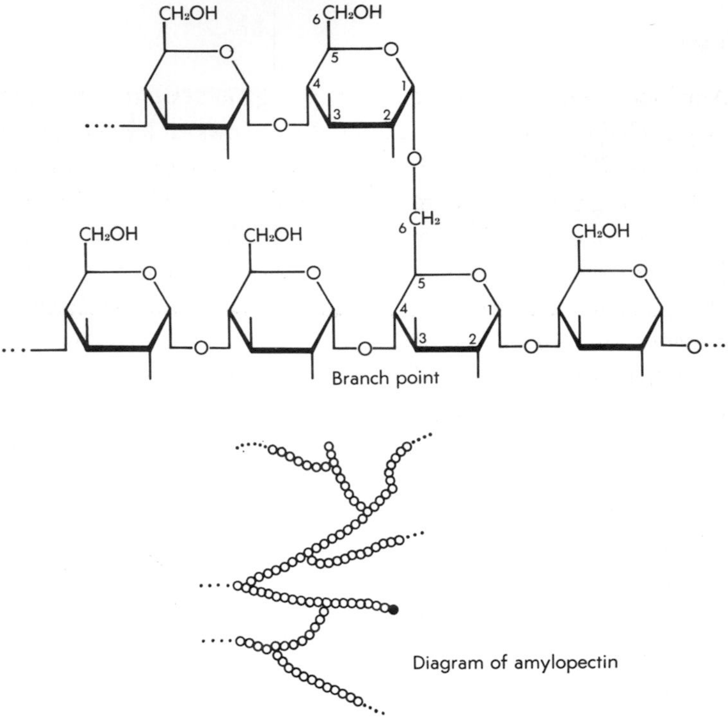

Diagram of amylopectin

FIGURE 7–3   *The structure of amylopectin and glycogen.   The glucose units are shown in abbreviated form.*

a-D-$(1 \to 4)$ linkage (see Figure 7–2), amylopectin has those chains but in addition has branch chains of similar nature.   The branch points in amylopectin are a-D-$(1 \to 6)$ linkages (see Figure 7–3).

AMYLOSE

Amylose prepared from potato starch has a molecular weight of approximately 35,000, which means that it is composed of some 200 glucose units.   It makes up about 20 per cent of the total starch.   The chain length of an amylose molecule is not definite, but rather we find a distribution of chain lengths around a preferred length.   This is in direct contrast to the proteins and the nucleic acids, both of which are also long-chain molecules but which do have a very definite number of units making up their chains.

AMYLOPECTIN

Amylopectin has branched chains that are much shorter than the single chain of amylose. Figure 7–3 shows a branch point $[\alpha\text{-D-}(1 \rightarrow 6)]$ in amylopectin. All the reducing groups of the individual glucose units are linked in glycosidic linkage, except the single one at the extreme right-hand side. Amylopectin has just one reducing end, one reducing glucose unit per molecule. It is possible to determine the complexity of a molecule such as amylopectin. In the method developed originally by Haworth,[1] dimethyl sulfate $(CH_3)_2SO_4$ reacts with free —OH groups to form stable methyl ethers. Acid hydrolysis gives monosaccharides that are methylated to an extent depending upon the number of —OH groups originally *not* involved in glycosidic linkages. By complete methylation of the polymer, one obtains 2,3,6-trimethyl glucose from the interior of the chain, 2,3-dimethyl glucose from each branch point and, in principle at least, 1,2,3,6-tetramethyl glucose from the reducing end. However, from the end of each branch one gets a molecule of 2,3,4,6-tetramethyl glucose. By separating and quantitatively estimating these individual methylated derivatives of glucose, one can obtain an estimate of how many branch ends there are per molecule. This is an important characteristic of the amylopectin molecule, since the utilization of the glucose units

FIGURE 7–4 *The repeating unit in the polysaccharide chondroitin sulfate c of connective tissue. The subunits are composed of a glucuronic acid residue and an N-acetyl-galactosamine-6-sulfate residue.*

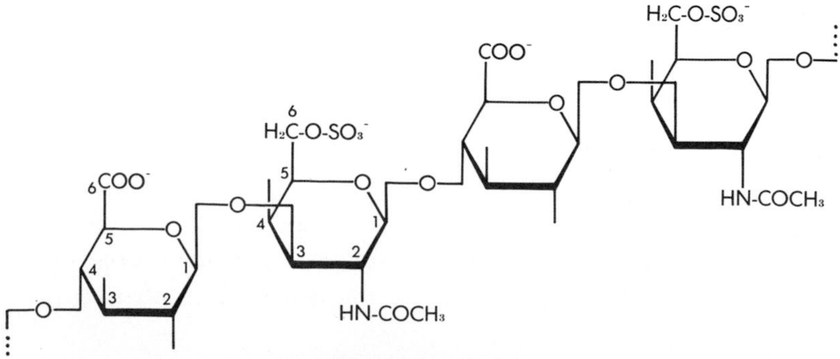

Chondroitin sulfate C

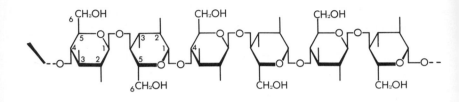

(a)

(b)

FIGURE 7–5   (a) *Structure of cellulose, using an abbreviated formula for glucose.   [Note the* β*-D-*$(1 \to 4)$ *linkage.]*
(b) *Diagram of the unicellar structure of cellulose.*

it contains depends to a considerable extent on the ability of specific enzymes to release glucose starting from the ends of each branch.   Therefore, the more branches a molecule has, the more rapidly it can be degraded.

In the case of amylopectin from rice starch, we have a molecule of molecular weight of 500,000 with about 80 to 90 branch points between connecting chains, each one of which has some 30 glucose units.

GLYCOGEN

Glycogen is the glucose-storing molecule in animal tissues. It is similar to amylopectin, having the same kind of branched-chain structure. However, glycogen is considerably larger in size and has a molecular weight of 1×10^6 in the case of muscle glycogen and about 5×10^6 in the case of liver glycogen. Again the chains of glucose units are linked in a-D-$(1 \rightarrow 4)$ linkage and they branch by a-D-$(1 \rightarrow 6)$ linkages at the branch points. In addition to having a higher molecular weight, glycogen is more densely branched than is amylopectin, having only some three to four glucose units between branch points in the center of the molecule with some six to eight glucose units at the ends of each branch. Again, as in amylopectin, a glycogen molecule has only a single reducing glucose unit per molecule. The function of glycogen is to store glucose and the glucose has to be readily available inside the cell, for example, inside the muscle cell for

FIGURE 7–6   *The conformation of the amylose chain.*

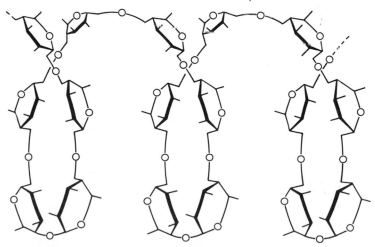

muscle contraction. A densely branched-chain structure is advantageous in such a situation, since the degrading enzymes act on the ends of the branches; the more ends there are the more rapidly the glycogen molecule can be degraded and, by the same token, the more rapidly glycogen can be built up again during periods in the cell's metabolism when glycogen neogenesis occurs. Actually, during glycogen resynthesis it is found that after a short time even the inside of the molecule is newly built up. Presumably through the action of internally acting amylases, like α-amylase, glycogen is fragmented as well as sequentially degraded at the branches. New, small "priming" molecules are therefore formed continuously and on these glucose can also be added.

DEGRADATION OF STARCH AND GLYCOGEN DURING DIGESTION

The enzymatic breakdown of glycogen and starch during the digestion of food proceeds by a totally different set of enzymes than does the intracellular breakdown of glycogen. Digestion begins through the action of amylases in the saliva and continues with the further breakdown by pancreatic enzymes in the intestine. The amylases concerned in this breakdown fall into the general class of hydrolytic enzyme known as the glycosidases, and Figure 7–7 illustrates the hydrolytic mechanism in a particular case. The amylases are enzymes that are highly specific for glucose linked in the α-D configuration.

FIGURE 7–7   *The hydrolytic action of β-glucosidase. The enzyme has no specificity for the nature of the R group.*

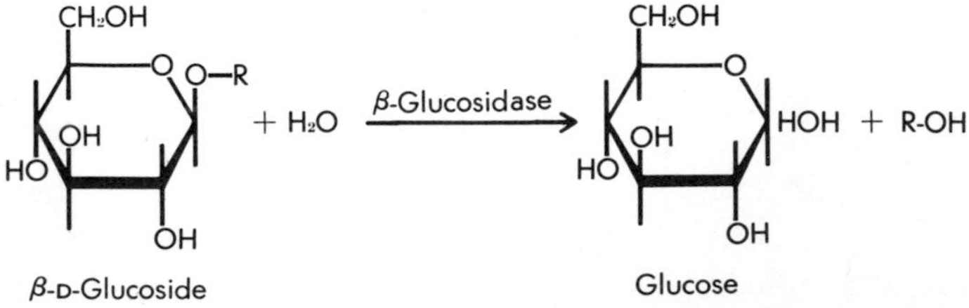

β-D-Glucoside   Glucose

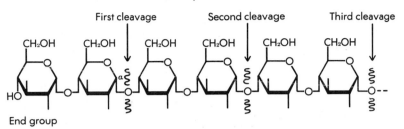

FIGURE 7–8   *The mechanism of sequential hydrolysis by β-amylase, producing maltose units.*

β-AMYLASE

This enzyme is found in the pancreas, the saliva, and it can also be prepared from potato.   It is a sequential enzyme hydrolyzing the α-D-(1 → 4) linkages to be found in the straight chains of amylose and in the branches of amylopectin (Figure 7–8). Beginning at the free nonreducing end of such a chain, β-amylase hydrolyzes every second glycosidic linkage, thus liberating units of maltose. The sequential digestion of the long chain of amylose can proceed to give 100 percent hydrolysis to maltose units.   Actually a small amount of glucose is also produced.   On the other hand, the reduction in molecular weight is relatively slow, because this is a sequential enzyme beginning at one end.   To complete the digestion of amylose, another enzyme also present in the intestine will hydrolyze maltose to glucose units.   In the case of the digestion of amylopectin or of glycogen, β-amylase will attack the nonreducing ends of the branch chains; it will proceed along the chains liberating maltose units until it comes to a branch point.   At this, β-amylase action stops so that, with pure β-amylase, we get a limited hydrolysis of amylopectin or of glycogen, the extent of hydrolysis depending on the order of complexity of a particular molecule.

α-AMYLASE

This enzyme is also found in the pancreas, in the saliva, and in the potato. Like β-amylase, α-amylase also hydrolyzes α-D-$(1 \rightarrow 4)$ linkages, but internally (see Figure 7–9). This causes the rapid breakdown of large molecules of amylose, amylopectin, or glycogen into relatively large fragments, thus rapidly reducing the molecular weight. If both amylases are present, the action

FIGURE 7–9   *Schematic diagram of hydrolysis of starch by α-amylase, an enzyme acting internally.*

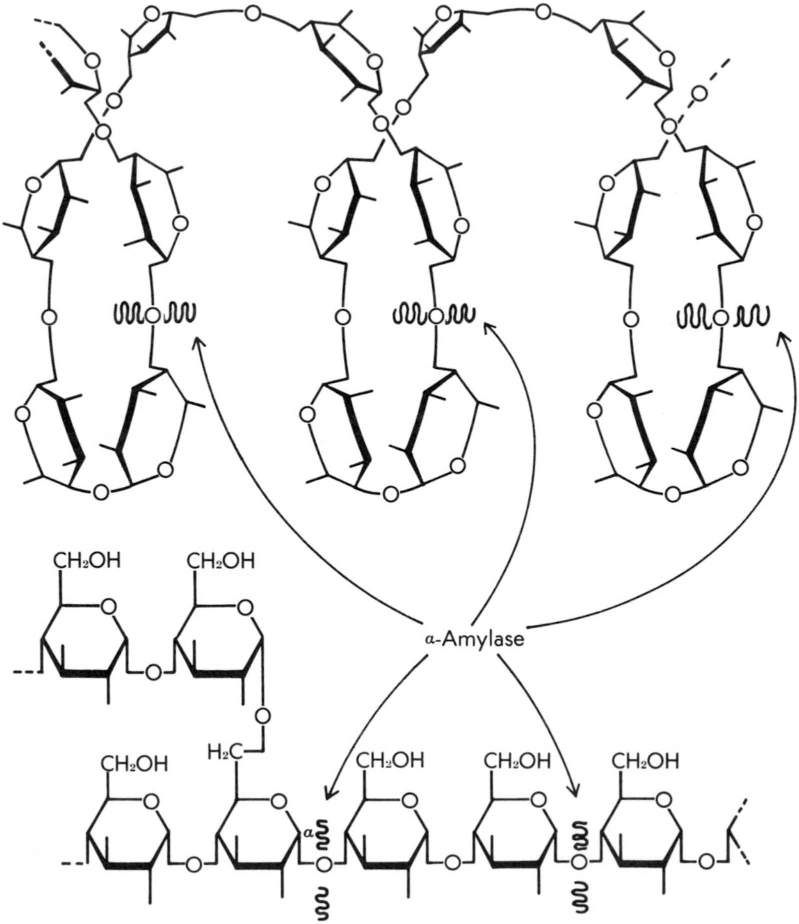

of α-amylase will create new points of attack for β-amylase, so that between the two of them these enzymes can degrade the polysaccharides quite rapidly.

α-Amylase cannot hydrolyze the α-D-$(1 \rightarrow 6)$ linkages found at the branch points any more than β-amylase can. For this purpose another enzyme is present, the so-called α-$(1 \rightarrow 6)$-glucosidase, whose specific function it is to liberate glucose from the α-D-$(1 \rightarrow 6)$ linkage found in amylopectin and glycogen. Four enzymes are required for amylose, amylopectin, and glycogen to be broken down completely during digestion. It should be noted that these digestive enzymes are not capable of dealing with the more unusual carbohydrate-storage polysaccharides, such as inulin, which is found in artichokes and which is almost entirely composed of fructose monosaccharide units. Neither can these enzymes deal with the very common constituent of food, cellulose, in spite of the fact that it is also a polysaccharide composed entirely of glucose subunits. The reason for this is that cellulose is linked in β-D-$(1 \rightarrow 4)$ linkage. The specificity of the amylases and the two other glycosidases we have just discussed is, however, strictly for α-D-linkages. On the other hand, many microorganisms do possess cellulases that are specific for the β linkage. For example, symbiotic microorganisms living in the digestive system of the cow will digest cellulose by means of cellulases which they secrete. Again, such animals as the shipworm and the termite are capable of digesting cellulose, because they either have a cellulase of their own, as in the case of the mollusk, or they have living within their digestive systems symbiotic microorganisms which perform the hydrolysis for them.

SYNTHESIS OF A DISACCHARIDE

Before considering the biosynthesis of a polysaccharide, we shall look at the mechanisms by which a disaccharide can be made. As our example we shall take the common disaccharide sucrose (Figure 7–10), which is composed of one residue of glucose and one residue of fructose. Sucrose is hydrolyzed to its component monosaccharides by an enzyme such as the invertase of yeast. A

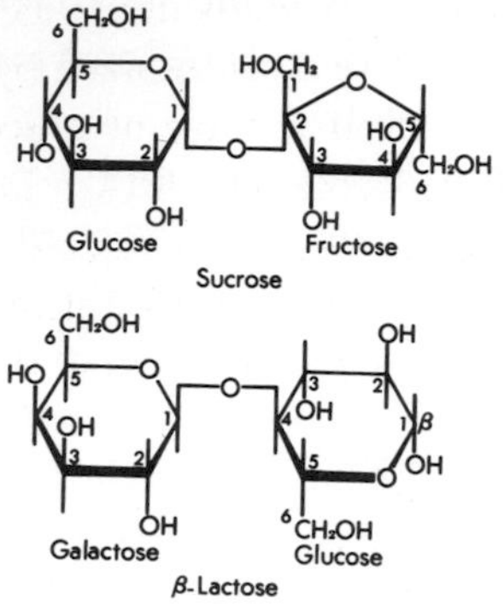

FIGURE 7–10   *The structures of the disaccharides sucrose and lactose.*

similar enzyme exists in the digestive systems of the higher animals. Although this is a reversible reaction, the reversal of hydrolysis is really the least efficient way for making sucrose.

Through the action of invertase, sucrose is split into glucose and fructose. If the reaction is carried out in the presence of water containing oxygen-18, we find on isolating the products that the oxygen isotope is on carbon atom number 2 of the fructose molecule. Therefore, the oxygen atom that originally formed the glycosidic linkage is now to be found on glucose. The reaction greatly favors hydrolysis and only traces of the disaccharide can be produced by the incubation of high concentrations of glucose and fructose together with the enzyme. Under physiological conditions no synthesis would be expected, particularly since the concentration of water would be very high.

Although it has been reported[2] that the synthesis of sucrose can be achieved in some bacterial systems by the reversal of a phosphorolytic reaction, it is doubtful whether this mechanism is of much importance. As can be seen in Figure 7–11, the phosphorolysis reaction of sucrose in the presence of inorganic phosphate leads to the production of glucose-1-PO_4 and one equivalent of fructose in the furanose configuration. The latter is in equilibrium with its pyranose form, which is the normal configuration of fructose in solution.

In higher organisms, particularly in plants such as wheat germ and potato sprouts, sucrose is synthesized by a different mechanism[3] involving the activated form of glucose, namely, UDP-glucose. This UDP-glucose (UDPG), illustrated in Figure 7–12, transfers its glucose to a molecule of fructose in the presence of an enzyme, thus directly forming the disaccharide sucrose, and liberating UDP [Eq. (7–1)]. The equilibrium

UDP - glucose + fructose $\rightleftharpoons$ sucrose + UDP

$$7–1$$

constant for this reaction at 37°C is between 2 and 8, indicating that the equilibrium lies in favor of the synthesis of the disaccharide. It should be noted that this equilibrium favors synthesis, because an activated form of glucose is used in the

FIGURE 7–11   *The hydrolysis of sucrose by bacterial phosphorylase.*

Sucrose   HO-PO$_3^{2-}$

Bacterial phosphorylase

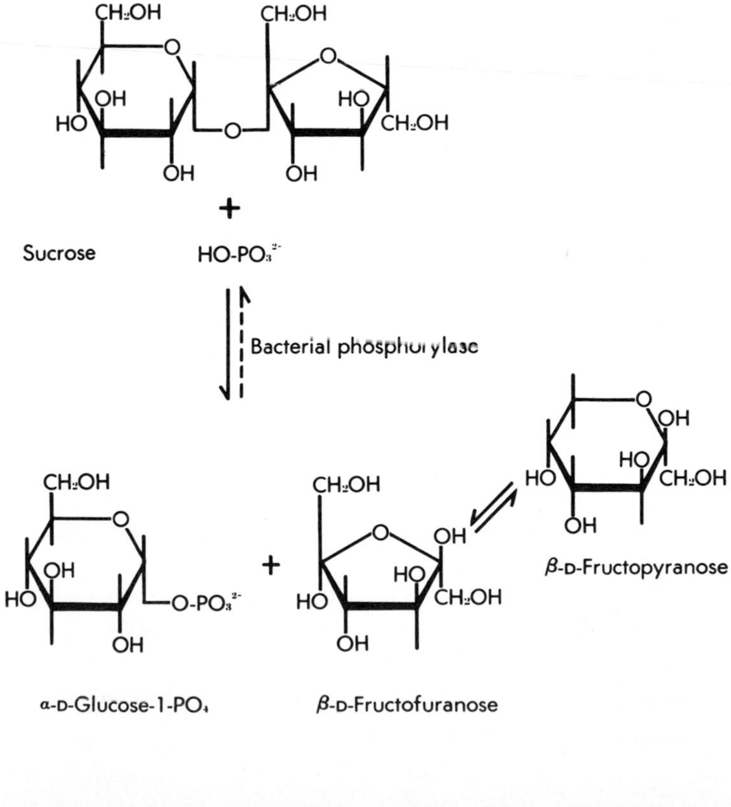

a-D-Glucose-1-PO$_4$ β-D-Fructofuranose   β-D-Fructopyranose reaction. The energy in fact is probably derived from the ionization of an additional phosphate acid group when UDP is liberated. Originally the energy needed to produce this activated form was derived from ATP in the production of glucose-6-PO_4; this in turn formed glucose-1-PO_4, which reacted with one molecule of UTP to form the UDP-glucose (see Figures 7–13 and 7–14). The UTP itself requires another equivalent of ATP for its formation from UDP.

A slightly different pathway for the synthesis of sucrose in some plants involves the transfer of glucose from UDP-glucose to fructose-6-PO_4, thus forming sucrose phosphate together with UDP. A separate phosphatase is required to release free sucrose. As will be seen later, the transfer reaction involving an activated form of glucose as in UDP-glucose is the most favorable way of synthesizing a glycosidic linkage. The same process is used many times over when polysaccharides are synthesized. Analogous UDP compounds involving other sugars are known and are used in the biosynthesis of polysaccharides containing these sugars.

PHOSPHOROLYSIS OF GLYCOGEN

In contrast to the digestive pathway where glycogen underwent hydrolysis to its component glucose units, glycogen is degraded in the muscle cell or in the liver cell by a phosphorolytic pathway (Figure 7–15). The muscle phorphorylase requires inorganic

FIGURE 7–12   *The structure of UDP-glucose.*

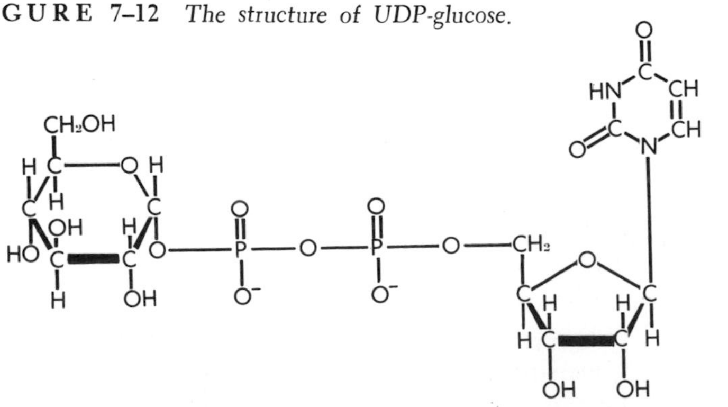

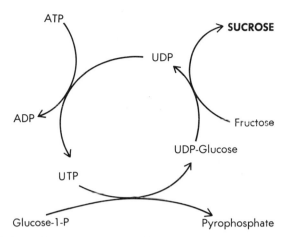

FIGURE 7–13   *The formation of sucrose, involving three enzymatic reactions.*

phosphate to form glucose-1-PO$_4$. The glucose-1-PO$_4$ so formed may then enter the glycolytic pathway and be broken down for the release of energy or for conversion into smaller carbon compounds needed in biosynthetic reactions.

Glycogen is a branched-chain molecule and the phosphorylase reaction, which is a sequential reaction, can only work on the ends of branches. In other words, phosphorylase degrades the free ends of the branched glycogen molecule sequentially until a branch point is reached; shortly before this point is reached, phosphorylase action has to stop. In any case the *extent* of phosphorylase reaction will be dependent upon the conditions inside the cell and on the demands for glucose-1-PO$_4$.

By the reversal of the phosphorolysis of glycogen and given a glycogen primer, one can resynthesize the chains of glycogen in vitro. However, it appears that this reaction, which has been well studied in vitro, is of much less importance in vivo. For the in vitro reaction, a phosphorylase such as muscle phosphorylase *a*, needs a glycogen primer[4] to add glucose units from glucose-1-PO$_4$. After a long lag, some glycogen can be synthesized in the absence of primer. The rate and extent of conversion of the glucose-1-PO$_4$ to polymer is dependent upon the number of free chain ends available to the enzyme. Glycogen, which has very

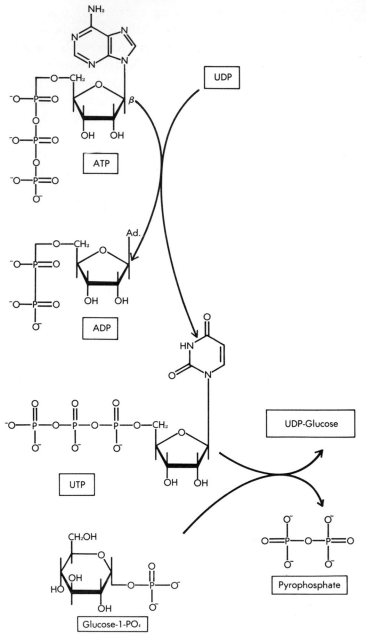

FIGURE 7–14 The enzymatic formation of UDP-glucose.

many branches, is a good priming material, since it provides many end groups on which to build chains. From the specificity of the enzyme it is clear that no new branches can be formed by the phosphorylase reaction. The bonds that are synthesized are entirely of the a-D-(1 → 4) glycosidic type and muscle phosphorylase *a* is specific for glucose-1-PO$_4$, in the pyranose form. The per cent conversion of monomer to polymer depends on the quantity of primer present.

The phosphorolysis reaction cannot lead to a complete breakdown of glycogen, since it can only degrade glycogen to a limit dextrin, being limited by the branch points. These branch points can themselves be further broken down by a specific a-D-(1 → 6) glucosidase.

For the in vitro synthesis of a long-chain polysaccharide by the phosphorylase enzyme, a great deal of information is available on the nature of the primer required. Table 7–1 shows the Michaelis constants that have been determined for the priming ability of various polysaccharide primers. Clearly, the Michaelis

FIGURE 7–15   *The phosphorolysis of glycogen.*

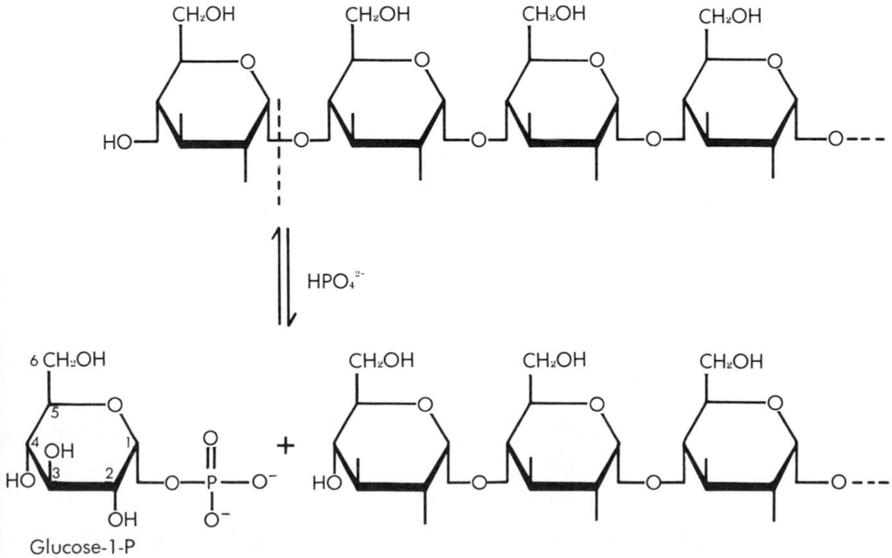

Glucose-1-P

TABLE 7-1 *Primer in the in vitro synthesis of amylose by phosphorylase*[a]

Primer	Average chain length	Michaelis constant Km, moles end group/liter
Dextrin	7	17×10^{-5}
Dextrin	23	5
Corn amylose	100	3.6
Tapioca amylose	650	0.9
Potato amylose	1450	0.4
Dog glycogen	15	71
Corn amylopectin	26	10

[a] From Reference 5.

constant is inversely proportional to the chain length of our primer, at least for these straight-chain primers. A similar relationship holds for the amylopectin and glycogen mentioned in the last two lines of Table 7-1. In order to work at all, a primer has to have at least three to four glucose units; however such a short chain is a very poor primer.

GLYCOGEN SYNTHETASE

For in vivo synthesis of glycogen, it was shown by Leloir,[6] in 1957, that from liver, a *glycogen synthetase* enzyme can be prepared that catalyzes the transfer of activated glucose residues from UDP-glucose to the nonreducing ends of a glycogen primer. The result of this reaction is a lengthening of the chains of glycogen and the stoichiometric release of UDP. The reaction is closely parallel to the synthesis of the disaccharide sucrose, which we have already discussed. The glycogen synthetase requires a primer, as does the phosphorylase, for the lengthening of glycogen chains. Quantitatively, the UDP-glucose pathway is the important one in the synthesis of glycogen in the liver. The same pathway exists in muscle, where Robbins et al.[7] showed in 1959 that glycogen is made from UDP-glucose. The release of free energy for the transfer of one glucose unit to glycogen is approximately equal to 3000 cal. On the basis of this figure, a conversion of UDPG to glycogen of better than 99 per cent was expected and was found.

Figure 7–16 indicates the various ways in which glycogen is degraded and is built up again in a tissue such as muscle. Through the action of phosphorylase *a*, glycogen is degraded to glucose-1-PO$_4$, and this in turn can enter the glycolysis pathway; at the same time a limit dextrin is produced. Glycogen is degraded to the extent to which the glucose is required. On the other hand, when the supply of glucose in the muscle increases (here we should note that the glucose arrives via blood glucose), increasing amounts of glucose-6-PO$_4$ are formed which in turn give rise to glucose-1-PO$_4$. This together with UTP allows the formation of UDPG, the activated form of glucose. The synthesis of UDP-glucose requires also a supply of energy in the form of ATP, provided by oxidative phosphorylation. As well as providing the glucose-1-PO$_4$ required for the synthesis of UDPG, the increasing amount of glucose-6-PO$_4$ in the cell has an activating effect on the glycogen synthetase. Therefore, this enzyme not only has the UDPG available to carry out its synthetic function, but it is also activated by the precursor of its substrate. In addition, UDP-glucose itself can act as a competitive inhibitor of the reversal of the phosphorylase reaction, thus additionally directing the pathway of glycogen synthesis to the UDP-glucose pathway. Perhaps we can regard what happens to the breakdown or resynthesis of glycogen in the muscle cell as a function of whether glucose-6-PO$_4$ is drained away in the glycolytic pathway, or whether the supply of glucose-6-PO$_4$ is increased by the abundant supply of energy and of glucose.

Phosphorylase is required for the release of monomer units from glycogen. But the enzyme in muscle exists in two forms, *a* and *b*, of which *a* is the active form with a molecular weight of 500,000 and phosphorylase *b* is relatively inactive (molecular weight 250,000). A kinase exists which, in the presence of ATP, converts phosphorylase *b* into phosphorylase *a*. Muscle phosphorylase *a* differs from phosphorylase *b* in being active in the absence of 5′-AMP and in being stimulated by much smaller concentrations of 5′-AMP. The degree of stimulation of the phosphorolytic activity of phosphorylase *a* by 5′-AMP depends on the substrate concentration. This is a consequence of a decrease in K_m for substrate when 5′-AMP is added, while there

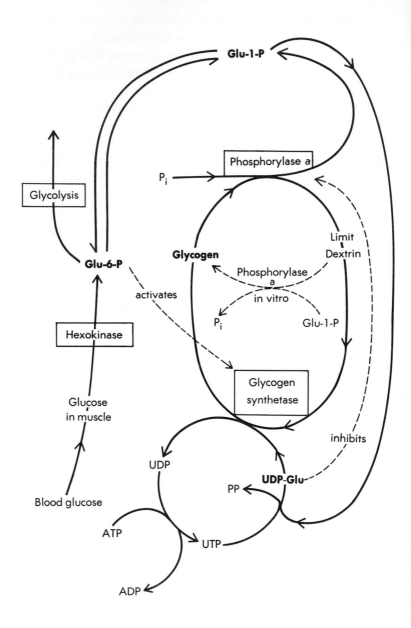

FIGURE 7–16   *The over-all scheme of glycogen breakdown and synthesis.*

is no significant change in V_{max}. One suspects an allosteric effect. The dependence of muscle phosphorylase on 5'-AMP for activity, absolute for b and relative for a, is explained in either case by increased affinity of the enzyme-AMP complex for the substrate.[8]

Although the breakdown of glycogen and the release of glucose may be controlled by the demands made for glucose, there exists a hormonal system that controls the mobilization of glycogen. Under conditions of excitement or when the blood level of glucose is low, the adrenal medulla secretes a hormone, epinephrine (Figure 7–17). When this hormone reaches the cell (e.g., the muscle or liver cell), it stimulates the enzymatic conversion (Figure 7–18) of ATP to a 3',5'-cyclic adenosine phosphate together with the release of one equivalent of inorganic pyrophosphate. This cyclic adenosine phosphate in its turn catalyzes or stimulates the conversion by the specific kinase enzyme of inactive phosphorylase b (two molecules) together with ATP to the active phosphorylase a. ADP is liberated in this conversion. In turn the active phosphorylase a can carry out the breakdown of glycogen to glucose-1-PO_4. Thus we see, as illustrated in Figure 7–18, that in times of excitement or when the glucose level is low, additional glucose is furnished to the muscle by this system of hormonal control. It is of interest that analogs of epinephrine act as antagonists and will block the activation by epinephrine.

Low blood-glucose concentrations stimulate also the secretion of the hormone glucagon from the alpha-cells of the islets of

FIGURE 7–17   *The formula for epinephrine (adrenalin).*

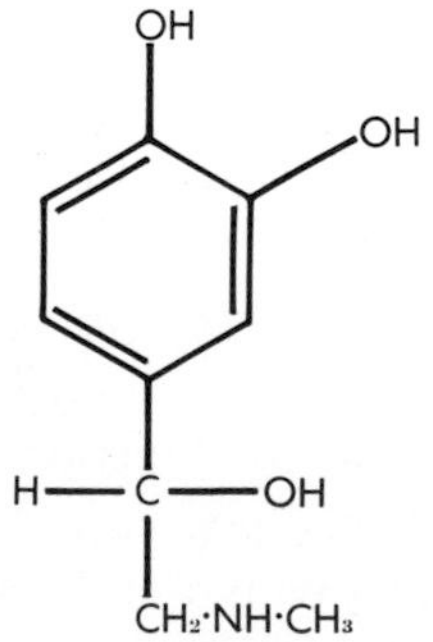

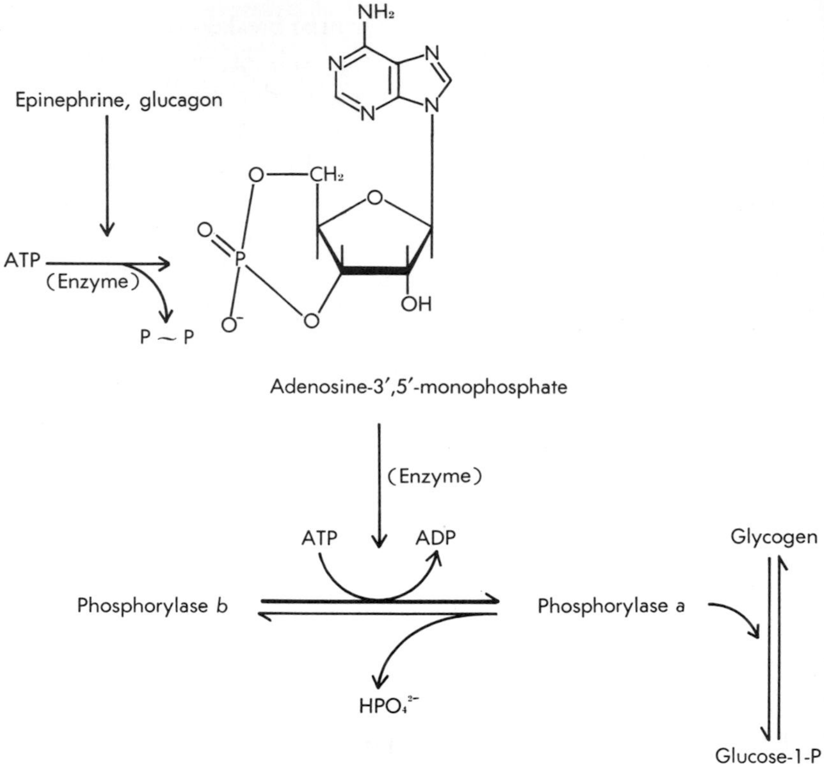

FIGURE 7–18 *The effect of epinephrine and glucagon on the release of glucose-1-phosphate from glycogen.*

Langerhans in the pancreas. Glucagon acts only in the liver cells much as epinephrine acts in the muscle *and* liver cells following the scheme shown in Figure 7–18. Therefore, low blood glucose leads, via the secretion of glucagon, to the mobilization of the glycogen reserve of the liver, which in turn leads to the liberation of glucose into the bloodstream. When the level of glucose is sufficiently high, the β cells of the islet tissue in the pancreas secrete another hormone, insulin. Exactly what the function of insulin might be is not quite clear, but its over-all effect is to lower the blood level of glucose. Thus glucagon and insulin work antagonistically and between them control the amount of glucose in the blood.

SYNTHESIS OF BRANCH POINTS

So far we have only discussed the sequential breakdown and the building up of straight chains at the ends of the glycogen molecule. Other enzymes are required to produce branch points with their a-D-$(1 \rightarrow 6)$ glycosidic linkages. In the liver, a so-called branching enzyme exists whose function it is to form new branch points from straight polyglucose chains. The branching enzyme transfers segments of a-D-$(1 \rightarrow 4)$ linked straight chains to a 6 hydroxyl group of a glucose residue elsewhere in the chain. To show that the formation of branch points by the liver-branching enzyme occurs through the transfer of sections of chain and not by the addition of single glucose units, the in vitro experiment illustrated in Figure 7–19 can be performed.

In step (a), phosphorylase in the presence of inorganic phosphate partially degrades glycogen. The remaining polymer is isolated and purified. Next, in step (b), more phosphorylase is added together with radioactive glucose-1-PO_4 labeled with ^{14}C. Under these conditions the chains of glycogen are lengthened again and, if we use purified phosphorylase enzyme for this

FIGURE 7–19 *Branch-point synthesis in glycogen with a radioactive-labeling technique, (a) incompletely degraded glycogen segment at nonreducing end, (b) glycogen segment with labeled outer chain, and (c) glycogen segment after action of branching enzyme. (After Reference 9.)*

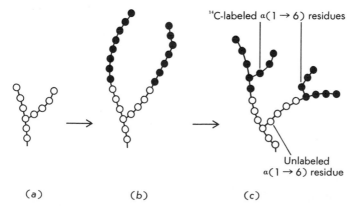

^{14}C-labeled $a(1 \rightarrow 6)$ residues

Unlabeled
$a(1 \rightarrow 6)$ residue

(a)   (b)   (c)

reaction, no branch points are formed at this stage. The previously existing nonreducing ends of the polymer have been lengthened with radioactive glucose units. Again the polymer is reisolated and purified; it is incubated in step (c) with the purified branching enzyme. After incubation and (presumably) formation of new branch points, the polymer is repurified and incubated with purified phosphorylase, inorganic phosphate, and the so-called debranching enzyme. The last is an α-D-$(1 \rightarrow 6)$ glucosidase. As the result of the combined action of both these enzymes, the polymer is broken down completely. Phosphorylase degrades the straight-chain portions to a mixture of unlabeled and labeled glucose-1-PO$_4$. The debranching enzyme produces free glucose.

If the branching enzyme in step (c) can transfer sections of straight chain, new branch points are formed and some of the free glucose formed in the last step of the experiment will be labeled. On the other hand, if the branching enzyme requires free glucose, which it attaches to the 6' positions, no new branches could have been formed in step (c) since no glucose was available. In the experiment, the glucose liberated in the final step was radioactively labeled and therefore the branching enzyme can transfer segments of chain to the 6 position of glucose units in the chain.

CELLULOSE

The polysaccharide cellulose (Figure 7–5), which is the structural material of plants, is also composed entirely of glucose units, but these are linked by an β-D- $(1 \rightarrow 4)$ glucosidic bond. The polymer forms long chains of no definite length. Presumably the insoluble cellulose fibers are formed by the parallel alignment of the long molecules and are resistant to disturbance and attack by virture of their close packing. Breakdown of cellulose is by cellulases, such as those that occur in snails, the shipworm, and in microorganisms. The biosynthesis of cellulose is supposed to occur via GDP-glucose, the guanine-containing analog of UDP-glucose, but the mechanism of the synthesis is not at all understood. It should be pointed out that, although the glycosidic linkage in GDP-glucose is α-D-, inversion must occur, because the glucose units in cellulose are in the β-D-configuration.

REFERENCES

1. Haworth, W. N., and Percival, E. G. V. (1926), "Polysaccharides, Part XI. Molecular Structure of Glycogen." *J. Chem. Soc.*, page 2277

2. Hassid, W. Z., and Doudoroff, M. (1950), "Synthesis of Disaccharides with Bacterial Enzymes." *Adv. Enzymol.*, **10**, 123.

3. Cardini, C. E., Leloir, L. F., and Chiriboga, J. (1955), "The Biosynthesis of Sucrose." *J. Biol. Chem.*, **214**, 149.

4. Cori, G. T., Swanson, M. A., and Cori, C. F. (1945), *Federation Proceedings*, **4**, 234.

5. Hassid, W. Z. (1960), in *Metabolic Pathways*, Vol. I, page 273, ed. D. M. Greenberg (Academic Press, New York). Potter, A. L., and Hassid, W. Z. (1948), "Starch. I. End-Group Determination of Amylose and Amylopectin by Periodate Oxidation." *J. Am. Chem. Soc.*, **70**, 3488; and "Starch. II. Molecular Weights of Amyloses and Amylopectins from Starches of Various Plant Origins." *J. Am. Chem. Soc.*, **70**, 3774.

6. Leloir, L. F., and Cardini, C. E. (1957), "Biosynthesis of Glycogen from Uridine Diphosphate Glucose." *J. Am. Chem. Soc.*, **79**, 6340.

7. Robbins, P. W., Traut, R. R. and Lipmann, F. (1959), "Glycogen Synthesis from Glucose, Glucose-6-Phosphate, and Uridine Diphosphate Glucose in Muscle Preparations." *Proc. Natl. Acad. Sci.*, **45**, 6.

8. Helmreich, E., and Cori, C. F. (1964), "The Role of Adenylic Acid in the Activation of Phosphorylase." *Proc. Natl. Acad. Sci.*, **51**, 131.

9. Larner, J. (1953), "The Action of Branching Enzymes on Outer Chains of Glycogen." *J. Biol. Chem.*, **202**, 491.

GLOSSARY

Active Site. The active site of an enzyme is that portion of the enzyme protein molecule where the substrate molecules combine and where they are transformed into their reaction products. It is thought that in general the active site is part of the surface of the enzyme molecule.

Allele (Allelomorph). One of a pair of alternative hereditary characters (genes) which occupy the same locus on a particular chromosome.

Allosteric Effect. The result of interaction of a small molecule with a protein molecule which leads to changes in the conformation of that protein with consequent alteration in the interaction of that protein with a third molecule.

Angstrom Unit. An angstrom unit equals 10^{-8} cm and is written as Å.

Antigen. A substance which causes a series of changes in the organism resulting in the formation of antibodies specific against the particular antigen and in the phenomenon of immunity.

Bacteriophage. A virus which infects bacteria.

Carboxypeptidase. Two enzymes (A and B) from pancreas which hydrolyse peptide chains *sequentially* beginning from the carboxy-terminal end of the chain and liberating amino acids one at a time. Carboxypeptidase A will liberate most types of amino acids, except for proline, arginine, and lysine; it has a marked preference for amino acids with an aromatic or a long aliphatic side chain. Carboxypeptidase B will only liberate the basic amino acids arginine and lysine, when these are carboxy-terminal.

Chymotrypsin. A proteolytic enzyme from pancreas which hydrolyses peptide chains internally at peptide bonds on the carboxyl side of various amino acids, with pronounced preference for the aromatic amino acids phenylalanine, tyrosine, and tryptophane.

Coding Triplet. The genetic message which provides for the sequence of amino acids in specific proteins is contained in the sequence of nucleotides of DNA. The particular nucleotide sequence specifying a particular amino acid is the "code" for that amino acid. It is currently thought that a sequence of three nucleotides in DNA is a coding unit or a *coding triplet.* The term is also used loosely for the corresponding (and complementary) sequence of three nucleotides in the template (messenger) RNA, into which the original DNA sequence is transcribed as an intermediate step in protein synthesis.

Collagen. The chief structural protein of connective tissue fibres.

Counter Current Distribution. A process for the separation of mixtures of substances, which takes advantage of differences in the distribution of these substances between two immiscible solvents. The apparatus is an ingenious assembly of many (up to 2,000) vessels, each one of which is like a separatory funnel for the mixing and separation of two immiscible liquids. The apparatus provides for the automatic mixing of liquids in each vessel and the automatic transfer of the lighter of the two liquid phases from one separatory unit to the next.

C-Terminus. That end of the peptide chain which carries the free α-carboxyl group of the last amino acid; usually, written on the right-hand side of the peptide chain.

Degeneracy in Coding. A genetic code is said to be degenerate if more than one nucleotide sequence "codes" for the same amino acid.

Density Gradient Centrifugation. (1) *Equilibrium Method:* A method for characterizing the buoyant density of a macro-molecule and thereby its chemical composition. Used in biological research mainly to characterize DNA, RNA, and their complexes, in terms of the three-dimensional structure and the base composition of these molecules. (2) *Zone Centrifugation:* In this technique macromolecules are characterized by their velocity of sedimentation through a preformed concentration gradient, usually of sucrose. Sedimentation velocity in a given medium is primarily a function of molecular size.

Elastase. A proteolytic enzyme from pancreas, originally detected through its ability to hydrolyse the unusually resistant structural protein of tendon—elastin. Elastase hydrolyses peptide chains internally at peptide bonds formed between two neighboring amino acids with nonpolar aliphatic side chains.

Electrophoresis. The movement of charged particles and molecules in solution in an electric field.

Furanose-Pyranose Forms of Sugar. The monosaccharide glucose, for example, exists in solution largely in the form of a ring compound which is in equilibrium with a small amount of the corresponding open-chain form. The six-membered ring in this cyclic form is related to the heterocyclic compound pyrane and is termed a *pyranose* ring. Under certain conditions, another form exists in which the ring is five-membered and related to the heterocyclic compound furane. Such a ring is called a *furanose* ring.

Genetic Map. The arrangement of the genetic loci (genes) belonging to a particular chromosome in a linear fashion, using the results of recombination between these loci to assess their relative positions and their distance apart.

Genotype. The genetic constitution of an individual or of a group of identical individuals.

Glucagon. A polypeptide hormone produced by the α-cells in the islets of Langerhans in the pancreas which causes a rise in blood sugar and counteracts the effects of insulin.

HeLa Cells. The oldest strain of human cells carried successfully in tissue culture for over twelve years, originating from a specimen of tissue from carcinoma of the human cervix.

Homopolymer. A polymer composed of identical monomer units, e.g., amylose, polyuridylic acid, polyphenylalanine.

Hydrogen Bond. The bond which may form between a hydrogen atom and an atom containing an unshared electron pair—for example, between a hydroxylic hydrogen and an oxygen atom of either the same or another molecule (intramolecular and intermolecular hydrogen bond, respectively). Hydrogen bonds are much weaker than ordinary covalent bonds, but stronger than the van der Waals attractive forces between molecules.

Hyperchromic Effect in Nucleic Acids. The increase in absorbency of ultraviolet light in a solution of DNA or RNA, observed when these substances are denatured by heat, alkali, low ionic strength, etc. The denaturation implies a disturbance of a regular three-dimensional structure.

Insulin. A polypeptide hormone produced by the β-cells in the islets of Langerhans which causes a fall in blood sugar and counteracts the symptoms of diabetes mellitus and the effects of glucagon.

Islets of Langerhans (α- *and* β-Cells). Spherical or oval bodies scattered throughout the pancreas and concerned with the secretion of the hormones insulin (β-cells) and glucagon (α-cells).

Keratin. Structural protein forming the basis of epidermal structures such as horns, hair, and nails.

Lysozyme. An enzyme, originally discovered in egg white, capable of dissolving the polysaccharide cell wall of many bacteria.

Meiosis. The process of reduction division of germ-cell chromosomes which halves the number of chromosomes (from diploid to haploid number).

Microsome. Ribosome particle still attached to a membrane—the endoplasmic reticulum. It is in this form that ribosomes are found in most cells of multicellular animals.

N-Terminus of a peptide chain is that end of the chain which carries the free α-NH_2 group of the first amino acid; usually written on the left-hand side of the peptide chain.

Oxidative phosphorylation. The transformation of respiratory energy into phosphate bond energy.

Paracrystalline Aggregate (*Tactoid*). A regular arrangement of molecules, as in a crystal, but in one dimension only. Such linear aggregates line up and pack parallel to each other.

Pepsin. A proteolytic enzyme from gastric mucosa which at low pH hydrolyses peptide chains internally at various peptide bond sites.

Phenotype. The characters of an organism or a group of individuals due to the expression of genotypic characters in response to the environment.

Polyribosome (Polysome). An assembly of ribosomes, presumably on the template (messenger) RNA, found in the cytoplasm of cells. It is thought that this is the form in which ribosomes are active when producing soluble proteins *in vivo.*

Prosthetic Group is that portion of a complex protein which is not polypeptide in character—for example, the heme groups of hemoglobin, which are iron-containing porphyrin molecules. Usually the prosthetic group is the active site of such a protein or is part of the active site.

Radioautography on the microscopic scale is a technique for localising within a cell, or other biological preparation, the site of the incorporation of radioisotope. Usually an isotope which emits short-range particles is chosen, for example, tritium-^{3}H. The preparation or section is fixed and a film of photographic emulsion placed on top of it. The area of radioactivity then exposes the film directly above it and this appears as black dots or blackened areas after development of the emulsion. The section can be stained through the photographic film. Microscopic examination now shows the sites of radioactivity in the exposed film superimposed on the usual stained specimen.

Recombinant. The new individual or cell arising as the result of recombination.

Recombination. Any process which gives origin to cells or individuals associating in new ways two or more hereditary determinants in which their ancestors differed—for instance, cells with determinants A*b* or *a*B descending from other cells with AB or *ab.* Although this process can be due to the Mendelian reassortment of chromosomes, it can also occur as the consequence of genetic exchanges between a pair of homologous chromosomes. The term *recombination* is used in the latter sense in this book.

Recombination Frequency. The total number of recombinants divided by the total number of progeny individuals. Used as a guide to assessing the relative distances between loci on the genetic map.

Revertant. An allele that arose through mutation of a gene can in turn mutate back to the original form of the gene or to a closely related and functionally similar form.

Ribosome. A cytoplasmic nucleoprotein particle found in all cells which are capable of synthesizing proteins. Composed of high molecular weight RNA and of several kinds of basic protein, the ribosome is the site of protein synthesis (see polyribosome).

Sedimentation Constant.   This may be determined by subjecting a protein solution to a strong centrifugal field and by observing the rate of movement of the protein outward from the center of rotation.   The rate of sedimentation is expressed in terms of the sedimentation constant *s*, which is the velocity for unit centrifugal field of force.

$s = \dfrac{dx/dt}{\omega^2 x}$, where *x* is the distance of the boundary of sedimenting protein from the axis of rotation, and ω is the angular velocity. Using also the value for the diffusion constant for the protein, a molecular weight of the protein may be calculated from the sedimentation constant.

Transformation.   The heritable modification of the properties of one bacterial strain by an extract derived from cells of another strain.   In most cases, the *transforming agent* appears to be DNA.

Trypsin.   A proteolytic enzyme from pancreas which hydrolyses peptide chains internally at the peptide bonds on the carboxyl side of the basic amino acids lysine and arginine.

Zone Centrifugation.   (-Zone Sedimentation)   See *Density Gradient Centrifugation.*

READING LIST

Acides Ribonucleiques et Polyphosphates: Structure, Synthese et Fonctions. Strasbourg, 1961. (CNRS.)

Annual Review of Biochemistry, 1961.

Berg, P. *Specificity in Protein Synthesis.*

Levinthal, C., and Davison, P. F. *Biochemistry of Genetic Factors.*

Annual Review of Biochemistry, 1962.

Cavalieri, L. F., and Rosenberg, B. H. *Nucleic Acids: Molecular Biology of DNA.*

Grunberg-Manago, M. *Enzymatic Synthesis of Nucleic Acids.*

Simpson, M. V. *Protein Biosynthesis.*

The Biochemistry of the Nucleic Acids. Davidson, J. N. 4th Edition. (John Wiley, New York) 1960.

The Chemistry of Nucleosides and Nucleotides. Michelson, A. M. (Academic Press, New York) 1963.

Cold Spring Harbor Symposia on Quantitative Biology. Volume XXVI. 1961.

Cold Spring Harbor Symposia on Quantitative Biology. Volume XXVIII. 1963.

Control Mechanisms in Cellular Processes. Editor: Bonner, D. M. (Ronald Press, New York) 1961.

Enzymatic Synthesis of DNA, Kornberg, A. (Wiley, New York) 1961.

Enzymes: Structure and Function. Bernhard, S. A. (Benjamin, New York) 1966.

The Hemoglobins in Genetics and Evolution. Ingram, V. M. (Columbia University Press, New York) 1963.

Horizons in Biochemistry. Editors: Kasha, M., and Pullman, B. (Academic Press, New York) 1962.

Informational Macromolecules. Editors: Vogel, H. J., Bryson, V., and Lampen, O. J. (Academic Press, New York) 1963.

Introduction to Molecular Biology. Haggis, G. H., Michie, D., Muir, A. R., Roberts, K. B., and Walker, P. M. B. (Wiley, New York) 1964.

Vth International Congress of Biochemistry. Volume I. 1961. (Pergamon Press.)

Molecular Basis of Evolution. Anfinsen, C. B. (John Wiley, New York) 1959.

The Molecular Basis of Neoplasia. (University of Texas Press, Austin) 1961.

Molecular Biology of the Gene. Watson, J. D. (Benjamin, New York) 1965.

The Molecular Control of Cellular Activity. Editor: Allen, J. M. (McGraw-Hill, New York) 1962.

Molecular Genetics. Volume I. Taylor, J. H. (Academic Press, New York) 1963.

Progress in Nucleic Acid Research. Volume I. Editors: Davidson, J. N., and Cohn, W. E. (Academic Press, New York) 1963.

Proteins and Nucleic Acids. Perutz, M. F. (Elsevier, New York) 1962.

Techniques in Protein Chemistry. Bailey, J. L. (Elsevier, New York) 1962.

INDEX